# Technical Drawing
# for Stage Design

*Gary Thorne*

THE CROWOOD PRESS

First published in 2009 by
The Crowood Press Ltd
Ramsbury, Marlborough
Wiltshire SN8 2HR

**www.crowood.com**

**British Library Cataloguing-in-Publication Data**
A catalogue record for this book is available from the British Library.

ISBN 978 1 84797 151 7

**Dedication**
This book is dedicated to my dear parents Peggy and Gordon, and to Wojciech Trzcinski with gratitude for the remarkable personal support and patience.

Typeset by Jean Cussons Typesetting, Diss, Norfolk
Printed and bound in India by Replika Press Pvt Ltd.

# CONTENTS

Acknowledgements . . . . . . . . . . . . . . . . . . . . . . . . . . . . . . . . . . . . . . . . . 4

Introduction . . . . . . . . . . . . . . . . . . . . . . . . . . . . . . . . . . . . . . . . . . . . . . 5

1  The language of technical drawing . . . . . . . . . . . . . . . . . . . . . . . . . 9

2  Drawing tools and equipment  . . . . . . . . . . . . . . . . . . . . . . . . . . . 15

3  Freehand sketching . . . . . . . . . . . . . . . . . . . . . . . . . . . . . . . . . . . 31

4  Types of drawing . . . . . . . . . . . . . . . . . . . . . . . . . . . . . . . . . . . . . 40

5  The scale rule . . . . . . . . . . . . . . . . . . . . . . . . . . . . . . . . . . . . . . . 44

6  Geometry and technical drawing exercises . . . . . . . . . . . . . . . . . 48

7  Venue drawings or theatre drawings. . . . . . . . . . . . . . . . . . . . . . . 91

8  Lettering and printed matter . . . . . . . . . . . . . . . . . . . . . . . . . . . 104

9  Orthographic projection . . . . . . . . . . . . . . . . . . . . . . . . . . . . . . 113

10  Line characteristics and drawing up. . . . . . . . . . . . . . . . . . . . . . 137

11  Scenic elements and terms . . . . . . . . . . . . . . . . . . . . . . . . . . . . 146

12  The orders of architecture . . . . . . . . . . . . . . . . . . . . . . . . . . . . 179

Glossary . . . . . . . . . . . . . . . . . . . . . . . . . . . . . . . . . . . . . . . . . . . . . . 182

Further reading. . . . . . . . . . . . . . . . . . . . . . . . . . . . . . . . . . . . . . . . 189

Index . . . . . . . . . . . . . . . . . . . . . . . . . . . . . . . . . . . . . . . . . . . . . . . . 190

# ACKNOWLEDGEMENTS

Thanks to the support of staff at RADA, Director Edward Kemp and in particular Director of Technical Training Neil Fraser, whose trust promotes professionalism in all areas of teaching and technical theatre practice; to my colleagues Gill Salter, Dave Agnew, Mark Tweed, George Orange, Daniel Collins, Matt Prentice, Deryk Cropper, Davy Atkinson, Diane Favell, Natasha Mackmurdie and Chris Mock; with gratitude to RADA design students Laura Cordery and Sarah-Jane Prentice, whose support with technical drawing and text material greatly enabled this book to meet completion; and to students Lo Wipp, Grace Stonehouse and Jessica Walsh; to Motley Theatre Design teaching staff, in particular colleagues Alison Chitty OBE, Ashley Martin-Davis and Catrin Martin, whose professional approach to design projects makes the most appropriate demand on technical drawing for stage; to Central School of Speech and Drama staff, in particular colleagues Jessica Bowles, Caroline Townsend and Keith Orton, whose investment in technical problem-solving drives forward good practice; and to the following young cohort of RADA designers for applying taught principles to personal practice – Lorna Ritchie, Chryssanthy Kofidou, Ingrid Tønder, Regina Fraas, Katie Lias, Jennifer Maiseloff, Piera Lizzeri, Trudi Molloy and Alison Neighbour. Further thanks to Central St Martin's College Artscom Short Course staff Steve Whalley, Chris Ball, Ashley Palmer, Shamain Nelson and Mauro Di-Pasquale, whose initiative for creating opportunities for learners permits development of personal ambition, and also to David Neat, Jeremy Lindon, Charles Russell, Neil Peter Jampolis, Debra Hanson, Ann Curtis, Stephanie Howard and the Stratford Festival Archive Canada.

# INTRODUCTION

Why is it that the designer, draughtsman and model maker place themselves before the drawing board or computer for days or weeks producing accurate technical scaled drawings? Who requires the drawings and what is to be included within a package of drawings? With finely scaled models available why cannot construction take proportion and measurement directly from them, especially as they deliver remarkably precise detailing? In the pages that follow are answers to the many questions that arise when trying to mentally shape ideas, to problem solve in 2D, to construct precise 3D models, and to deliver with clarity and precision design intention for production and construction. Herein are techniques, methods and applications, which serve the designer and model maker in problem solving in anticipation of the 'build' or construction realization.

A design presentation is not only about a finely executed model box, with its scaled figures and intended visual effect on the eye of the audience. Those working in production know that the outcome of a model box is through understanding the crafted balance between creative and practical decision making, and although they take the view that the model is a true representation of designer and director intention, it is understood that the way in which the design is to be integrated into the architecture of the venue cannot exclusively be depicted within the scale model box.

The preliminary white card model is often considered the aim of design at an interim period, and by its very nature delivers structural concerns of a technical kind in respect of the particular theatre, alongside delivering aspects of stagecraft, construction, lighting and sound requirements, and the role of stage management. Technical drawings accompanying such a presentation inform production there is more to consider than the model. The venue is represented in the form of ground plan and theatre section, each depicting the detailed inter-relationship between set, architecture and audience.

The scale model cannot fully articulate the very practical nature of design for the 'build', nor can it comprehensively communicate how design has become integrated into the architectural framework of a specific venue or theatre. Design in technical terms facilitates moving production forward through supplying a comprehensive package of technical drawings, clarifying the number of elements to be built and how proportionally these dimensions form a workable relationship with the venue. The package of drawings delivers in a precise manner that which production and construction require; relationships between:

* design and the venue architecture
* audience and design
* lighting requirements and design
* actor and design – offstage and onstage
* stage management and design
* materials and production construction processes
* build and technical stagecraft
* build and engineered components
* cost and feasibility
* cost and a production budget.

The drawings describe not only an overview of all the elements to be built, but include measurement and dimension details along with notes on designer preference for material and/or finish. The package of drawings initiates or facilitates a comprehensive costing. To budget effectively, the drawings and the model are consulted to plan the

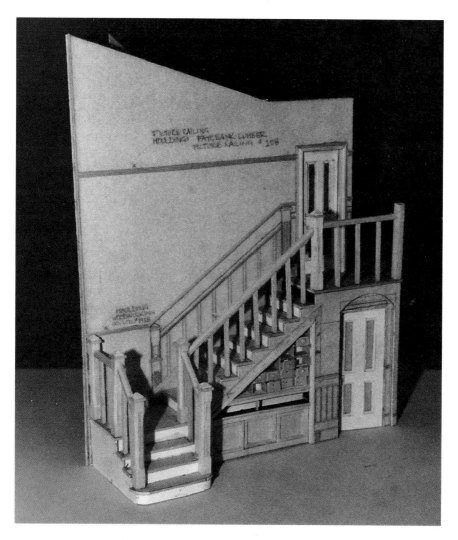

*From technical drawing into model design. Dye-line or photocopy prints from technical drawing are glued onto card, using elevation front view and side views. Further detailing is added. Scale 1:25. Design: Neil Peter Jampolis.*

schedule for a build; to put structure to form; to put material to structure; to engineer requirements; to meet health and safety standards; and to meet the needs of scenic art in application and decoration.

The material content of this book offers guidelines, exercises, references, principles of good practice and techniques, approaches to problem solving, and a glossary of terms useful to the designer and draughtsman. The reader gains understanding through practical application, as first-hand experience in board-drawing leads on to familiarity, confidence, and competence in problem solving in two dimensions in anticipation of three-dimensional outcomes. Learning to use principles of good practice, while problem solving, encourages both the proper use of tools and equipment and the appropriate approach to shaping ideas in 2D. A drawing that is clear and precise supports making an accurate 3D model.

Drawings serve the function of 'thinking something through' as much as they may serve 'shaping a decision' formally. Knowing why one is drawing and what is to be achieved helps sort out which approach to use. There is little benefit in jumping ahead and missing out part of a process to achieve a quality image, which is not yet thought through. As there may be a choice of options for approach, method and technique it is good practice to become familiar with as many as possible, as each may be used either on its own or in combination with another.

## A GUIDE TO THE EXERCISES

The exercises within this book should be considered task work as they inform the learner of process and lead on to evidence of training, with the evidence becoming portfolio material. As an archive it is invaluable for future reference. Exercises ease the reader into good drawing practice. Through on-the-board practice, the learner applies practical aspects of drawing plane and solid geometry to achieve determined outcomes. Chapter 2 introduces the reader to correct use of draughting tools and equipment. Through practice, ease in handling equipment encourages an ever more efficient manner where precision and accuracy become a discipline well ingrained. Proceed through the exercises to best understand the dynamic of tools while gaining confidence in handling them. It may sound simple enough, yet when tools are used in combination they involve skill. Knowing just how to manipulate the adjustable set-square leads to using it with great efficiency and speed when applied to more complex drawings.

To comprehend fully the ground plan and theatre section, it is recommended an actual venue plan and section be acquired. Approach a local theatre to request them, but avoid a venue that is too architecturally sophisticated. Follow the guidelines in Chapter 7 (venue drawings), as layout is an important factor in ensuring the drawing makes sense.

## THE USE OF ILLUSTRATIONS

The illustrations in this book speak about the actual process involved in arriving at a predicted outcome, as well as – often through an alternative choice – offering a different way to solve the same problem. In such a case the different technique or method introduced is worth knowing. In anticipa-tion of a career full of technical problems a designer is constantly in need of choice. In having the ability to weigh up one method over another, a mental agility is exercised, encouraging dexterity of the mind.

Illustrations describe how drawing-up should proceed, with different processes for specific outcomes. It is the nature of many drawings (as is generally evident in all technical orthographic drawings) that the process is left as evidence of how something has been thought through. The inclusion of two types of line: lines that reveal how a problem is solved (construction lines) and lines that clarify the outcome (finished lines), help illustrate the relationship between process and outcome.

All illustrations have accompanying captions or text. Each explains to the reader the necessary stages involved in drawing-up. Where complex problem solving is involved, the illustrations help to explain the process as much as the caption does. As a reader, approach both with keen interest, as it is often the case that one process is easier to comprehend than the other, or through cross-reference the illustrated process can be better understood. Many exercises have an element of a puzzle about them or come across as a mental challenge, yet it is often the same in drawing-up for production, where new ideas are designed and presented; the nature of the challenge first appears as unfamiliar territory. Approach problem solving with a healthy attitude and with a keen interest in taking on the challenge. At the planning stage of any drawing it is good practice to keep the approach simple.

There is a parallel between what the reader observes in an illustration and what needs to be delivered to construction. The process of thinking through relationships from one view to an adjacent view helps inform construction of logical inter-connecting relationships. When a drawing is comprehended as a whole, it facilitates the formation of a mental picture in the mind of the viewer. As drawings often depict something new and different, being partially of invention, they make complex reading. It is the nature of the theatre business to take risks and to adapt form to meet new purpose, and in so doing makes draughting a varied job.

Work through exercises chronologically. It is good practice to keep drawings flat, as once rolled they become difficult to handle. For the learner the process of accomplishment is in completing a drawing in a precise manner, with a developed understanding of what has been achieved in the skill of equipment handling, in clarity of lines, and in accuracy, and foremost in learning the principles. All techniques learned become a foundation for future practice when problem solving. The more on-board practice one has, the more skilled one becomes at effective proposing, planning, and promoting of calculated decision making.

## FREEHAND SKETCHING

Ideas of the mind often become something quite different once expressed, when transformed into visual form. Designers often grapple with finding the right form and material for ideas. Drawing is a means to an end, as it serves a purpose; thoughts can be expressed, promoting discussion, which may lead to the development of an idea to an eventual realization. It is often said, 'a drawing proves more effective than words'. Sketching is a quick means to an end. It facilitates presenting an impression of something imagined. A sketch is not a technical drawing bound by principles, yet confidence in drawing is important in putting across a proposed thought successfully. Freehand drawing can be most effective when delivering ideas to a craftsman in the property (prop) making department. The rough sketch, usually found bound in a sketchbook, supports the direction of Sketch Model development. Yet it may well work the other way round, where a Sketch Model is further developed through sketching.

## EFFECTIVE COMMUNICATION

Communication is essential for the successful development of design. Through effective collaboration, technical developments complement performance developments, ensuring the design intention reaches specified aims. Because produc-

tion often involves the management of sizeable teams, including construction, stage technicians, engineers, lighting and sound technicians, stage management, scenic artists, and prop makers, there is every likelihood of misinterpretation. Therefore a designer and draughtsman needs to be both a confident leader artistically, and technically competent.

Working to a brief demands knowing that brief well. When delivering preliminary drawings to accompany a white card model, a rough ground plan and section will be required, along with rough orthographic drawings for all proposed scenic elements. Preliminaries support an estimate for costing. In this instance a white card model may only have proposed mouldings and relief drawn in 2D upon its flat planes or surfaces, yet the suggestion passes on intention. Drawings should support the overall volume of a build, with overall dimensions.

## REFERENCING

As the designer works from a wide range of reference, including the world of architecture, interior design, product design, manufacturing, art and design, mechanical engineering, material and processes for construction, it stands as good practice to pass on influential references to back up design interpretation and technical decision making. Research may effectively introduce material, handling and manufactured specifications, including methods for binding or adhesion to other materials. Such information transferred through to construction saves valuable time and opens out round-table discussion.

Regardless of the challenging nature material and processes of construction present, the grammar of graphic representation serves to convey calculated decision making within an appropriate format and manner readily accessible to production and technical management. Guidelines within this book assist the draughtsman in making simple and effective proposals, regardless of how complex they may at first appear. Ideas delivered with clarity and precision allow production processes to move forward in a constructive manner.

# 1 THE LANGUAGE OF TECHNICAL DRAWING

## THREE TYPES OF DRAWING

Three types of drawing serve design. Each drawing type serves in a practical way to accomplish particular aims.

### Drawing – ideas in a process of development

Drawing is a tool and as a tool it offers the potential to reveal. Drawing can represent, as 'we draw to see what we observe'. Through representation a better understanding of what it is we observe can be made, as in the study to discover inherent truths. Drawing also supports putting shape to ideas; something imagined takes shape through drawing. Putting pen to paper facilitates visualizing the process of thinking something through. Ideas on the page once formed provoke or initiate a response in the viewer. In practical terms ideas presented invite or welcome comment and criticism. The act of drawing is in itself problem solving; for example, applying practical building geometry to formulate the surface development of a cone or pyramid (*see* pages 70–71).

### Drawing – ideas as a presentation medium

A drawing facilitates communication: an idea in progress, a proposal formulated, or a calculated intention. As a drawing it may appear very much unresolved. Through being interpreted a drawing may initiate the process of construction; to initiate 'bench drawings' and later the 'build'. A drawing therefore initiates both the discussion necessary to move production forward, and the production processes. A presentational drawing generally does not explain how realization is achievable; therefore drawings facilitate a feasibility study.

Many ideas conveyed in a drawing deliver a desirable intention, where design ideas may outweigh actual practicalities. The ideas behind a drawing may promote something new or unique. A drawing may only present a proposal for possible inter-relationships. Drawings that represent the intended form may not address the structural concerns that actually support form. Drawings may be developed freehand, as technical board drawings, or they may be computer-generated.

### Drawing – ideas as a guide for construction

Technical drawings inform construction through a scaled representation of how a scenic element or prop should look to the eye once built. As there is typically a scaled model or prototype in 3D to accompany a drawing, the viewer has the opportunity to see the aesthetic intentions in both 2D and 3D. Whether the drawing is a preliminary or finished drawing it should convey scaled proportional relationships, defined by overall dimensions and internal intermediate dimensioning. Technical drawings are generally presented in the same scale as the scenic elements built within either a 'sketch model' or within a 'presentational model'; the scale is typically 1:25. Technical drawings facilitate the making of the model. The model box with its set design is complemented by the 'package' of technical drawings. This package of technical drawings, which amounts to the full collection of drawings for a show, once delivered to the construction department informs them of calculated intentions. The precise nature of technical drawings facilitates production management, at the first stage, costing the build. Yet before construction can begin to build they must first interpret the package of drawings to convert them into 'construction drawings'. This is something that the Head of Construction will process, and involves turning all the designer's draughted information into drawings that define the actual materials to be used and the processes for construction. The result is the 'construction drawings', a set of technical drawings that communicate directly to those on the shop floor involved in the build. The development of construction drawings does involve and engage the designer, as all materials and methods to be used will have a knock-on effect. The aim of the designer's presentational drawings is to guide construction through to a build, with designer drawings offering clear and precise intention. For design the enlargement from scale to real size should be of no surprise.

> **Form and structure: Definitions**
>
> * Form (noun): a shape, outward aspect or shape of a body, the mode in which a thing exists or manifests itself.
> * Form (verb): to make or fashion into a shape or form, take a certain shape; be formed.
> * Structure (noun): a whole constructed unit, especially a building. The way in which a building is constructed, a set of interconnecting parts of any complex thing, a framework.
> * Structure (verb): give structure to; organize.

## GRAPHIC REPRESENTATION

Technical drawing is a graphic language and it is characterized by fine line pencil or ink drawing, delivered in a mechanical way. As a form of language, communication is established through using applied methods, principles and techniques for representing objects technically. An object as drawn in orthographic projection appears represented two dimensionally (in 2D), and is perceived through presented 'views'; the multiple views of an object in 2D enable the viewer to formulate a mental picture of the object in the mind as three-dimensional (in 3D) – see Chapter 8. Graphic layout includes depicting the front view, side view, top view, plan and rear view, all of which add up to the formation of a 3D impression. Production and construction teams are well experienced at reading the graphic language of technical drawings to formulate those mental pictures, which support them in anticipating a build and realizing that build.

The graphic nature of technical drawing in 2D facilitates constructing the scale model in 3D. A drawing showing the different views of a 'dresser' (see page 123) can be copied or dyeline printed, and the resulting copy can be pasted to card, and once fixed is then cut and assembled, much like a kit. Scale models are typically the centre of attention at production meetings. The drawings that accompany a model back up the accuracy of the model. Precision and clarity are essential elements in technical drawing.

## FORM AND STRUCTURE

The designer considers form as the geometrical configuration of structure. Form presents itself with having structural concerns. To make an assessment of structure it is necessary, but not easy, to remove the form to reveal what is giving it shape. Designers often seek to discover the material form that works best to complement ideas related to the play text. Their interest may focus more on form than structure, with the aim that structural concerns do not play an active role visually. In contrast to this they may seek to discover a structure supportive of ideas in the play text. Either way, any discussion between design and construction which occurs over the design will require judgments to be made on material and the relevance of the proposed construction processes.

Research often leads on to studying structural form as witnessed in the natural world. Designers may, like engineers, be particularly interested in stress factors as found within natural formations, in understanding principles of how form is affected by structure. Nature may be a key resource for design, and through observation, inspiration may be found. Such an interest may invite the design to be more organic, or to be interested in tensions and compressions as discovered in the real world. The construction department ensures that adequate strengths be applied to the build through the production process. A key or primary aim will be to satisfy strict health and safety standards.

Set design also needs to consider expectations or demands that will take place during a performance. It will also embrace the demands made when design is in any way transported. With touring productions there is a unique demand upon the build, where the importance of materials and their capacities – along with relevance of construction processes – must be factored in. How scenic units are to dismantle or break apart into component parts suitable for transporting is of typical concern for design. The aesthetics of scenic breaks in a set need disguising in some form or other, as no designer wants visible break-lines. Financial or budget considerations help both the designer and construction choose one method of construction over another.

> **The aim of technical drawing: Clarity**
>
> * Know who needs the drawing.
> * Know the purpose of the drawing.
> * Know what it is they need to know.
> * Know how best to communicate the information.
>
> **Precision**
>
> * Accurate drawings save time and money.
> * To cost a production effectively, all scenic elements must be included.
> * Each scenic element needs calculated measuring and dimensioning.
> * Views included within a drawing give all information required.
> * Drawings speak for themselves.
> * Accuracy is achieved through attention to detail.

## THE AIM OF TECHNICAL DRAWING

The technical drawing aims to depict with clarity and precision how the object will look. How an object is represented is typically through representation of its different views. Accompanying measurements detail height, width and depth. A drawing might clarify formal concerns for proportioning and dimensioning, while detailed drawings clarify component parts or internal relationships. Accompanying text will flag up intentions as further required, and may well inform construction on scenic art effects to be applied once built, and how actors or stage crew will handle the object. All of this informs construction of the practicalities of a design. The two key principles of technical drawing are clarity and precision.

## THE BRIEF

Knowing the brief makes drawing up all the easier. Understanding why a particular view should be included informs construction of required information. Delays in production usually occur when error or discrepancies appear. To avoid error it is good practice to make revisions of drawings prior to handing them over. An interest in practical problem solving forges good working relationships with those on the shop floor. Observing processes of construction encourages knowledge transfer, in favour of a well-informed designer working to maintain constructive interrelationships. Knowledge of material and processes of construction leads to better forward planning at the drawing-up stage, where a sensibility for budgeting informs both design and its decision-making. Knowledge of the role and responsibility of the designer enables the delivery of clear and precise information, meeting expectations. Above all else, a technical drawing serves a purpose.

## THE ROLE OF DESIGNER AND DRAUGHTSMAN

The role of designer and draughtsman is to provide leadership. Good leadership includes an aptitude for creative and practical decision making.

Evidence of leadership is found in how effectively the processing of design relates to presentational proposals. The production process is therefore supported by well-defined practical problem solving in 2D and in 3D. Thereafter the skill of teamwork and negotiation becomes all-important. Production management expects the competent designer to drive intention forward. The designer or draughtsman is expected to be both creative and technically aware. As design embraces creative risk-taking, flexibility is paramount. Production management initiates risk assessment for the design. Aspects of health and safety carry on right through the production period on a daily basis. Once actors arrive on-stage for the technical period there are guidelines for health and safety to be implemented. Where design becomes technically engaging for an actor, it is not unusual for the actor to be called to the shop floor to interact with specific scenic elements. This visit may actually enable construction to solve issues that can only be addressed with the actor present, as any such engagement should help make the transition to on-stage all the easier. Where floor traps may drop an actor through to sub-stage, or where lifts carry them to on-stage, or where harnessing enables an actor to fly, the technical demands to achieve risk-free results require team members to engage in clear and precise communication. Planning in advance for risk assessment meetings and anticipating what issues will arise is part the process of proposing design ideas technically. The designer/draughtsman maintains a constant interest in all aspects of production development, to support negotiations and enable design to serve performance needs.

To present the most effective representation of an object or scenic element, the draughtsman needs to follow guidelines for good practice. Thereafter reasoning becomes second nature when working through problems. More sophisticated levels of reasoning are developed through using reference books on subjects such as construction geometry, building geometry and technical engineering and architectural drawing. It is expected that some areas of technical expertise come through referring to the knowledge established by others in specialist fields. The use of such references assists the draughtsman to acquire an appropriate language for those interpreting the design.

## COMMON TERMS

### The technical sketch

The term 'technical sketch' refers to both freehand drawings (those made traditionally without the use of instruments) and drawings made using technical equipment to render an idea through to a visible form. The sketch conveys ideas as they occur in the mind of designer, showing how ideas are developed. Throughout the pre-production and production periods, where teams come together to discuss developments, the ability to sketch proves remarkably useful. Sketching is a form of thinking aloud, as it is both quick and direct in clarifying ideas. Where scale is central to understanding a sketch, it is recommended to include within the drawing some recognizable form which clarifies the proportions; this may be a figure standing alongside the form or other such familiar proportional item.

### Technical drawing

The term 'technical drawing' applies to drawings that are not artistic but are used to convey information represented for building or constructing. A technical drawing represents the appearance of form for the purpose of construction, wherein true measurements can be found including height, width, and depth. Proportion in relation to physical human proportion is factored in to most technical drawings for performance, as design centres on the actor.

Those involved with the production process will respond to technical drawings through questioning material choice and processes of construction. Where a drawing indicates construction material the concerns will focus on stress engineering and costing issues. A technical drawing can present comprehensively calculated technical information.

A drawing for a scenic flat may only depict door and window positions, but might also include: door frame and casing details and the practical nature of door hinges; window sash mechanics; period detailing; cross-section views of all moulding such as skirting boards, chair rails, picture rails, and cornices to be applied; wall surface finish such as wallpaper or paint effect; and notes describing material finish including glaze treatments. The reason for including scenic art finish as notes within a drawing is to draw construction's attention to the concern for using the best possible materials in support of those scenic art treatments.

## Construction drawings, working drawings or bench drawings

Drawings produced by Head of Construction are referred to in different ways, although they amount to the same thing. All the terms refer to the technical drawings that the Head of Construction generates to be passed on to the shop floor. Through interpretation made based on the designer's technical drawings, detailed drawings are produced as appropriate for the shop floor. The emphasis is on the true dimensions of structural materials to be used in the build, and on construction methods including joinery techniques. These drawings are typically produced with Computer Aided Design (CAD) programs. Structural information will include drawings for mechanical and engineered parts. Such drawings also define assembly methods with particular attention to the hardware used when applied to stage fixings.

## Detail drawings and the engineer

A detail drawing is generally at a larger scale than the layout drawing. For construction purposes a cross section drawing will be included, defining the details as component parts. The term 'engineering drawings' applies to industrial modification of technical ideas. These specific and highly detailed drawings are accurate and precise for the manufacture of engineered components. The graphic language of engineering drawings is very specific. Complex scenic units that engineers design on behalf of set designers include mechanisms for movement such as: revolve, hydraulics, pneumatics, or where power control is required or where motion control functionality is needed.

## Venue drawings: the theatre ground plan and theatre section

Theatre or venue technical drawings define the architecture of the performance venue. This consists of two drawings: 'theatre ground plan' and 'theatre section'. Each defines the architectural relationship of auditorium seating to on-stage and off-stage areas. Off-stage areas may include wing space, dock area for scenic storage, get-in facilities such as dock doors, lifts, actor entrances from dressing rooms or as cross-over behind or under the stage, and access to sub-stage including orchestra pit. The amount of technical detail included on a theatre ground plan or theatre section can be significant, often making them complex maps to read. Additional elements within a venue facility may include: fly-floor and flying system with its grid and pulley system and the counterweight cage; trap access; dimmer traps; lifts; heating and cooling systems; electrics for sound and lighting or lighting bridges; winch mechanisms; fire hoses or extinguishers; permanent vertical ladders and safety cages; safety curtain; house tab or track system; and permanent or sliding tormentors, to name but a few. To fully comprehend a technical ground plan or section it is always recommended to visit the site for a survey, taking along a camera to record features that may not appear in the drawings. An 'alternative venue' or that which is classified as 'site-specific' demands a comprehensive survey by the design and production team. Where there is interest in the unconventional space, the technical team made up of designer and production manager may need to generate its own survey, measuring the space to draught up a ground plan and section. Such a visit is typically called the 'recce', which refers to a survey.

## Recce

The term 'recce' (derived from 'reconnoitre') is used to indicate a survey, that is, a pre-production visit to a site for purposes of surveying its facility, a visit prior to making the model box. Items to take include a camera, tape measure, scale rule, plan and section.

## Model box

The theatre model box refers to the 3D card model version of the venue, representing the architecture of the theatre. The designer is responsible for making the model box, although theatres may offer the designer one already prepared. The ground plan and section facilitate making the model box, as dimensions are transferred across to card, then cut and assembled. The designer's photographic record (from the recce) supports its development. Depending on features found within the architecture, there can be embellishment applied at scale to compliment it; for example, the carved relief often found in a proscenium surround with its gold leaf can be applied. Once the model box is complete, the designer begins establishing a set design. On-stage features greatly affect design therefore it is not unusual to include details such as brick walls. A portion or all the auditorium seating is to be included.

The designer will begin working through ideas in 3D alongside developing sketches, rather than on the drawing board first. A plan and section will be on the board while design is being introduced in the model. While experimentation in 3D is explored, ideas are transferred to the board drawings. Problem solving on the board supports redefining ideas within the model. A logical sequence for exploration might be:

* Design development in 3D is passed across to the plan and section.

* Practical problem solving of a technical nature is then explored on the board in 2D, with results altered within the model.

The ground plan and theatre section support solving problems in respect of constraints and limitations of the architecture, and audience sight-lines. Shape ideas in 3D, record them in 2D and test them out; avoid getting too far ahead where it might be difficult to alter 3D design which has become too rigidly fixed.

## Building geometry

Basic knowledge of building geometry, which can be found in many reference books, is essential as it provides reference for the solution of practical problems designers are likely to encounter within the construction industry. Practical building geometry includes tools and how to use them, drawing practice, lines and angles, geometric shapes, areas, mouldings, arches, loci, orthographic, isometric and axonometric projections, geometrical solids, auxiliary projection, sections, interpenetration, and stair casing. The solving of seemingly complex problems such as a spiral staircase is easily comprehended through such reference books on building geometry. An understanding of the principles of practical plane and solid geometry is essential for technical drawing.

# 2 DRAWING TOOLS AND EQUIPMENT

With clarity and precision being the objective in drawing, all tools, instruments and other studio equipment need to support the draughtsman in achieving standards of excellence. With proper care and maintenance, quality tools of a professional standard stand a good chance of lasting a lifetime. Effective handling of draughting tools and instruments facilitates working at speed; yet the initial aim when learning is to maintain accuracy through regular practice, with the objective being consistency.

Successful drawings reflect discipline, through their adhering to principles of good practice, combined with an approach reflecting clear thinking, and calculated decision making. Professional quality draughting tools may prove marginally more expensive than college quality, but the expense usually pays off in the long run. Seek advice prior to making a purchase, by asking a draughtsman what is preferred. Quality tends to deliver quality, making it a good investment. A quality Bow Compass Set, if constantly maintained in good working order, never lets one down. Once purchased and tested, mark or inscribe tools with your name or initials, as this makes for easy identification in shared studio practice.

There are ways to cut costs when setting up the studio, such as using a table for a drawing board with T-square instead of a parallel motion board and built-in arm. As with any expenditure for tools, instruments and equipment, keep receipts and test out accuracy as exchanges may be necessary due to manufacturing faults. It is not unusual to find that even professional quality set-squares or rotary sharpeners have faults.

The exercises within this book refer to specific tools and instruments to assist in the process of problem solving. The list below is comprehensive; not all items need to be purchased initially, but some may become regularly used. Some tools remain a luxury, such as the electric rotary eraser.

## KEY TOOLS

Key tools include the set-squares of 45 degrees, and of 30/60 degrees, and the adjustable set-square. These are essential, as is the T-square

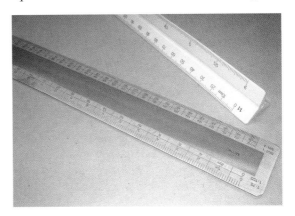

*Scale rulers.*

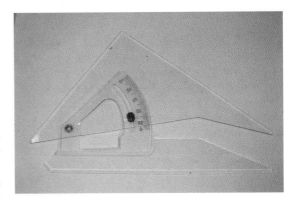

*An adjustable set-square.*

| Paper sizes | |
|---|---|
| A0 | 1189 × 841mm |
| A1 | 841 × 594mm |
| A2 | 594 × 420mm |
| A3 | 420 × 297mm |
| A4 | 297 × 210mm |

when working on a flat board without parallel motion. The mechanical clutch pencil and its rotary sharpener, the erasing shield and draughting eraser are as crucial as scale rule, a compass set, masking tape, a supply of tracing paper and a flexible curve.

## Paper and board size

Drawing paper size is of standard dimensions; therefore each paper size requires a board size proportionally larger. Once drawing paper is positioned on a board, the space around the drawing permits the positioning of T-square, use of drawing tools such as set-squares and gives allowance for slightly larger paper as underlay beneath a tracing paper drawing. With ground plan and theatre section typically plotted or printed on larger page sizes (A1), the smaller boards tend to become less useful except for detail drawings. A board of A1 size is most typical for theatre work. An A2 drawing board is versatile when working on orthographic drawings (multi-views of objects).

## Table and drawing boards

An ordinary table is perfectly acceptable when its surface has no irregularities, and it has no raised metal edge. The table's side (vertical) edge, where the T-square head connects, must have no irregularities to impede a smooth run of the head, up and down its length. Any smooth surface, even an old door on trestle legs, can serve the designer's needs. It is not unusual for designers to find themselves in situations where the facilities are less than professional and a form of ingenuity is called for with portable T-square and set-squares at the ready.

The drawing board should be used exclusively for technical drawing. Avoid using it for cutting, even when using with a cutting mat, and avoid the habit of using the board as a shelf for models or books. Keep the board covered with a light cloth between sessions, to protect it from dust.

Boards can be cut out of a sheet of plywood or MDF (medium density fibre board). The board edge, with which the T-square connects, must be evenly cut and smooth, without chamfer or rounding. As a portable board it can be positioned on a tabletop, either by laying it flat or by propping it up slightly beneath the top horizontal edge, to achieve a slight angle to the working surface. Avoid making it too steep, as the T-square will constantly slide down. Place the board in landscape format, with the long sides positioned as top and bottom. When it is placed on a table, position the bottom horizontal near to the bottom edge of the table, to minimize strain when drawing.

| Drawing board size |
|---|
| A0 paper requires minimum 1270 × 920mm drawing board size. |
| A1 paper requires minimum 920 × 650mm drawing board size. |
| A2 paper requires minimum 650 × 480mm drawing board size. |
| Drawing paper requires space around it. Too small a board and it becomes difficult to tape down a drawing, shift a T-square out of the way, or for set-squares to work close to paper edges. |

*The portable drawing board*
*with parallel-motion arm*
Portable drawing boards have a parallel-motion arm attached – this is a horizontal drawing arm attached through cables connecting to pulleys positioned at all four corners. The arm rides or slides up the board, maintaining a consistently accurate parallel to a horizontal.

Boards are manufactured as laminates, to achieve a high-quality hard surface, resistant to warping and surface damage. Manufacturers offer a choice in quality, with variations most evident in the parallel arm mechanism. Most portable drawing boards have a built-in stand, which allows for giving the board angle. Depending on the type of stand one may be more portable than another. They are useful, being easy to store away, with some brands supplying a travel case. As most venue ground plans are on A1 it is recommended to invest in this size.

*Floor stand drawing board*
If studio space permits, the floor stand with attached board should be considered. They can be purchased second hand, more economically. The advantage is the built-in adjustable height mechanism, the sturdy pulley system for the parallel-motion arm, and the adjustable feature giving the board gradients, allowing for working flat right through to a near-vertical plane.

*Board maintenance*
When not in use, cover with a cloth or sheet to prevent a build-up of dust. Good practice involves never leaving masking tape attached between sessions and never using it twice, as it has less strength to adhere. As tape dries out, it rapidly results in the gum backing being transferred from tape to board and onto paper. To remove graphite from the board surface use a putty eraser; where more grime builds up, wipe the board using a clean cloth dampened only with water. Never use any washing-up liquids or soaps, as the residue from cleaners will not permit masking tape to stick. Cleaners with alcohol tend not to interfere with masking tape adhesion. However, beware of 'safety warnings' and read carefully all manufacturing guidelines for use before applying it to the board. Establish the habit of removing masking tape at the end of each day. To remove old masking tape first peel all the tape off, then with a soft cloth and a small amount of either methylated spirit or lighter fluid gently wipe off the gum. Both fluids are a fire hazard and are toxic: use in a well-ventilated room and never near an open flame.

## T-square
The T-square is so called as it resembles the capital letter 'T'. This instrument is comprised of an extended arm forming the horizontal, fastened to the head, which is precisely set at a right angle to the arm. The arm will likely have a bevelled or chamfered edge, to facilitate seeing clearly when drawing all horizontal lines. The head sits aligned to the side vertical of the drawing board. Through maintaining contact, as it slides up and down the board, any number of horizontal lines drawn will remain in 'true' parallel to one another (*see* pages 24 and 49).

*Left-handed and right-handed T-squares*
A left-handed draughtsman should buy a left-hand T-square. The T-square head will be positioned to run along the right-hand vertical edge of the drawing board. The simplest and most typical plain wood version of T-square will not serve the left-hander, as one edge on the arm is not set at a true right angle to the head, so when the head is in position, on the right side, the arm angle ends up as the top horizontal edge. This type of T-square can only be used with its head on the left side of the board, making it suitable only for the right-handed user. There are other T-squares that accommodate flipping from left side to right side, and it is these the left-hander must shop for.

For a right-handed draughtsman the T-square head is positioned along the left vertical edge of the drawing board. Place the arm horizontally across the board, align the head connecting it to the left vertical edge. Slide the T-Square up and down the board, maintaining the connection of the head with the outer edge. Any time the head is not true in its alignment, the horizontal becomes untrue, and the accuracy of the draughtsman fails.

*Maintenance*
The mechanical precision built in to the T-square is set by four screws or rivets, joining both components. This join is vulnerable to knocks; at intervals gently tighten the screws. Protect from damage, as dropping or knocking may also put a chip or gouges into the horizontal arm, affecting the quality of line. Clean by wiping over with a

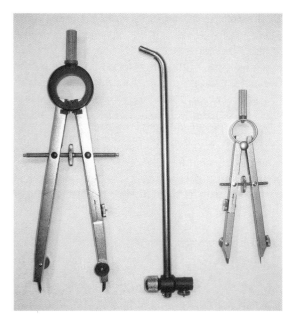

*A bow compass.*

### Bow compass and mechanical drawing instruments

The compass is for accurate drawings of circles, arcs or chords of a circle. The bow compass has a centre wheel, which when spun opens and closes the arms with fine precision. A compass should be of a solid metal nature, and of a professional standard, to produce consistency. A model of bow compass is available with centre wheel and push-button mechanisms, to enable quick changes from one size to another for radius, and once roughly set the wheel refines the distance as required.

A compass set should include: small bow compass, large bow compass, extension arm for drawing large radii, ink pen attachment, compass leads at 2H, spare needle points, and a divider. The divider is a measuring device; both arms have needle point ends.

putty eraser to remove the build-up of graphite then use a lightly dampened cloth to remove grime, and an alcohol-based cleaner, such as lighter fluid or methylated spirits, for removal of gum tape. Read 'safety warning' instructions thoroughly.

*Sharpening compass lead*

The 2mm-thick lead, inserted into the arm end, is the same diameter lead as in the mechanical clutch style pencil, allowing for interchange of lead types. Snap off a length of lead between 15mm and 20mm, and insert into the holding mechanism on the arm and gently tighten the fixture. Using a fine 'sandpaper block' (*see* page 22) or scrap of sandpaper, position the lead at a 30-degree angle and with even strokes pass the

*Sharpened compass lead.*

*Dividers and
a compass.*

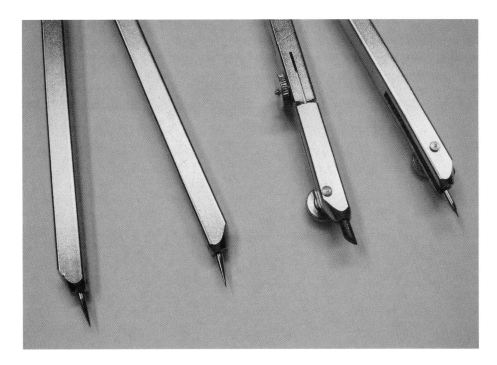

lead back and forth across the sandpaper. The bevel produces a point or sharp edge. Close the compass arms all the way, so both lead and needle point are aligned – they should almost meet. Gently loosen the mechanism holding the lead, and rotate the lead in its housing so the bevel is facing out, away from the needle, then tighten. The compass is ready for use. A 4H lead should be used for construction lines, and an H or HB lead for finished lines.

*Handling a compass*
A compass boxed set allows for drawing circles from an approximate radius 10mm to 250mm when the extending arm is employed. Place the needle point at the circle centre and, with a little downward pressure to secure the point into the page, proceed as follows. Right-hander: hold the compass in the right hand by pinching the top shaft between thumb and forefinger, lean the compass slightly towards the forward direction, rotate the compass shaft between finger and thumb, drawing the circle in a clockwise direction. Left-hander: hold the compass in the left hand and draw circles counter-clockwise.

Use the scale rule to set off radius measurements, yet do this on a page rather than allowing the needle point to make contact with the scale rule, as the rule (being made of plastic) will damage. Mark off the intended radius (use 4H lead) and draw the circle as in a lightweight construction line, aiming for consistent pressure throughout. Once the entire drawing is completed, darken the circle using H lead, with firm pressure. Where the diameter is given the radius needs to be calculated (divide the measurement in half using instruction for dividing a line into two equal parts, *see* 'Using a divider', below).

*Beam compass*
A ruled arm with a fixed compass point at one end and a slide mechanism along the rule which holds lead. This tool permits drawing larger diameters or arcs than is possible on a bow compass. The sliding mechanism may be the needle point rather than the lead holder.

*Using a divider*
Dividers are typically used to create sub-divisions, or to produce calculated unit measurements that

require repeating. It is a particularly useful instrument for transferring measurements and greatly assists in division of a line into equal measured units.

To divide a given line (A-B) into equal subdivisions, for example into thirds:

Approximate a third of the distance from A, with the dividers. Trust the eye to calculate this third. Place a divider point on A, the other on the ray of line and proceed to 'walk' the instrument along the line, towards B. Hold the divider top shaft between thumb and finger. If the final position lands beyond C, then the arms need closing to reduce their span. Make a slight adjustment and try again. Once successful, mark with a pencil the points where the needles make contact with the line. This method may take several trials to perfect.

Both compass and dividers are to be operated with one hand only. This avoids likelihood of inaccuracies where the other hand may alter the mechanism.

*Scale rule*

Made either in a flat format with a selection of scaled rules on two sides, or in a triangular scale format with a selection of six scales (*see* page 15). The designer working with performance will require a scale rule with the following scales: 1:1 or 1:10, 1:50, 1:25 and 1:20. Avoid the architect or engineer scale rule. The selection of scales they require is inappropriate for theatre draughting. Do not mistake a 1:25 for a 1:250 or 1:2500

(*see* Chapter 5 for a detailed explanation on how to use it).

**Set-squares**

These are clear plastic right-angled triangular tools for drawing lines. They may be used either independently or together to form prescribed angles of a nature relevant to the principles of building geometry (*see* pages 50–51). As with all plastic tools when inking, the tool needs flipping over, with beveled edge face down, to avoid ink touching the tool itself, as ink will run under a tool if it makes contact with the plastic surface. Always hold the ink pen perpendicular to the page.

*The 45-degree set-square*

The 45-degree triangular set-square is made of clear plastic, and comprises two 45-degree angles and one 90-degree angle (the sum of which is 180 degrees) (*see* page 50).

*The 30 × 60-degree set-square*

The 30 × 60-degree triangular set-square is made of clear plastic and comprises a 30-degree, a 60-degree and a 90-degree angle (180 degrees in total). Note that combining the 45-degree set-square with the 30/60-degree set-square results in angles of 15 degrees and 75 degrees (*see* page 50).

*The adjustable set-square*

This clear plastic 45-degree triangular set-square has a precision mechanism for making adjust-

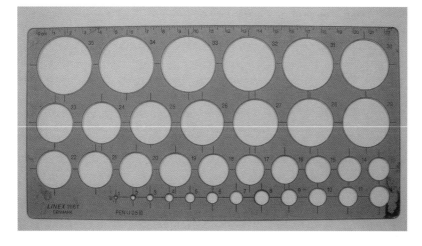

*A circle template.*

ments to enable the formation of determined degree angles (degree markings are clearly indicated for accuracy). It is a masterful tool when working to achieve aligned views of irregular angles found in objects. It is also invaluable for plotting on the raked stage in theatre section, for squaring to a line set at any angle on the page, and when formulating a series of parallel lines set to an angle (*see* page 15).

## Circle template

A clear plastic tool offering templates for circles of different diameters, ranging from 1mm to larger. It is a useful template for all work on the board (*see* page 20).

## Protractor

A clear plastic 180-degree or 360-degree tool, used to define accurate angled degrees. The adjustable set-square has the same advantage, yet a protractor makes for easier placement of degrees off a line that is not set vertical or horizontal.

## Pencil types

### Mechanical drawing pencil

These are manufactured with a push-release shaft mechanism at one end and a claw or clutch mechanism gripping a 2mm lead at the other end. For added security of grip a finely textured shaft is part of the design. The release mechanism shaft can be removed, allowing for coloured shafts to replace it, as colours relate to the type of lead. With each new purchase of twelve leads of the same type, the manufacturer includes a new colour shaft. Clutch style pencils are manufactured with component parts that unscrew, enabling access to the internal components; this facilitates servicing, cleaning and installing new lead. It is a well-manufactured instrument and is highly recommended for all technical draughting. To maintain a consistent thickness to pencil point when drawing a line across the page, slowly rotate the mechanical pencil between the fingers while drawing the line across.

A comprehensive range of 2mm-thick lead types are available, ranging from soft 2B through to hard 4H. As few as three leads may be purchased at one time, as they are sold in tubes. The

*Protractor.*

claw or clutch grip with its spring mechanism creates a firm grip on the lead, to withstand firm pressure on drawn lines. Clutch mechanical pencils usually have their own brand of rotary sharpener.

### Mechanical or propelling pencil

Known as propelling pencils, they contain specific lead widths of a fine 0.7mm or 0.9mm that are of use to a draughtsman. A full range of lead types is available from soft to hard. They do not require sharpening as the lead widths complement the particular line widths required. There is a disadvantage however in that the leads tend to slide up the inner shaft when pressure is applied when line drawing. As the lead types for technical drawing range only from 4H to H, and all use 2mm-thick lead, it does prove an advantage to use the mechanical clutch pencils, as variation in thickness of line may be achieved though the rotary sharpener. The lead in a propelling pencil proves too weak when applying firm pressure.

### Rotary sharpener for clutch mechanical pencil

The mechanical pencil rotary sharpener is sold separately, and is made of two component parts for easy care and cleaning. On the rotary lid are two guide holes with corresponding symbols noting the two types of point available (sharp point and dull point). The cavity, or base well, collects the graphite, and within is the built-in grinding file. The rotary sharpener is designed for 2mm lead only (graphite or colour). The lid slides off, permitting the well to be emptied.

## How to use a rotary sharpener

1. Press the shaft to release the lead, allowing it to drop into the 2mm hole. Once it hits the bottom, with shaft still pressed, slide the claw down to touch the lid. Release the shaft mechanism. The length of lead is appropriate for producing the intended point.
2. With claws firmly holding the lead, carefully slide the pencil down into the large hole, the one with protruding mouth opening. Slide down all the way (it may require a gentle rocking to sink all the way down).
3. Firmly hold the base container in one hand on a table top. The other hand holds the pencil with finger and thumb close to the lid mouth. Grip the mechanical pencil and very gently rotate clockwise, with no downward pressure on the pencil. Keep rotating until the grinding sound disappears. As it becomes more free-wheeling, apply a slight downward pressure and keep going until no grinding is heard.
4. Remove then slide the lead into the cotton filter that is built in to the lid. This removes all graphite residue. Remove.
5. Press the shaft to release the lead, yet do so with either the table top or the palm of the hand beneath the point and once the claw releases the lead gently slide the lead in until the bevel of the sharpened lead is touching the claw. Release the shaft. The pencil is ready for use.

*Wood pencils*

Traditionally wood pencils were used for technical drawing. A selection of wood pencils with three lead types is recommended: the hard lead pencils (4H and 2H); mid-range lead pencils (H); or F. With firm pencil pressure using H or HB there should be no need for Bs as their softness increases the risk of smudging. The disadvantage in use of wood pencils is in their constant need to be sharpened as consistency in point is necessary at all times.

Traditionally, sharpening was done using a scalpel or small box-cutter blade to strip off the wood around the lead, before sharpening with a block of sandpaper. The wood is shaved or whittled off at an angle from 2.5cm up from its end. This produces a bare lead of 1cm in length. The lead is sharpened to a cone, by rotating it as you pull it towards you across the sandpaper, with the aim of maintaining as much as possible of the 1cm length of lead. Loose graphite particles are wiped off with a soft cloth.

Graphite filings easily attach themselves to tools, instruments, and equipment. Sharpen well off to the side of the drawing board. As good practice, at the start of the day, wipe down tools from T-square to set-squares with a damp cloth, and dry thoroughly before placing on the page. To remove graphite from the board surface, use a putty eraser. To wipe the board use a clean cloth dampened only with water. Never use any washing up liquids or soaps as the residue from cleaners will not permit masking tape to stick. Cleaners with alcohol, once air dried, do not interfere with masking tape adhesion.

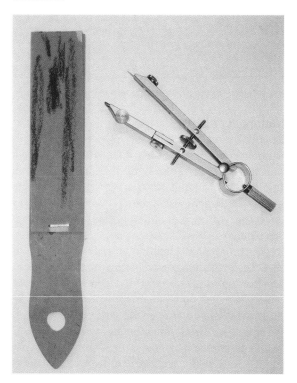

*Compass and sandpaper block.*

*An eraser brush.*

*An erasing shield.*

## Sandpaper block

This is a small, palm-sized pad with fine quality sandpaper stapled onto a thin wooden block, used to sharpen 2mm compass leads and wood pencils. It is possible to cut costs by making your own, by gluing fine sandpaper to a small wood block.

## Technical drawing eraser

This may be used for graphite on paper, and for matt draughting film, such as tracing paper. Quality brand names produce minimal residue waste, due to their resistance to crumbling. The lightweight card packaging is designed as a practical sleeve, to expose only a small amount of eraser at a time, and to protect the eraser from the likelihood of build-up of grease or oil from the fingers. It is recommended for tracing paper and as a general drawing eraser.

## Erasing shield

This thin shield of metal is a template with a variety of cut out circles, used to shield areas from being erased when erasing specific details. The series of small circles which run across the whole plate enables erasing a solid line to produce a series of dashes. This is considered an essential tool, for maintaining accuracy and precision.

## Electric eraser

A rotary-type electric eraser, with accompanying cylindrical vinyl erasers.

## Dust or eraser brush

A bristle brush with wooden handle, this is particularly useful for avoiding smudges caused by wiping the hand or cloth across the page to clear off fine dust or eraser residue. It should be used regularly to help tools remain as graphite-free as possible.

## Masking tape

Tracing paper is fixed to a drawing board with masking tape only. Masking tape designed for the building industry, especially for painters and decorators, tends to have much less adhesion and should therefore be avoided. Professional draughting tape or quality tape is more expensive yet holds for longer periods.

### Removing dried tape

Masking tape soon begins to transfer gum to both board and paper. Gently peel off old tape; that which has hardened and will not budge requires scraping off. Avoid any tool that might damage the board surface. Once scraped away, remove the glue residue using a soft cloth and a small amount of lighter fluid or methylated spirit. Note that this must be done in a well-ventilated space, where the circulation of air will avoid build-up of fumes. Both fluids are highly flammable: never use near an open flame or where something is burning. Read packaging instructions carefully before use. Once clean, the tools and instruments will require airing. Put all used cloths in a plastic bag, and dispose of as recommended. Establish the habit of removing tape from the board at day end, as tape dries out.

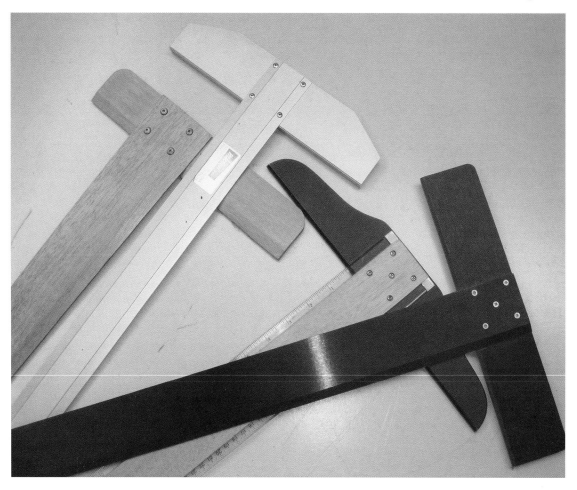

*T-squares.*

## Cartridge paper

This is used as underlay between board and tracing paper. The board surface is usually too firm for a compass point to bite into. Cartridge paper also affects pencil quality on tracing paper, in a positive manner. 140gsm is a good average weight cartridge paper.

*Positioning cartridge paper*

Position the T-square arm with the horizontal arm flat on the board. Align the head with the edge of the board. The base of the arm should align itself with the base of the drawing board. Place the cartridge paper onto the board, being sure the paper is sitting in line with the top horizontal of the arm. The paper's vertical edge nearest the head should be positioned approximately 20mm from the board's side edge.

Cut masking tape in short lengths of 50mm, and place each diagonally across the page corners, and press firmly. To avoid tape having wrinkles or any unevenness, it is recommended tape be cut with scissors. Do not use any other tape, such as clear tape.

## Tracing paper, detail paper and technical drawing film

Tracing paper is the recommended drawing paper for all technical drawing. Tracing paper is a manufactured standard paper for ink drawings, yet also serves pencil drawing. Tracing paper is available in various weights ('gsm', or grams per square metre), with the thinner being 60gsm and the heavier 116gsm. Heavier weight tracing paper at 116gsm is ideal for finished presentational drawings, either inked or in pencil. Tracing paper permits overlay onto ground plans and theatre section drawings, those supplied by the venue. With ability to position drawings one over the other, the transferring of information from sketch to preliminary to final is easy. Tracing paper meets dyeline printer requirements (*see* Dyeline Printing, pages 27–28). It is sold on pads, in sheets, or on a roll, in either 25m or 50m lengths.

*Detail paper*

A semi-transparent lightweight tracing paper at

---

### Tracing paper type

* For rough stage drawings use detail paper (53gsm) or tracing paper (63gsm).
* For preliminary stage drawings use tracing paper (63gsm).
* For presentation or final-stage drawings (inked and pencil drawings) use film/tracing paper (90gsm or 116gsm).

---

53gsm weight. Ideal for roughs and all preliminary drawings as it is inexpensive. It is sold in pad form or by the roll, in 25m or 50m lengths. The thinness demands extra care while drawing as edges are susceptible to tearing, but it is highly recommended as an all-purpose paper, suitable for sketch, rough plan and orthographic planning.

*Tracing paper*

This professional drawing paper is a semi-transparent film available in three weights: 60gsm, 90gsm and 116 gsm. Note that tracing paper at 60gsm and 90gsm is prone to creasing and tearing more than 116gsm. Tracing paper ages well without becoming brittle.

*Technical drawing film*

Where drawings are likely to be used for long-term reference, the use of film is recommended. It is an appropriate surface for ink, with a durable and permanent character, since film will neither become brittle with age nor tear. The film is very smooth, of a translucent nature, maintains flatness even after being rolled for long periods, resists creasing, and is recommended for dye-line printing.

*Storage tips*

Rolled drawing should have the drawing facing out. This permits easy feeding of paper into the printing machine. Also, when drawings are placed flat for viewing, the curl is towards the table surface rather than away from it, making it easier to weigh the corners down. Avoid rolling a drawing tight; it is advisable to roll with a 100mm diameter.

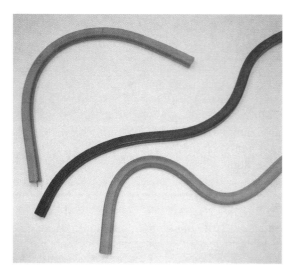

*Flexible curves.*

*Effects of humidity*

All tracing paper is affected by change in humidity: the subtle changes in moisture cause the paper to expand or contract. Avoid leaving tracing paper taped onto the drawing board overnight, as over extended periods humidity will cause the page to pull away from tape or begin to buckle when expanding. Any tool or instrument left on the surface overnight, such as set-square or T-square, will cause the page to wrinkle permanently across the surface where the tool edge made contact; once affected it is no longer useable. Where the page is simply softened by humidity it becomes unsuitable for hard lead, making softer lead pencil types necessary to compensate, as harder lead types do not produce a quality line.

*Positioning tracing paper*

With cartridge paper secure and squared to the board through use of the T-square, place tracing paper over it, align, and tape the corners diagonally with masking tape. Use the T-square to 'iron' the page flat as the tape is applied from first the bottom of the page to the top, or vice versa.

## Flexible curve

A rubberized drawing rule, with internal mechanical spine structured to permit the drawing of curves from plotted dots upon the page. Useful for drawing an ellipse or to produce organic shaped curvilinear lines that are not possible to create using a compass. The internal mechanism is susceptible to damage, through flexing the tool in an opposite fashion, as it can only be flexed across one plane, the one where it sits on the flat page.

## French curve or irregular curves

A clear plastic tool, with an elaborate range of curves designed in its shape, used by architects and engineers to produce curves through having plotted dots on a page. Sold in a set of three or individually, they are comprised of irregular arcs which a compass could not achieve without a complex range of established radii. The calculation of the curve is done independently. The tool joins dots; where the curve is compounded it is achieved through drawing part arcs. Avoid trying to achieve one long curve with the tool, as it is intended to join up short stretches of arcs.

## Calculator

Ideally an all-purpose, desktop solar-powered calculator to facilitate easy problem solving using basic calculations. Functions need to include addition, subtraction, division, multiplication, and percentage. An eight-digit screen will be enough capacity.

## Lettering guide

A clear template with an inner rotating disc, which is used when drawing a series of equidistant parallel lines across the page for lettering. The disc has a prescribed series of holes running in line with one another; these are guidelines for the pencil. With the series of holes set in a vertical manner the lines are furthest apart; through rotation the angle produces the effect of lines becoming closer together. Rotating the disc determines the line distances.

## STUDIO EQUIPMENT

### The draughting studio

Acquiring quality equipment and maintaining its condition is essential for good practice. A studio ideally should have a permanent space set up for the drawing board. Adequate levels of lighting, an adjustable height chair, and control over the surrounding levels of distraction are all important. As high levels of concentration are required, working between the model box and drawing board, control over the working environment becomes of particular concern. Simple mistakes are easy to make, and it is often the simplest of mistakes that have the greatest knock-on effect in drawing. Directional lighting is achieved with an angle-poise lamp. A plan chest is ideal for storing drawings, but since it takes up a lot of room drawings can be hung off the wall using bulldog clips on a wire or cord. Rolled drawings make for awkward viewing later on, so be sure to roll no smaller than a diameter of 100mm.

As orderliness requires planning, seek the best and most convenient arrangement for equipment. Personal preference comes into it, yet the main issues are touched on herein. The board needs be ready for use at any time. Keep instruments within easy reach of the drawing board; place them to one side while working by positioning a small table or chair to your immediate right (if right-handed) or left, where drawing equipment is stored during use. Avoid stacking instruments one upon another, as they have a tendency to slide off one another. The studio set-up should avoid becoming cluttered, and the board should never become a shelf for model boxes, or for books. The table height for the board should be fixed in relation to what suits the individual; however, make allowance for plenty of leg room beneath, as the body is constantly shifting while drawing, with the chair needing to move from right to left with ease.

## Adjustable seat

All drawing boards demand that the body shifts position, as no single position works over all. A swivel or castor-legged chair facilitates the demands from left to right while a height adjustment permits working comfortably from top of page to bottom, without undue strain on the back. When drawing for extended periods frequent adjusting of the chair is required. Less fatigue in the body supports more focus on the board. Avoid

standing over the drawing board when it is in a near horizontal position, unless the board is raised to above waist height. When seated keep legs placed forward beneath the table with both feet on the floor.

## Lighting

A reading lamp with articulating joints or elbows allows easy manipulation to achieve the best possible position of directional lighting. The angle-poise lamp is best positioned at the top of the board, within arm's reach (attaching the angle-poise to the table or to a wall backing the board is ideal). Adjustment promotes sustained focus, and facilitates working with speed and accuracy. The angle can be altered to avoid any casting of shadow in the area where the drawing is ongoing. Even a set-square will cast shadow, making it difficult to locate precise points of reference to the side of its edge. With this lamp it is easy to adjust the light to avoid glare from the page to the eye.

## Printing process

The dye-line or blue-print process is the traditional method used for reproduction from tracing paper. Drawings can be in pencil or ink. Dye-line printing has a dark blue line quality and a pale blue background. The paper used in printing is chemically treated and light sensitive. For dye-line printing to produce high quality lines it is advisable to work in ink. If this is not possible due to time constraints a drawing in pencil firmly drawn will print successfully.

*Process of dye-line printing*
The tracing paper drawing is placed on top of the light sensitive paper, with the drawing face-up. Both sheets are feed through the first set of rollers in the dye-line machine, exposing the pages to ultra-violet light. Light passes through the tracing paper except where there are drawn lines. The machine then passes the two sheets back out. The original tracing paper drawing is removed and stored aside. The chemically treated paper is then fed through another set of rollers exposing it to the vapour of ammonia. The vapour chemically transforms all yellow lines into dark blue, and then it

passes the page out of the machine. Pencil lines or ink lines which have variation in thickness and in variation of weight (darkness) show up as variants in mid to dark blue. The page itself has a pale blue colour. Dye-line printing produces a precisely accurate copy, as the rollers restrict the tracing paper and chemical paper from shifting, during the first process. Although the machines are expensive the process of printing is inexpensive.

*Commercially produced copies*
The commercially available photocopying process has become the more readily available method today, although colleges have dye-line machines. Commercial printing companies have switched from dye-line to photocopying almost exclusively. Photocopying is vastly more expensive and has its shortcomings; for example, distortion in precision occurs.

## Light box
A light box is ideal for working in overlay to trace copy and generally transfer information from one drawing to another. A box unit safely supplies an electric light source from within, set beneath a translucent white plexi-glass sheet on which drawings are placed.

## Plan chest and drawing storage
A plan chest consisting of A1 or A0 size drawers makes it ideal for storing drawings, as they are placed in flat. They do take up considerable room, but the top surface is an ideal table top for a model box. Drawings can also be hung off the wall or rolled for storage.

# GUIDELINES FOR GOOD PRACTICE

* To reposition the T-square: tilt the head downward, which raises the arm off the page, then slide the head along the board edge.
* When making slight adjustments to the T-square, simply shift the arm across the page flat with little to no downward pressure.
* Graphite lead in compass and in pencils deposits a light residue over tools, the drawing board and page, with smudging occurring once residue adheres to the underside. Wipe equipment regularly with a dry soft cloth. For built-up residue lightly dampen a cloth with warm water and wipe thoroughly. Be sure to wipe equipment bone dry, and air before re-use.
* Pick up a set-square by its tip, then move it.
* Be sure the studio is stocked with draughting eraser, erasing shield and putty eraser.
* Never sharpen pencil leads (either with a rotary or regular sharpener) near to the drawing board.
* Remove graphite from a sharpened lead by rolling it on a soft cloth and avoid using the same cloth for cleaning tools.
* A draughting brush used regularly sweeps aside graphite and eraser residue. Brush to the left and right and off to the sides of the board, never upwards as the residue accumulates beneath the page at the top. Avoid wiping a drawing with your hand or a cloth as it causes smudging.
* If possible start a drawing at the stage of 'finished lines' at the top left, working down and across to the right (the reverse if left-handed).
* A perfectly smooth drawing board, with no surface irregularities, reduces the chance of black marks from tools sliding across its surface.
* Place a plastic-lined waste paper bin near the drawing board for pencil shavings and for the collection of eraser residue.
* Use the sandpaper block for sharpening compass lead; position it over an open envelope.
* Avoid placing items on the drawing board other than the instruments in use at any one time.
* Avoid the T-square falling, as the joint will work itself loose, causing the right angle to fail in accuracy.
* Avoid dropping set-squares, as the angled corners crack and splinter.
* Place an A4 sheet of paper under the wrist when applying text and dimensions, to avoid smudges and to reduce the chance of natural oils or sweat being transferred to the page.

✳ Avoid tools falling to the floor, as plastic attracts dust through static.

✳ At regular intervals wipe the base of the T-square arm or parallel-motion arm with a soft clean cloth.

✳ To wipe under a parallel-motion arm: slide the arm to mid-board position. Lift it gently off the board and place a roll of masking tape or similarly sized item beneath to prop it up. Wipe across the base surface with a clean cloth. The cable linking the arm to the mechanism is under the least amount of strain when the arm is mid-board, putting the least amount of strain on pulleys and cabling.

✳ Keep compasses within boxed sets between uses.

✳ Wipe hands regularly with a separate clean cloth, one allocated only for this use, to avoid damp or natural oils affecting the page.

✳ Cover the drawing board overnight with a light cloth to avoid build-up of dust.

✳ Before commencing a drawing session clean tools and instruments.

✳ Put set-squares into their plastic/vinyl sleeves after use.

✳ Tidy away all erasure residues.

✳ Avoid putting fingers through the hair, since moisture or perspiration can come into contact with tracing paper in this way.

✳ Avoid brushing away eraser compounds with the hand; use a draughting brush and be sure the T-square is positioned above the area being cleaned.

✳ When pointing at areas in a drawing, flip the hand and use the fingernail edge or a dry clean instrument.

✳ Remove tape after every drawing session.

✳ If a drawing needs to remain on the board overnight, position it horizontally, remove all tape and avoid any tool being placed on its surface.

✳ Cover a drawing with a dry sheet of cartridge paper to protect it from reacting to a change in temperature or humidity.

✳ Clean a T-square with a putty eraser, not water. Then use a clean cloth very slightly dampened or sprinkled with water, dry immediately and thoroughly.

✳ All plastic tools need flipping over, with beveled edge face down when inking a drawing, to avoid ink touching the tool itself, as ink will run under a tool if it makes contact with the plastic surface. Always hold the ink pen perpendicular to the page.

✳ Place drawings flat in drawers.

✳ Never use the drawing board as a cutting table.

✳ Do not fold tracing paper.

✳ When storing tracing paper drawings rolled, roll with the drawing on the outside, with diameter at 100mm, protect from smudges once rolled by wrapping in a sheet of cartridge paper rolled round them.

## Orderliness

Plan using common sense and the studio will take shape to work efficiently, providing a practical place to problem solve. Sort the position of the drawing board first in consideration of the best place for lighting. Tools and instruments should have a home or station, and through practice things are always placed back from where they were taken; even in a drawing session establishing such a habit serves working efficiently. Tools are expensive and delicate, and parts are easily mislaid. At the end of every session tighten the screw mechanisms on compass sets, empty contents of a rotary sharpener, and generally tidy up. The larger drawings supplied by a venue as in ground plan and theatre section should be either pinned to a wall or suspended on clips, as they are called for regularly.

## Neatness

Naturally when working with graphite it tends to accumulate on everything in the studio. Page smudging occurs mostly from residue adhering to instruments. Investment in a draughting brush reduces the risk, yet at day end there is an accumulation of residue on the studio floor and table top, which needs attention. Efficiency and accuracy is helped when things are kept clean. Take pride in the studio space, in the execution of drawings, in their storing and filing. When rolling drawings for storage, label a sheet of cartridge paper wrapped round the outside. As the designer and draughtsman is under considerable pressure of time, the neatness of the studio assists in reaching deadlines, where having something at hand gets quick results.

## Precision

A professional approach is in knowing the aim of a drawing; what is required in the detail and when it is due. Knowing processes of construction supports a drawing in communicating what the shop floor need to know, making the transition from page to the build all the more realistic. Develop the habit of checking and rechecking measurements, calculations and sums. Drawings showing accuracy save both time and money. As the draughtsman is prone to error at the initial stage of planning the page, it is good practice to approach the early stages with a critical mind. Page layout and overall dimensions for an object need attention, as simple errors of miscalculation lead to drawings that are not true. When taking measurements from the model to transfer them to the board, always write them down, or use the ticket stub method: a scrap of card whose edge is used to mark off measurements, with letters correspon-

ding to the marks for easy recall. Read scale measurements in millimetres, and it also helps to say the number out loud when reading it and when writing it down, before transferring it. Keep a record of measurements noted on a separate page attached to the side of the drawing for reference. Having to write the number confirms the reading, and creates trust between what one sees, reads, and formulates. Initially take time over producing a set of drawings.

Anticipating the build is partly showing concern for material, size and proportioning, but also having the capacity to understand how something drawn will be built. Experience on the workshop floor proves invaluable when proposing ideas through technical drawings. Understanding construction requirements increases awareness of what purpose a drawing has to fulfill. Get to know the role of Production Manager, along with the workings of construction, through reading about it, asking questions, listening, getting experience first-hand and making the investment to gain close working relationships. Skill development in technical drawing comes largely through knowing what the design expectations are in meeting construction and prop-making requirements.

# 3 FREEHAND SKETCHING

The importance of sketching to the designer, draughtsman, engineer, and craftsman in both technical and non-technical work is that there is nothing quite as immediate for expressing and formulating ideas. Where verbal descriptions tend to fail in their inability to create concise mental pictures, communication through the graphic language of pictures becomes a valuable method of formulating, expressing, and recording ideas in more concrete terms. Sketching offers a way to articulate that which is in mind; it supports thinking something through, and offers up an instant impression of process when problem solving.

Freehand is not to be viewed as an untidy or crude form of drawing, as the style of rendering, although not mechanical, conveys care in the drawing with good line weight and character. The nature of the term 'sketch' implies quickness, yet accuracy is often as important as the expression.

With ability to transform familiar objects into simplified geometric form the designer/draughtsman achieves likeness through representation. Experience with drawing basic geometric form, such as a cube, prism, cylinder, cone, pyramid or sphere, supports freehand drawing especially when making observations from life. Familiar objects are a good starting point for sketching; drawing exercises initially start with simple familiar objects such as a cup and saucer, mug, glass, bottle shapes, teapot, bowls, boxes, vases, and forms of packaging.

Making a mark on a page begins to convey something, and although sketching or drawing is monochrome by nature there is opportunity to add in shading to give more vividness to the image.

Drawing in design has a purpose, and the immediacy of plotting a line to define an edge for a plane facilitates moving quickly on to formulating shape and form through interconnecting or intersecting lines. Construction lines in a sketch consist of: horizontal and vertical lines, central axis, diagonals and tangents, curves, arcs and circles. Lines may be plotted through placing points on a page and joining dots, or through more freehand sketching rays.

## NEGATIVE SHAPE

Negative shape (that which is surrounding solid form) becomes as interesting as positive shape (that which makes up the volume space within a solid form) when drawing aims to establish relationships between forms and the space they occupy. Drawing form without due attention to the shape of space around it tends to lead to objects having no context – or at least no substantive feeling of occupying space. To concentrate on the space discovered beneath a four-legged chair, and the outer shape where it inter-relates to the floor or wall it is against, supports giving the representation a proportional relativity. It also reminds the draughtsman that nothing exists on its own; everything has relationships.

Freehand drawing of lines should consist of light, freely drawn lines, as in a sketchy manner, without the aid of a rule or straight edge. A sketch may start with formal concerns for the mass of the object or may focus on internal proportions, arriving at a formal shape through discovery of internal relationships. Construction lines conveniently remain as evidence, giving the drawing a clear indication of the process.

## ADVANTAGES OF SKETCHING

1. A verbal description tends to have its limitations in creating effective mental pictures.
2. The graphic language of representation is a practical approach to formulating, recording and expressing ideas.
3. A sketch often outweighs the mechanical drawing for the purpose of considering aspects of engineering.
4. It provides further information to oral descriptions.
5. A sketch can prove practical even when rough and incomplete.
6. Sketching is employed professionally by the artist, designer, draughtsman, builder, and engineer.
7. A sketch effectively conveys proportional relationships.
8. Sketches are achievable using only pencil, paper and eraser.

## SKETCHING MATERIALS

* Soft pencil leads (HB and 2B) for shade effect.
* Putty or gum eraser
* Cartridge paper (140gsm offers a suitable matt surface)
* Tracing paper
* Graph paper

### Graph paper

Graph paper provides guidelines for those less experienced and encourages speed for the more experienced. Place the tracing paper over the graph paper. Tape down paper onto a pad or drawing block, begin plotting points for lines to connect to. Where the drawing also includes angled lines, as in rendering freehand perspective, the purchase of graph paper with diagonal lines supports this. Where proportioning may need more precision, the grid squares on graph paper can easily serve as a form of value – a measurement is then assigned to the proportion of one square within the grid.

## CHARACTER OF LINE

1. Sketching should have a quality of freedom and show variety. Avoid allowing sketching to become rigid or uniform.
2. Avoid a mechanical or technical quality line, as it will add to rigidity.
3. Natural-type lines are characteristically wavy; they search out form while continuing on a pathway, as found in growth patterns within nature.
4. Add variety to a straight line by using broken shorter lengths or strokes end-to-end, with the hand stroking the page. Allow for small gaps between the strokes.

### Types of line used in freehand drawing

Dimension, Extension, Centre line: very thin lines
Hidden line: thin dashed lines
Object line: heavy dark lines for the object to stand out
Construction line: a rough light line with overlapping strokes

## TYPES OF SKETCH

Both technical drawing and freehand sketching conform to a range of standard type drawings, these include:

* Multi-view: comprised of geometric planes or elevation views; front, side, top, bottom or plan, rear (*see* page 114).

### Pencil point

Pencils should be sharpened to a conical point.
There are three desirable pencil lines: thin, medium and thick.

* thin and black: sharp
* medium and black: nearly sharp
* thick and black: slightly dull

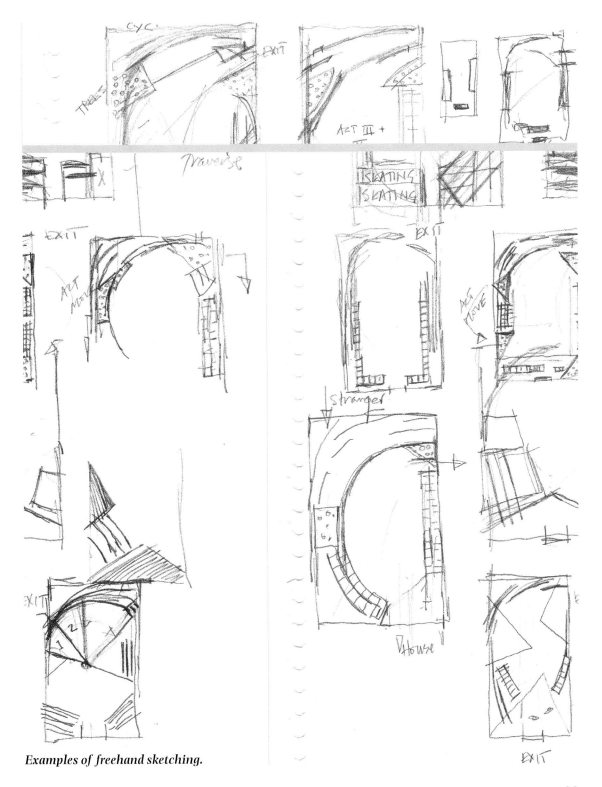

*Examples of freehand sketching.*

*Examples of freehand sketching.*

* Isometric freehand: this drawing, like the axonometric drawing, depicts three sides of an object in one view, very much looking down on the object, yet in a more perspective fashion than axonometric. This drawing shows the true plan of the object. The sides of the plan of the object are drawn set off the horizontal at an angle of 30 degrees. Circles appear as ellipses whether in elevation or in plan. Vertical measurements are true, yet depth measurements need converting (*see* page 133).

* Axonometric freehand: a view looking downwards on the object, with the drawing containing the true plan of the object. The sides of the plan of the object are drawn set off the horizontal at an angle of 45 degrees. Vertical lines are drawn as true. Circles on plan are drawn as true, but circles on elevation are drawn as ellipses (*see* pages 131–132).

* Oblique: surfaces which are a plane not set perpendicular to any plane already established, it cannot appear as a line as it is not parallel to

*Examples of sketching techniques.*

any plane, therefore cannot appear in true size. An oblique surface is one that appears fore-shortened in all views.

* Perspective: concerned with vanishing points within a cone of vision established by a specta-tor position at a pre-determined distance from the object. Plane surfaces converge on the van-ishing points.

## SKETCHING TECHNIQUES

### Establish a line
First indicate with dots the beginning and end points. Through making repetitive short strokes, aim to project rays through a forward and back-ward motion faintly marking the page as you go. Maintain eye focus ahead of where the pencil point is at any one point. It is best practice to look at the final destination point while drawing. Draw verti-cal lines downwards or turn the page sideways to facilitate lines being drawn with ease, in a horizon-tal manner.

### Draw lines running parallel to the page edge
Allow the small finger to reach out and run along the page edge. Or place a rule at a comfortable dis-tance from the intended line and allow the small finger to run along the ruled edge. Do not use the rule itself to draw a sketched straight line.

### Draw lines running parallel to one another
Use the pencil as a measuring device to plot points of equal distance from a given line. Use the dis-tance between pencil point and position of the fin-gers, to determine a distance. Plot dots on the page as reference (two or three are often enough), and follow through by joining the dots.

### Proportions in life study
Draw using the mind to calculate relative propor-tions. Consider an object's overall proportions, consisting of detailed intermediate inner propor-tions that size up against one another to form a sum. Overall proportions are height, width and length.

### Estimating a dimension
The artist's technique makes use of the pencil as a measuring tool. Extend the arm to its full distance from the eye. Observe a large-scale object at some distance. Hold the pencil vertically with the lead pointing up. One eye needs to be partially shut for this exercise. Focus one eye on the lead point, aligning the point with a specific reference point on the object (for example the top of a human head). Position the thumb below the pencil point, sliding it down to a level where the thumbnail reg-isters with a specific point on the object (say the chin). The distance from the tip of the pencil to the thumb tip will represent one unit. Keeping the thumb secured on the pencil in this same position, and keeping the arm fully extended, lower the pen-cil until the lead tip aligns itself with the second point of reference – the chin. The thumb tip is now aligned or registered with another point on the object. Continue moving the pencil in a downward swing with arm still extended, counting up the number of units it takes to scale the object's full height.

To transfer this information to the page simply determine a unit length, and plot two dots one above the other vertically on the page. This meas-urement is the distance from the tip of the head to the chin in reality, yet it has its own scale on the page. Measure down the page units of equal dis-tance, plotting them by way of a series of dots (put in as many as were observed in the original form). A stub of paper with one unit marking indicated on one edge works well for this. The distance of one unit is then possible to plot as distances both verti-cally (height of object) and horizontally (width of object). Refer back to the object viewed in the dis-tance to clarify true measurements.

### Dividing lines into equal measured units
Use the pencil point and the position of the thumb on the pencil as a way of prescribing set distances along a given line span. Or approximate half the distance of a given line, using distance between pencil point and thumb as a measure, moving it from left of a proposed centre to right, adjusting the thumb distance until it is approximately cor-rect. Make a dot at centre when correct. The mid

point between centre and each end point can be done in the same fashion. With practice the draughtsman is able to approximate centre or sub-divisions without a tool but through a method of trusting the eye to proportion out units.

## Drawing circles and arcs

Sketch a square within which a circle is estimated to fit. Make sure each side of the square is of equal length. Draw in both diagonals from corner to corner. Along each side of the square plot the centre. The point where diagonals intersect is the centre of the circle. Using the pencil as a measuring device, plot the given radius from the circle's centre to where a mark was made along the side indicating half its distance. This radius measurement needs marking off from the circle centre along the diagonals. The square now has a series of dots along all lines. And the task now is to sketch (freehand) a circle joining the eight dots as plotted.

With large circles, draw in additional radials or 'spokes' and mark off radius points in the same fashion as above. This method enables more accurate sketching as there are more arcs to draw and they are of a shorter distance, making it easier to be accurate. When plotting an arc use faint construction lines, using a harder lead (3H) with light pressure. Once the circle appears uniform apply more pencil pressure. Note: prior to drawing the finished line (using H or HB lead) dab the page evenly with the putty eraser to dim the lines.

A useful tool for marking off the radius is a scrap of paper or 'ticket stub': note the required measurement unit as radius along one edge. Once the square has its radials with the circle centre plotted, the ticket stub is used to mark off the intended radius. Plot the radius along each radial from the centre. Freehand the arc lines from spoke to spoke.

## Drawing a freehand ellipse

If a coin is rotated between thumb and forefinger, first being set parallel to the eye where it appears a true circle, to being in a horizontal position by way of the pivot or axis running perpendicular to the eye (left and right), it can be observed that through rotation, the circle transforms into oblique views until it is a flat plane (like a horizontal line). The oblique views are elliptical, appearing foreshortened. The horizontal or central axis is its 'major axis'. The central vertical axis is its 'minor axis'. When the coin is observed partially rotated, the view is of an ellipse. First draw the enclosing rectangle; sides must run parallel and be of equal distance. Plot and mark the centre of each line forming the sides. Draw lines joining centre points

across to its opposite side. The intersection of these two lines (the major axis and the minor axis) forms the centre of the ellipse. Employ the use of a paper 'trammel' to assist plotting the points within the rectangle through which the ellipse will be drawn. (*See* page 80.)

## Geometric shapes

The most common geometric shapes are circles, angles, plane figures, and solids (*see* page 115).

*Angle*

The common symbol for an angle is indicated by <. This is to be followed by the degree of angle. (Note: there are 360 degrees in a circle.)

*Triangle*

A plane flat figure bound by three sides; the sum of the interior angles always equals 180 degrees. The triangle is the basis of the study of trigonometry, a branch of mathematics of much value to the engineer and draughtsman (*see* page 66).

*Quadrilateral*

A plane flat figure bound by four sides; regular polygons have equal sides. Regular solids have faces, which are regular polygons (*see* page 52).

*Pyramid*

A solid with plane triangular faces that intersect at a common point called the vertex (*see* page 70).

*Cylinder and cone*

A form comprised of single-curved surfaces, which also have straight-line elements (*see* page 71).

*Sphere*

A round ball. (The 'torus' is like a doughnut.)

# 4 TYPES OF DRAWING

## DRAWING AS A TOOL

The ability to differentiate drawing type supports planning and execution knowing the end result will fulfil specified requirements. Clarity for what should be included saves valuable time and energy. Drawings serve a purpose; knowledge of the recipient's needs makes the stages of work more clearly delineated.

Rough drawings help the development of design concept at the early stages of thinking things through and experimenting. The roughs solve initial relationship issues, introducing a floor plan into the model box of a proportion relative to the studio seating arrangement being proposed. This facilitates a sketch model that has some relation to the architecture in the ground plan.

Preliminary drawings complement a white card model, or a preliminary presentation of the design for a feasibility study, or for costing. The package is of scenic elements with key measurements included, with a workable or achievable design working to fit the constraints of the theatre section and ground plan. These drawings are in pencil and have a quantifiable amount of information for production staff to critically assess the proposal.

Presentational drawings are the finals that, once handed over, move design into production. These 'for construction' drawings deliver all requirements, comprehensively. They are only in need of developing to serve the shop floor construction staff. The comprehensive quality is in line with an acceptance that production has authorized the expenditure, based on the preliminary drawing and update on changes prior to delivery of these final drawings.

Where the draughtsman wishes to articulate material, text generally accompanies the image in printed form, on the drawing. Such notes and others are also included in the 'notes' box within a drawing.

## ROUGH LAYOUT DRAWINGS

As soon as design ideas take shape in the model box (in 3D) it is necessary to transfer material information to rough technical drawings. With the theatre ground plan and theatre section on the drawing board the habit forms to transfer information from card to floor plan. First place a sheet of detail paper (53gsm) or tracing paper (60gsm) over the ground plan, tape together with both aligned to the T-square arm or parallel-motion arm. Transfer key architectural features of the venue onto overlay, noting the centre-line and the edge of the stage as setting line. At this stage it is not important to draw all the architectural details: just a few key ones – such as proscenium opening, front row of seats, upstage wall position, and off-stage side walls – are enough to sketch in. Many more such drawings will be generated over time before finalizing the design. Use a 2H lead on overlay at this rough stage, as any mistakes will not need to be erased if the line is light. Include centre-line on the ground plan and plot sight-line points as indicated in both drawings. These are typically indicated by a small circle ('O') with a cross set within ('+'). This form of 'registration' should be comprehensive enough to enable drawings to be separated then put back together later on.

### Transferring the position of a unit from on-stage to ground plan

Scenic units, once positioned in the model box, need locating exactly on the ground plan. The model box with a centre-line added in makes the task easier. Having the setting line drawn on the model floor is also important; most typically it is the downstage edge of the stage. Where there is no downstage edge (as in a studio theatre), establish one that is clearly and easily recognizable; perhaps the edge of seating for the first row or a point in line with an overhead architectural feature such as a beam, as was included on the plan.

1. In the model box make a fine dot with a pencil where the ends of a scenic wall make contact with the theatre floor. Label the dots 'A' and 'B'. Remove the wall if possible.
2. Transfer these points across to the centre-line, by using a small right-angle set-square with one side of the right-angle positioned along the centre-line. Slide the set-square up the centre-line until its projecting right-angle makes contact with dots 'A' then 'B'. The set square may need flipping over, if the dots are either side of centre. Label 'A' and 'B' along the centre-line for

easy identification. Before removing the set square, measure in scale the distance from the centre-line across to points 'A' and 'B' respectively. Write this measurement down.
3. Measure the distance up the centre-line, from the setting-line to 'A' and 'B' as marked on the centre-line. Write this down.
4. Plot these same measurements, in the same way, onto the ground plan.

### The testing nature of roughs

Rough drawings depict proportions (width, depth, height) for scenic units. The inclusion of dimensions for the overall measurements can be as simple as drawing each unit as an outline, on A4 or even A5 scraps of tracing paper, with lines which represent base width and height. These same measurements can then be easily plotted in the ground plan and theatre section. Where and how they register within the architecture on plan and section will be more defined than in the model box. In addition the draughtsman is concerned with sight-line (what the audience can see from their seat). Issues relating to sight-line also include how design serves to 'mask' the surrounding theatre from the view of the audience (*see* pages 97 and 99).

### The practical nature of roughs

The practical nature of rough drawing encourages working in a flexible manner. The benefit being developments in design remain sketchy, lateral thinking is easily applied, and a sense of economy avoids becoming too fixed on detail too early on in the process. Rough drawings encourage the designer to work with speed and fluidity, they support quick thinking and facilitate proposing alternative ideas within restricted time periods. Flexibility in 2D ends up serving flexibility in 3D. Rough drawings encourage open discussion round the table and collaborative development. For this reason the drawings are likely to offer up possibilities for direction rather than deliver one option.

### Serving to engage the viewer

Rough layout encourages working in a free

---

Rough drawings serve to:

* Clarify imagined concepts.
* Maintain a check on 3D development through referencing 2D venue technical constraints.
* Record development in 3D for all scenic elements, their placement and size formats, before becoming fixed within the model and final.
* Support a feasibility study to ascertain if a proposed project can proceed.
* Propose options enabling costing to embrace variables.
* Plan and propose how a budget will proportionally divide to embrace set design, making allowance for sums for costume design, props, lighting and sound.
* Propose key structural elements as desired, without burden of refinement of detail.
* Break down or clarify component parts as integral to an overall design.
* Propose breaking down scenic elements into appropriate proportioned units for transport or touring purposes.

manner as exploration in 3D can be easily tested in sketch form on the ground plan, in the belief it will add to the design credibility. A rough for the development of an object that is more property (prop) than set – as in a dresser unit, a counter unit, or piece of furniture – makes in itself a contribution to discussions. Such discussion may include director, production manager, and department members. The visualization of multi-views for an object, as a rough, shapes the object into a near reality. Drawings no matter how simplistic initiate feedback as ideas are communicated. Scaled prop drawings as roughs can be achieved without being on the board, as a scale rule and small set-square serve adequately enough, with tracing paper over graph paper assisting greatly. Proportion, dimensions and three-dimensional aspects of form are quickly laid out in 'three regular views' (top, front and right-side). A rough technical sketch for a prop can move production on and is often enough, as long as measurements are carefully plotted.

### Accompanying text

At this stage any notes are generally reminders for design, rather than for the build. The things that are not in the drawing may be added in as text. Accompanying text also aims to avoid likely misinterpretation. Notes may elaborate on a scenic element's function; reveal how component parts might inter-relate; or describe actor needs. Text is added to communicate that which is beyond what is in the drawing. It is added in note form, and flags up possible concerns or possibilities wished for.

### Anticipating problems

Rough drawings with their key measurements, their note-taking and sketchy appearance partially speak for themselves. They reveal a thought process reflecting an attitude to design and its use. The reading of roughs and the viewing of the sketch model box is usually reserved for the director, production manager and lighting designer. Lighting often becomes involved at this stage, as feedback in the form of professional opinion encourages constructive development. By their sketchy nature, roughs invite questions and initiate discussion. The production manager may wish to embrace design aims and objectives as early as the sketch model to anticipate on behalf of the creative team how it might fit within the limitations of venue, for running in repertory or for touring purposes, for example. Every idea proposed presents problems. Technical ideas need to complement creative ideas, in support of actually resolving them; therefore sketch model and roughs may have a larger viewing audience. Budgeting is crucial even at the earliest stages. Production management juggles concepts between all departments and budget allocation is often derived from the visual presentations. Even rough costing empowers design to sort priorities with regard to how allocation could be spread across departments.

### Positive feedback

Constructive criticism is therefore welcome from departments at any time. Design proposals rely on calculated responses. The experience of heads of department in making judgments about costing is critical. Feedback is welcome news, enabling design to plan and prioritize. Feedback from departments on materials and processes of construction helps shape design decision-making. Geographically there may be the obstacle of limited materials available, or limitations of workshop in facility or staffing. These limitations presented or discussed over a sketch model and rough plan and section, may steer design to aim for slightly different outcomes. Points of view at any presentation are perceived as having an effect on design. Feedback may help decide whether scenic art will create wood grain through paint effect or if real wood should or could be more effective.

When approvals for sketch model, rough plan and section are received design moves development onto the preliminary stage. Re-modelling demands re-calculating the relationships on plan and section, through to orthographic projects examining technical inter-relationships.

## PRELIMINARY DRAWINGS

The preliminary drawings that traditionally accompany a presentational white card model serve the making of that model. Drawings once completed to the level of detail required are photocopied, spray glued to card, cut and then assembled. This model is undoubtedly more technically accomplished. The design on plan and section provides calculated detailed plotting to meet practical constraints and creative demands.

The process of 'preliminary costing' is thorough enough to judge whether the design can be authorized or not. The comprehensive nature of preliminaries avoids leaving out elements that would later complicate the build financially. These drawings display accuracy and precision. Clarity of intention is evident in the package of drawings. Successful costing relies on as complete a proposal as is possible. Knowing a sash window will be practical, for example, assists in making things very clear. Whether design can afford it depends on all the other demands.

### Time management

The package of drawings assists production management in draughting a proposed schedule in respect of deadlines. Quality has its own timeline, and the clarifying of a deadline may actually prohibit elements being achievable. Practical experience offers reference for planning and scheduling.

## KEY THINGS TO REMEMBER

1. Avoid overworking a drawing, yet suggest all features. Once approved, details can be added in the Final Drawing Package.
2. Consider that which is deemed 'essential' for clarifying intention; avoid over-communicating at this stage.
3. Give dimension details only if you are convinced that the budget will permit the build and there is no alternative means (hire, stock, adapting something already in existence).
4. Add detail knowing the effect is discernable to the eye of the audience.
5. Comprehensive costing requires the inclusion of all elements in the package.
6. The model is explained through drawings, although the focus on aesthetic is typically within the model; technical issues not readily visible will be calculated by the production manager.
7. Key dimensions and intermediate measurements must be clearly delivered.
8. The white card delivers structural concerns.
9. The ground plan and theatre section clarify how the venue serves the design.
10. The requirements for technical expertise are defined in the relationship between design and venue.
11. Sight-lines projected within plan and section describe how design decisions came about, promoting the inter-relationships between acting area, theatre architecture, auditorium or audience seating.
12. Preliminary drawings make demands on crewing or show staffing. Each scenic element requires handling: in the get-in, once on-stage, and throughout the run. A cloth being flown makes demands on man-power, so too the cyclorama, flown hard scenic flats, legs and borders, all of which for a schedule with prescribed deadlines.
13. A suggestion of real space off-stage, as viewed through an on-stage door opening, will have real width and height dimension, determined by section sight-line projections. Once drawn and calculated on section, real measurements can be applied, and costing can be realistically calculated.
14. The inclusion of a props list, with visual references and accompanying preliminary drawings, supports appropriate budget allocation.
15. The drawings delivered as a package present problems to solve, and technical discussions can become involved. Production Management should ensure department heads leave with drawings to cost, and that a comprehensive understanding goes with them.
16. Clarity in a drawing means effective communication.
17. Consistency in a drawing – even in lettering and dimensioning – minimizes any miscalculation or misunderstanding.
18. Errors lead to unnecessary expense.

# 5    THE SCALE RULE

A scale rule is a drawing tool designed to calculate reduction or enlargement. It is used to plot prescribed measurements onto the page either pro-

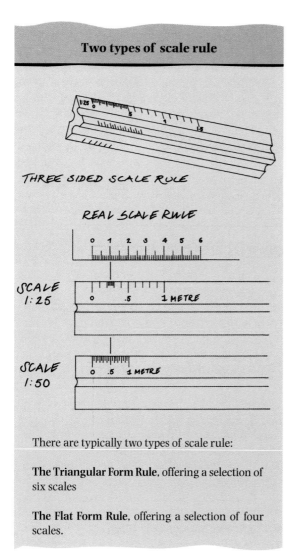

**Two types of scale rule**

THREE SIDED SCALE RULE

REAL SCALE RULE

SCALE
1:25

SCALE
1:50

There are typically two types of scale rule:

**The Triangular Form Rule**, offering a selection of six scales

**The Flat Form Rule**, offering a selection of four scales.

portionally larger or smaller than the original form. As long as the real measurements are known the process of scale conversion can take place. Establishing key dimensions for an object permits resolving proportional issues thereafter with the scale rule. Measurements taken from the real world inform design. The very nature of proportioning has been a study of architects and designers for thousands of years. The chair, for example, has gone through remarkable design processes and is still evolving to complement human requirements and designer whim. Most of the objects we employ are suited to human proportions. The height of a chair is figured in relation to the height of a table. Factors that influence design may derive from the study of ergonomics, where efficiency in the home, the workplace and world of business is what drives design decision-making.

Product design goes through a process of design, prototype and test products, with initial stages of design involving drawings. Being able to draw an object on the page very much depends on real dimensions and a scale that will enable it to 'fit the page'. The architect dealing with buildings and large-scale reality needs to reduce the original when fitting it to a page, whereas an engineer working on component parts may need to enlarge a small item to enable it to be viewed on the page.

When the original object to be drawn is much larger than the page, a scale needs to be chosen to re-proportion it, often taking into account the fact that there will be multiple views of the object on the same page. Knowing the original dimensions is essential, as is knowing what size of paper might be preferred. The scale rule offers a range of metric scales, yet once a paper size is chosen the possible range of scales is lessened. Ratios between paper size and scale become key options when plotting for printing from CAD (Computer Aided Design).

## UNDERSTANDING SCALE

### Scale 1:1

This is real size drawn as a replica or representation produced as 'true'. There is no reduction or enlargement. Details for production are often drawn 1:1. These drawings have no altered scale proportions. Drawings at 1:1 include: architectural mouldings, such as cornice, picture rail, dado rail, skirting board, or as door casing or framing of windows, and handrails.

The '1' which precedes the colon stands for one real centimetre. So it is necessary to draw a line 1cm long on the page. The number that follows the colon, in this case '1', is the measurement that is to be scaled to fit into the drawn centimetre-long line. Therefore 1cm drawn, will represent (or stand for) 1cm of reality. In other words, 'scale 1:1' means that 1cm (in reality, as indicated on a standard rule) represents 1cm.

### Scale 1:10

The '1' which precedes the colon stands for 1 real centimetre. So it is necessary to draw a line 1cm long on the page. The number which follows the colon, in this case 10cm, is the measurement which is to be scaled to fit into the drawn centimetre-long line. Therefore 1cm drawn, will represent (or stand for) 10cm of reality. In other words: 'scale 1:10' means that 1cm (in reality, as indicated on a standard rule) represents 10cm.

### Scale 1:20

One real centimetre drawn will represent (will stand for) 20cm. Therefore 20cm of reality will conveniently fit into 1cm on the drawing. In other words, 'scale 1:20' means that 1cm (in reality, as indicated on a standard rule) represents 20cm.

### Scale 1:25

One real centimetre drawn will represent (will stand for) 25cm. Therefore 25cm of reality will conveniently fit into 1cm on the drawing. In other words, 'scale 1:25' means that 1cm (in reality, as indicated on a standard rule) represents 25cm.

### Scale 1:50

1cm (in reality, as indicated on a standard rule) represents 50cm.

Further reductions include: 1:75, 1:100, 1:125 and 1:250.

### The preferred scale

Theatre work has preference for scale 1:25. This conveniently scales human figures down to a manageable and easily modelled size. Measurements found in reality, once reduced to 1:25, are easy to understand proportionally; a door opening, a chair and table, fireplace, unit detail are all easy to handle at such a reduction. With practice the scale becomes so familiar it is easy to critically assess proportions as right or wrong through making judgment by the eye only.

Note that 1:25 is not the same as 1:250. The scale rule with 1:250 or 1:2500 means something very different, as in the former 250cm (2.5 metres) is represented by the 1cm drawn. In the latter, 2500cm (25 metres) is represented by the 1cm drawn.

## DRAWING TO SCALE

Technical drawings are drawn on standard sizes of paper. It is typical for plan and section to be on A1, with orthographic projections of the scenic elements being on A1 or more usually A2.

Since the photocopying process can be expensive, with dye-line printing less so, the costs of many drawings (the package of drawings) can add up for production. It is good practice to work to a standard format as it is preferable to maintain a consistent size for the package of technical drawings, excluding the theatre plan and its section.

As the model box is most typically produced at scale 1:25, it is reasonable for technical drawings to complement this in scale. Drawings are used to build the model in almost all cases. However, there is every chance scales will vary within a package of drawings. The range of scales may include 1:25, 1:20, 1:10, 1:5 or full size at 1:1.

Drawings at 1:25 can be copied, spray glued onto card, cut out and assembled. Such drawings train the eye to respond to the same proportions in drawing as in model form. Larger-scale drawings can be reduced in size to 1:25 through photocopy reduction. Care must be taken to ensure accuracy.

---

### Experimenting with scale

Generally it is necessary to reduce large objects so they appear smaller on the page. Take from reality a measurement for, say, the height of a table. Observe that measurement as a vertical height on the A4 page, marking the base (floor level) and its height. Draw the table height at various scales and draw in the table top horizontal across part of the page. At scale 1:50 the table is impossibly small. At scale 1:25 it is twice the size and at scale 1:10 it is getting rather big for the page. Draw alongside the table a figure of average height in millimeters, standing with the feet on the same plane as the floor. Note the relationship between the scale of the figure and the same scale table.

---

## PLOTTING WITH THE SCALE RULE

Accuracy in draughting is essential for achieving a successful technical drawing. The accurate use of scale, in reading the unit measurements, determines correctness. Note the markings along any given scale appear small. Place the rule on the page, with the scale touching the paper. Make a dot for the '0' and another for a required length. Draw a line between these two points. Using the scale rule on the page to plot measurements can be done in this way, or through first having the line and applying dots to it for the unit length desired. The scale rule must not move when marking off such measurements. By marking the page with a small dot there is less chance of error, whereas a dash will have two ends to it.

Plant the dot on the page with a sharp pencil point, and with a hard lead such as 4H it may be necessary to rotate the point slightly, to leave a fine dot. To clarify that this is the measurement desired, double-check the reading on the rule before taking it away. To reduce the likelihood of error, position your eye above the rule to read it clearly, making sure there is no shadow cast where the dots are to be positioned. Place the pencil perpendicular to the page. To avoid accumulative error, when plotting units along a line, avoid moving the scale rule to establish each consecutive unit. Instead, to achieve 150mm increments along a line, for example, plot the first 150mm, calculate the sum of two (300mm), then calculate the sum of three (450mm) until the length is reached. Accumulative sums for different unit measurements will require good mental maths, a calculator, or long-hand sums on a scrap of paper. Avoid moving the scale rule along as there is every likelihood the total sum will not be a sum of all unit

---

### Figurative exercise

Draw a vertical line off a horizontal, and measure up from the base line a height measurement for yourself on A4 paper. This is for a figure drawing in a standing position, facing forward and at scale 1:20. Complete the drawing of yourself with arms at the side.

Once complete, draw another vertical line off the base horizontal, to the side of the previous drawing, measure off your height at scale 1:25. Complete the figure drawing. Finally, draw to the side of the previous two, another standing figure of the same height at scale 1:50.

Note the figure at scale 1:50 is complex and without much detail, unless it was drawn with a very sharp hard lead with careful artistic observation. Scale 1:20 in contrast encourages more detailing of features and such accuracy in detailing is not so very difficult to achieve, or becomes easier with practice. Through practice the designer and draughtsman achieve excellent detailed results at scale 1:25. Drawing such a figure at 1:25 helps enormously when modelling in wire and wax (or other medium) scale figures for the model box.

---

parts. The demand on mental maths is good daily exercise for the brain; it sharpens the mind.

## ADVICE

1. Avoid placing needle point of compass and dividers on to the plastic scale rule as the unit markings are susceptible to damage and scratching.

2. Where a measurement is to be repeated several times over across a page, a ticket stub marked with unit measure along one edge avoids error.

3. Avoid using the scale rule with it lying flat along the T-square arm; instead, use it independently.

4. Use a very sharp pencil point when plotting unit measurements, as the scale increments or half-centimetres are difficult to get accurate.

5. Note a technical drawing is not to be scaled from, as all dimensions on a drawing will clearly define the requirements for the build. It is unusual for a member of construction to measure from the drawing itself. Therefore a technical drawing may have inaccuracies in the drawing, yet it will not have any in the dimensioning as printed by the draughtsman.

6. Scale drawings also serve the properties department, as many objects are built rather than sourced.

7. Adding a scale figure, for an average height person, alongside the object being drawn supports understanding the relative proportions to human form. At times, such a comparison can make something unclear clear, as design often plays with distortion, heightening reality, and blowing things somewhat out of proportion.

8. The carpenter's expanding tape measure, at 3m long, is an ideal tool for making sure real measurements are as intended. Observing the real world offers great reference when considering proportions. And with such observation comes knowledge, useful in the long run for decision-making based on relationships to experience and study of life.

9. When proportioning dimensions for items of furniture, consider what effect these may have on real human proportions, as not all tables are of a suitable height for certain tasks, nor does the average person find low-seated sofas easy to get out of. How actors and their characters interact with such proportion should be of some interest to the draughtsman.

10. Construction does not require the finest of millimetre measurements in technical drawings, except where the material thickness or measurements matches the drawing. Calculating at scale tends to eliminate the chance of using finely defined millimetre increments. As a rule, discuss measurements with construction before finalizing, to avoid odd millimetre measurements that do not pertain to material sizes. Ask whether a table wouldn't be just as successful at 710mm or 720mm, as one drawn at 713mm or even 715mm. How engineered a measurement becomes is left to 'construction drawings' and it may be better to round to the nearest 5mm if at all possible.

11. Scale drawings at 1:25 are acceptable and are typical 'for construction' as long as details are clear. Where it is necessary to enlarge a detail in another scale within the same drawing, do so at a scale increase which just makes it articulate.

12. When plotting a circle it is more accurate to measure off the diameter on the page. Then divide the distance in half, to achieve radius, then compass in the circle.

# 6 GEOMETRY AND TECHNICAL DRAWING EXERCISES

## STANDARD PAPER FORMATS

The relationship between one paper size and its immediate reduced size is essentially the same as the first sheet folded. So A0 folded in half produces size A1, A1 folded in half produces A2, A2 folded in half produces A3, A3 folded in half produces A4, and so on.

A0 = 1189 × 841mm
A1 = 841 × 594mm
A2 = 594 × 420mm
A3 = 420 × 297mm
A4 = 297 × 210mm

## T-SQUARE AND SET SQUARE

The T-square comprises the head and the arm. Its head is positioned on the left-hand side of the drawing board for right-handed users and on the right side for those who are left-handed.

The T-square and set square can be used together on the drawing board to establish 90 degrees off the horizontal, being sure that they are married and that the T-square arm is secure against the board's side. To draw lines at angles, use the set squares independently to produce 30, 60 and 45 degree angles and in combination to achieve 15 and 75 degrees.

A 30/60 degree set square can be used with a T-square to produce a line 30 degrees off the horizontal or 60 degrees off the horizontal. A 45 degree set square can be used with the T-square to establish 45 degrees off the horizontal. Set squares are used in combination to create 15 and 75 degree angles. To achieve a 15 degree angle, place

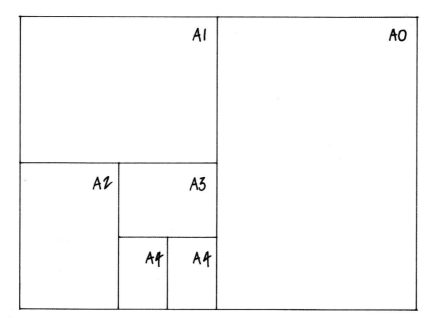

*Standard paper formats and the relationship between them.*

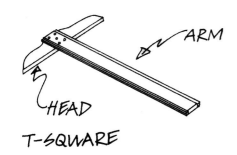

*The T-square.*

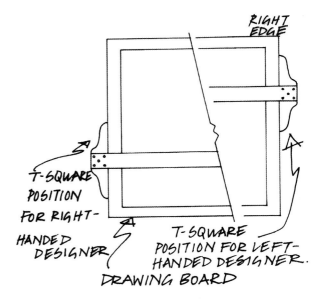

ABOVE: *The T-square positioned on the drawing board.*

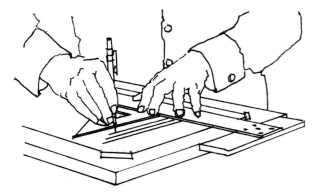

LEFT: *Combining the set square and T-square on the drawing board.*

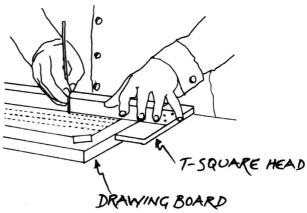

RIGHT: *Constructing horizontal lines using the T-square.*

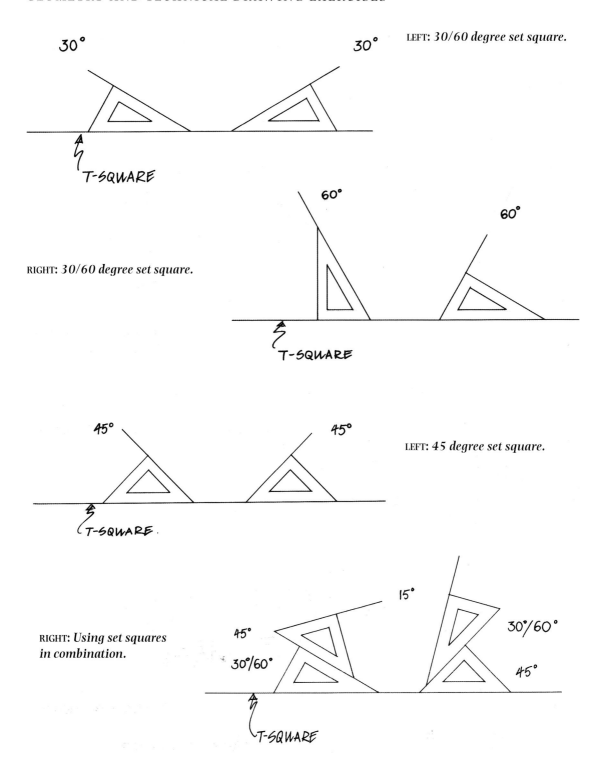

30°    30°

**LEFT:** *30/60 degree set square.*

T-SQUARE

60°    60°

**RIGHT:** *30/60 degree set square.*

T-SQUARE

45°    45°

**LEFT:** *45 degree set square.*

T-SQUARE.

**RIGHT:** *Using set squares in combination.*

15°

45°    30°/60°

30°/60°    45°

T-SQUARE

*Using the T-Square with the 30/60 degree set square triangle, the 45 degree set square, and combining the two.*

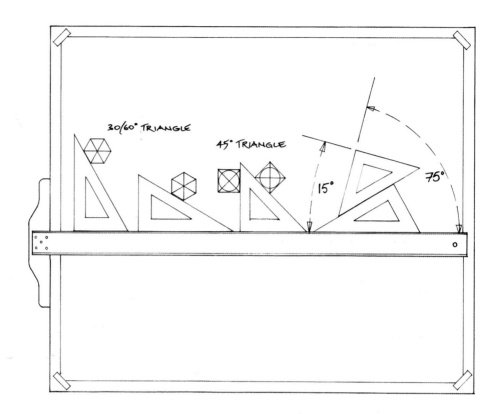

the 45 degree set square on the T-square, then slide in the 30 degree set square beneath it, literally subtracting 30 from 45, giving 15 degrees. To achieve a 75 degree angle, place the 45 degree set square on the T square, place on top of it the 30 degree angle, literally adding 30 to 45, giving 75 degrees.

## CONSTRUCTING QUADRILATERALS

In a square all angles are equal at 90 degrees. Diagonals drawn from the corners cross at the centre intersecting at 90 degree angles. To construct a square with T-square and 45 degree set square, first draw the base AB of the required square. Erect perpendiculars at A and B, then draw a line at 45 degrees from B to cut the perpendicular from A to establish D. From D draw a line parallel to AB cutting the perpendicular from B to establish C.

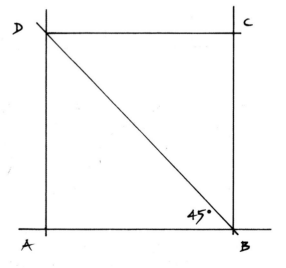

*Constructing a square with a T-square and set square.*

51

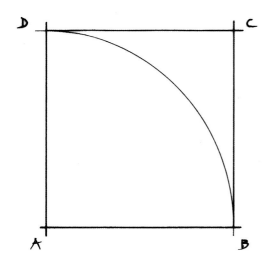

ABOVE: *Constructing a square with a compass.*

RIGHT: *A rectangle.*

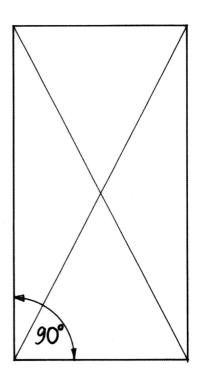

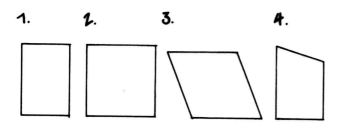

*Quadrilaterals and polygons.*

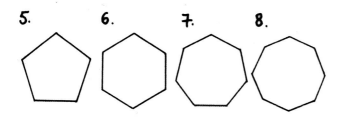

To construct a square using a compass, draw the base of AB of the required square. Erect the perpendiculars at A and B, then placing the compass on A, establish AB and draw a quarter arc to intersect the perpendicular at D. In order to confirm correct intersections, place the compass on B, using the established length AB, plot a quarter arc to intersect the perpendicular at C (not shown).

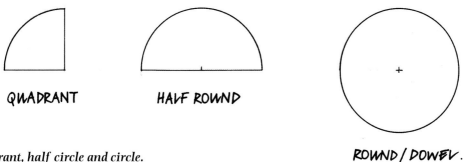

*A quadrant, half circle and circle.*

A rectangle is a four-sided figure with equal opposite sides and its angles all right angles. Opposite sides and all angles being equal; diagonals from the corners are equal yet where they intersect the angles are not 90 degrees.

A quadrilateral form is bound by four straight lines; when opposite sides are parallel it is a parallelogram. A quadrilateral can be a:

1. Rectangle: all angles are at right angles.
2. Square: if the sides are equal.
3. Rhombus: if all sides are equal yet angles are not right angles.
4. Trapezium: only two of the sides are parallel.

**Polygons**

Polygons are plane figures consisting of more than four sides. When sides are equal they are called regular polygons. Polygons include:

5. Pentagon: five sides
6. Hexagon: six sides
7. Heptagon: seven sides
8. Octagon: eight sides.

## QUADRANTS AND CIRCLES

The quadrant is a segment of a circle with a right angle at centre of the curve. The half circle has the radius of the circle forming the diameter line. The circle has a centre point. Radials can be drawn from the right angle point of a quadrant at degrees of 15, 30, 45, 60, 75 and 90 to form a quarter circle. This is established through using 45 degree and 30/60 degree set squares and a T-square.

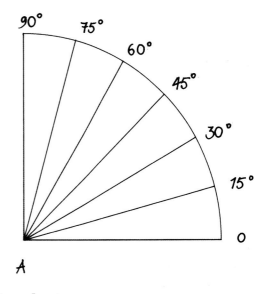

*A quadrant.*

## ANGLES

An acute angle is less than a 90 degree angle. An obtuse angle is greater than 90 degrees. It must be less than 180 degrees.

The supplement of an angle is the remaining degrees which when added equals 180 degrees. ABC (overleaf) is 110 degrees. Therefore the supplement to this angle is 70 degrees. The complement of an angle is the remaining degrees which when added together form 90 degrees. 70 degrees and 20 degrees = 90 degrees.

53

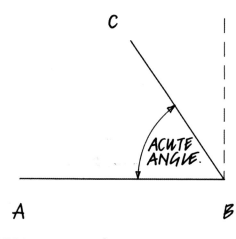

*ABC is an acute angle.*

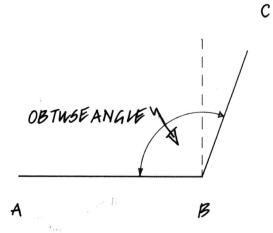

*ABC is an obtuse angle.*

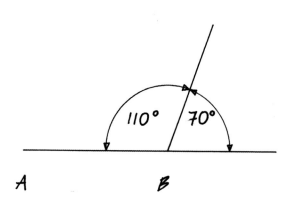

*The supplement of an angle.*

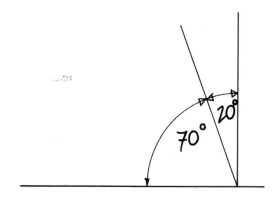

*The complement of an angle.*

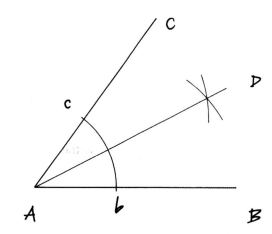

*Bisecting an angle.*

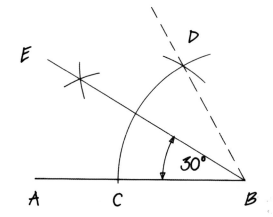

*Constructing a 30 degree angle.*

To bisect a given angle:

1. Draw the required angle ABC.
2. With A as compass centre, draw an arc intersecting AC and AB.
3. From the points of intersection draw two equal distant arcs beyond.
4. Join A with a line to the intersecting arcs.

To construct a 30 degree angle:

1. Draw a line AB.
2. With B as centre, draw an arc of any size through line AB.
3. With compass on C, and the same compass radius as previous cut an arc through to form intersection D.
4. Join D to B, and D to C and an equilateral 60 degree triangle is formed (not shown).
5. With compass point on C and then on D, draw arcs beyond to intersect.
6. Join by a line to the point of intersection to B.
7. ABE is a 30 degree angle.

## BISECTING LINES

To bisect any given straight line:

1. Draw a line AB, set the compass to a distance greater than half of AB.
2. With compass point on A, draw an arc above and below the line AB.
3. With the same compass setting, use B as a centre to scribe arcs to cut the first arcs at C and D.
4. With straight edge and pencil, join C and D. This line cuts AB at O making AO = OB, a true 90 degree angle. A right angle is made up of a line connecting to another line, with the adjacent angles formed being equal to one another. AOC and AOD are equal, each consisting of a 90 degree angle.

To establish a perpendicular to a given point C along line AB (*see* page 56).

1. With compass point on C, draw an arc as half circle intersecting with AB.

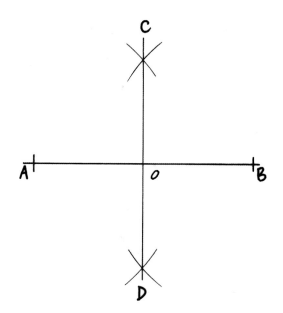

*Bisecting straight lines.*

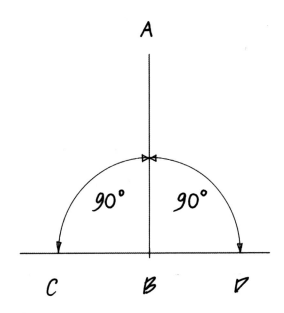

*A right angle.*

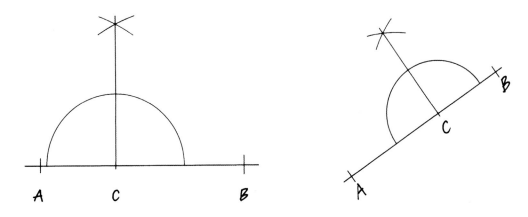

*Establishing a perpendicular.*

BELOW: *Dividing a line into equal parts.*

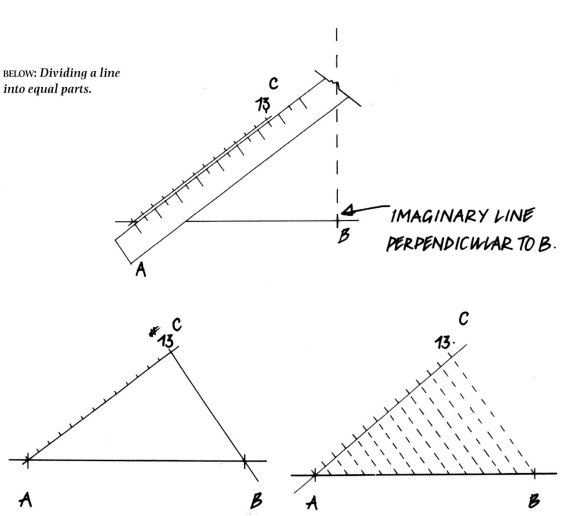

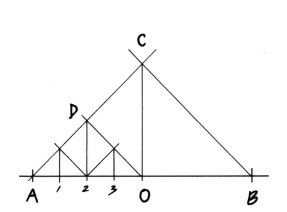

*Dividing a line into equal parts.*

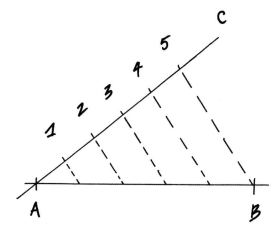

*Bisecting straight lines.*

2. With compass point on these two points of intersection draw arcs of equal distance above.
3. At the point of intersection draw a line through to C.

To divide any given straight line into equal parts:

1. Establish a line AB.
2. Plot a 45 degree angle from A and B to intersect at point C.
3. From point of intersection draw a line vertically to intersect with AB as a perpendicular to line AB, dividing AB in half.
4. Plot a 45 degree angle from O as centre, intersecting line AC to create point D.
5. Continue to repeat the process as described above to divide AO into further parts.

To divide a straight line into five equal parts:

1. Make AB the given line and draw AC at any reasonable acute angle from A.
2. On AC, mark off the required number of equal spaces by the scale rule, compass or dividers.
3. Join 5 to B using the adjustable set square, making sure the set square is securely married to the T-square.
4. Now slide the set square along the arm of the

T-square, projecting 4, 3, 2 and 1 to line AB, thus keeping all lines parallel to 5B. AB is now divided into 5 equal units.

If you do not have an adjustable set square, use the following method:

1. Join 5 to B.
2. Place a set square on the page along line 5B and a straight edge rule along the base of the set square.
3. Now slide the set square along the rule and join points 4, 3, 2 and 1 to line AB, thus keeping them parallel to 5B.

This method can be used to divide a line into any number of equal parts, marking off the required number of equal spaces along the acute angle and following the process as detailed. Line AB is thus divided into the required number of equal parts. When plotting an acute angle, the final number of units should not exceed an imaginary line set off B, as perpendicular to AB.

## CONSTRUCTING GEOMETRICAL SHAPES WITHIN CIRCLES

To construct a square with one side AB at a 45 degree angle:

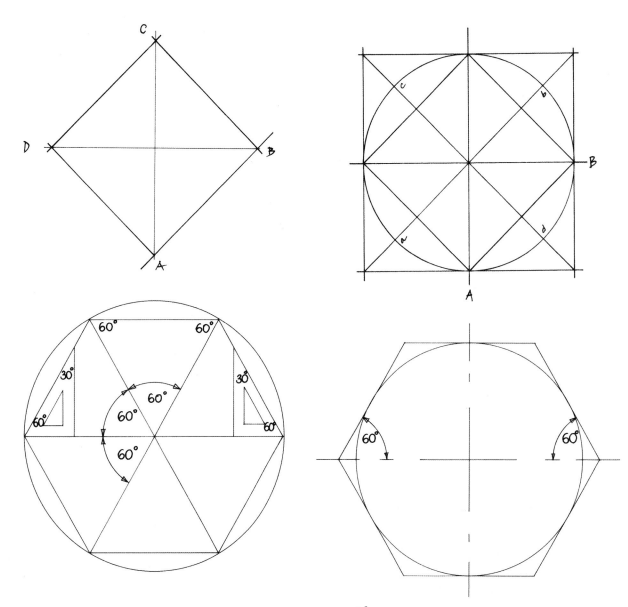

1. Plot AB of the required square at a 45 degree angle.
2. Erect perpendicular lines at A and B, these are also at 45 degrees.
3. Plot a horizontal line from B to intersect with the perpendicular to A to establish D at the point of intersection.
4. Draw a 45 degree angle at point D to intersect with the perpendicular off B to establish point C.

ABOVE: *A hexagon.*

TOP LEFT: *Constructing a basic square.*

TOP RIGHT: *Constructing a square within a circle and outside a square.*

BOTTOM LEFT: *A hexagon inside a circle.*

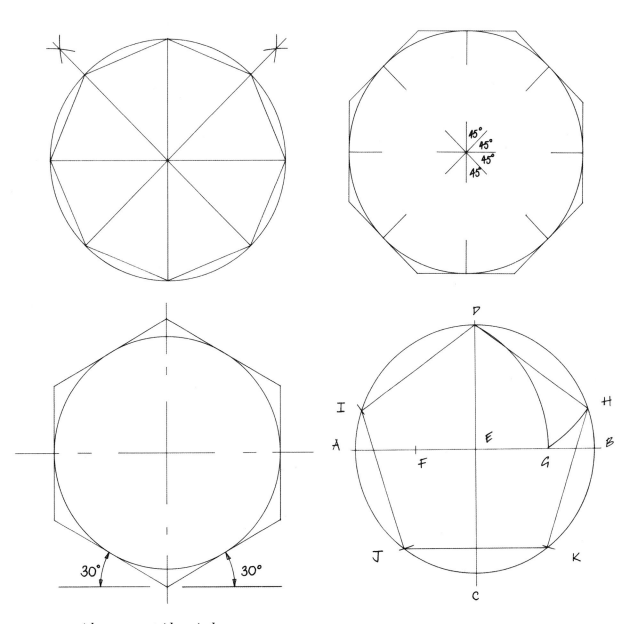

ABOVE: *A hexagon outside a circle.*

TOP, LEFT AND RIGHT: *Drawing an octagon inside and outside a circle.*

BOTTOM RIGHT: *Drawing a regular pentagon.*

To construct a square within a circle:

1. Draw a circle of the required diameter marking its centre.
2. Plot the desired angle for one side of the square using the adjustable set square, intersecting with the circle centre as a-b.
3. Produce the right angle to a-b at circle centre as c-d.

59

4. Bisect angle a-d to produce an angled line set 45 degrees intersecting circle centre to establish A.
5. Set the adjustable to angle a-b; extend point A on the circumference to produce B.
6. From A and B, at 90 degrees, draw lines connecting with the circumference.
7. Join the remaining marks on circumference to form a square.

To draw a hexagon, draw a circle of a determined diameter. Draw the horizontal axis to cross at centre. Off the horizontal axis draw in 60 degree angles to intersect with the circumference. At these points of intersection draw in the top and base sides as parallel lines to the circle's horizontal axis, both intersecting with the circumference. Then join all points (*see* page 58).

To draw a hexagon outside a circle, draw in 30 degree angles set off from the horizontal axis intersecting with the circumference. Draw in left and right sides as parallel lines to the central vertical axis, both intersecting with the circumference (*see* page 59).

To construct an octagon inside the circumference of a circle (*see* page 59):

1. Establish a circle of the required diameter.
2. Add in horizontal and vertical axes.
3. Plot diagonals through bisecting the 90 degree angles.
4. Draw in the 45 degree radials.
5. Join the intersecting points to one another, along the circumference of the circle.

An octagon can be constructed outside a circle using tangents to intersect and form the points of the octagon (*see* page 59):

1. Establish a circle of the required diameter.
2. Add the vertical and horizontal axes. Bisect the 90 degree angles to achieve 45 degree radials.
3. Tangents at 90 degrees off the radial make contact with the circumference.
4. The tangents intersect to form the points of the octagon.

To draw a regular pentagon with a given distance from the centre to each point.

1. Draw the vertical and horizontal axes AB, CD intersecting at E and draw a circle.
2. Bisect AE to find F.
3. With compass on F and radius FD draw an arc that cuts AB at G.
4. With compass on D and radius DG, draw an arc locating H on the circle, then pivot across to the opposite side to establish I.
5. With compass on H and then I, and radius DH locate J and K.
6. Connect with straight lines D-H, H-K, K-J, J-I, I-D.

## THE CIRCLE

Terms used relating to circles include the following:

* Circumference: a curved line equal distant from the point known as the centre that forms a circle.
* Diameter: a straight line drawn through the centre of the circle and ending with its points on the circumference.

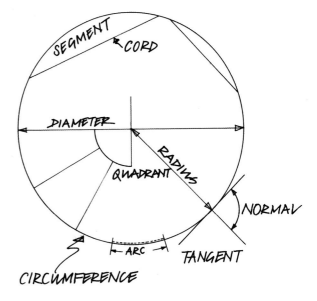

*The circle.*

60

* Radius: a straight line drawn from the centre point out to the circumference line.
* Radial: a line in the direction of the radius.
* Quadrant: a quarter circle.
* Arc: a part of the circumference.
* Segment: a part of a circle between a chord and its arc.
* Chord: a straight line drawn through a circle, having shorter length than the diameter.
* Normal: any line drawn from the centre point that is a radial to the centre of that circle.
* Tangent: a straight line drawn that touches the circumference and is at a right angle to a normal at that point. Draw first the radial and from that the right angle.

**Tangency points**

To locate tangency points for a right angle with a measured radius:

1. Plot a right angle and draw in a radius arc to establish tangency points.
2. Draw in perpendiculars to these points.
3. Where they intersect, use this as centre for arc. The same compass radius is applied as before.

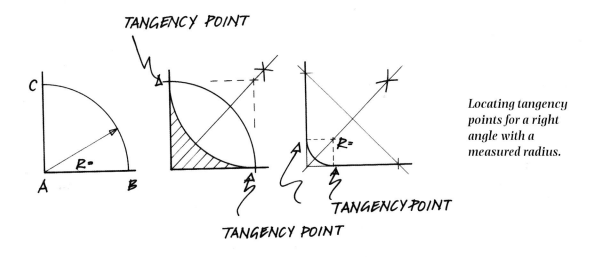

*Locating tangency points for a right angle with a measured radius.*

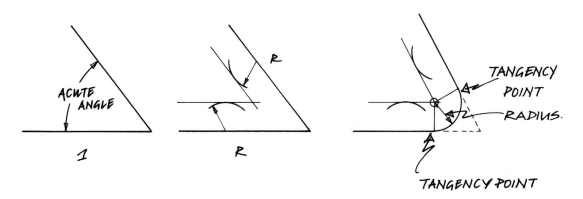

*Locating tangency points for an acute angle less than 90 degrees, using a compass to set off measured increments.*

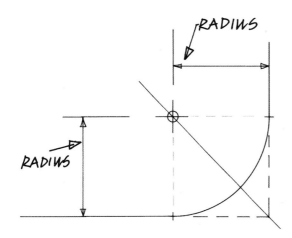

*Junction of a quadrant joining straight lines with radius as measured; used to form a square within which lines join and continue.*

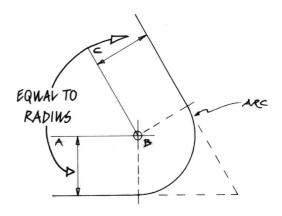

*How to form an arc joining an angle of less than 90 degrees.*

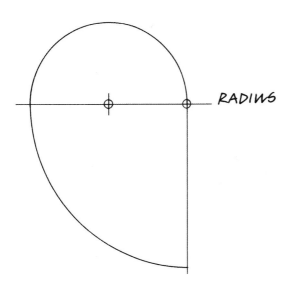

*Combination of arcs and arcs joining straight lines.*

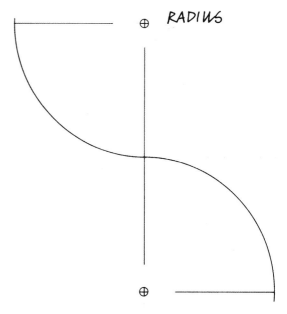

For locating tangency points for an acute angle (i.e. one less than 90 degrees), use a compass to set off measured increments. To form an arc joining an angle of less than 90 degrees:

1. From the straight angled lines forming ABC, measure the radius distance required away from each side at 90 degrees to each.

2. Draw parallel lines through these points.
3. The point of their intersection is the radius for the required arc.

A combination of arcs and of arcs joining straight lines can be achieved through establishing related centre points. Variations can be produced forming period tracery work.

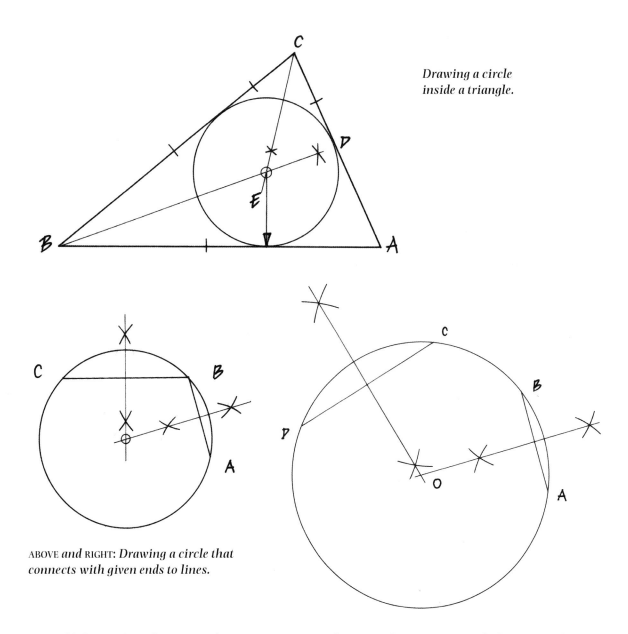

*Drawing a circle inside a triangle.*

ABOVE *and* RIGHT: *Drawing a circle that connects with given ends to lines.*

To establish a circle within a triangle:

1. Bisect ABC to establish BD.
2. Bisect ACB to establish CE.
3. At the point of intersection of BD and CE mark as centre.
4. Place compass point on centre, measure down to AB, perpendicular to AB, and draw the circle touching the sides of the triangle.

To draw a circle connecting with the given ends to lines, with lines intersecting to form an angle ABC:

1. Bisect AB to achieve the perpendicular to AB at its centre.
2. Then bisect BC.
3. The point of intersection of the bisectors is the centre of a circle that connects with points ABC.

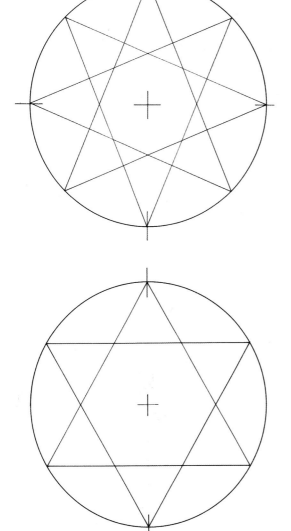

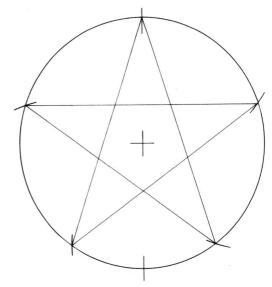

ABOVE: *A five-pointed star.*

TOP LEFT: *An eight-pointed star.*

BOTTOM LEFT: *A six-pointed star.*

## Stars

To draw an eight-pointed star:

1. Draw a circle of the required diameter.
2. Establish vertical and horizontal axes, marking the points of intersection with the circle circumference only.
3. Bisect the 90 degree radials, adding in the points of intersection connecting with circumference.
4. Join the points along the circumference all at 45 degrees.

To draw a five pointed star:

1. Draw a circle of the required diameter.
2. Mark off five equal points around the circle's circumference, using a compass or divider to achieve estimating the five segment arcs.
3. Join the points along the circumference.

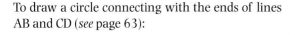

To draw a circle connecting with the ends of lines AB and CD (*see* page 63):

1. Bisect AB to find its centre and draw the perpendicular 90 degree angle.
2. Bisect CD and draw its perpendicular.
3. The point of intersection of the bisectors is the centre of a circle, which connects to each end point AB and CD.

To draw a six-pointed star:

1. Establish a circle of the required diameter.
2. Draw a vertical axis crossing the circle's circumference at two points.
3. Draw in 60 degree lines connecting to these points and project these through the circumference of the circle.
4. Join up each equilateral triangle.

To find the length of an arc:

1. Establish a circle of the required diameter.
2. Establish points C and D on the circumference defining the arc.
3. Establish AB as the horizontal axis.
4. Draw 60 degree angled lines from A and B, downward to intersect forming the vertical axis EF.
5. Project lines from E through C and D to intersect with a tangent to EF, now called ab (straightened circumference line).
6. To determine the circumference length for arc CD, measure cd along ab.

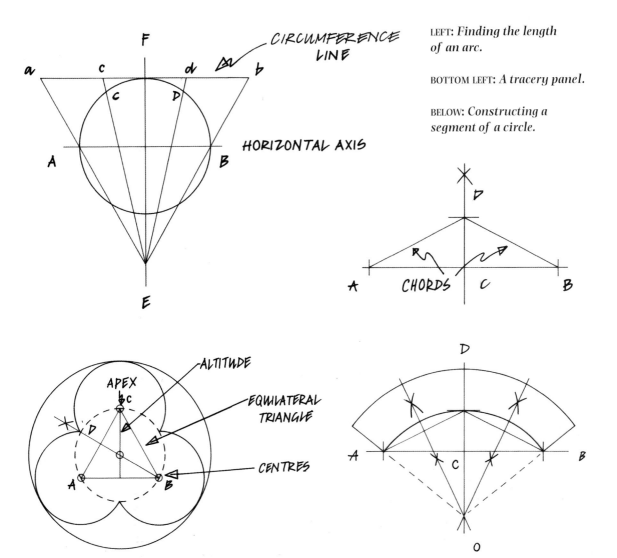

LEFT: *Finding the length of an arc.*

BOTTOM LEFT: *A tracery panel.*

BELOW: *Constructing a segment of a circle.*

To construct a segment of a circle that passes through a segmental arc (*see* page 65):

1. Establish AB as the span.
2. With CD as the altitude (height). Bisect AD, then BD, above and below to establish lines which intersect at O.
3. The normals to the tangent are the segment joins, which are radials from O.

To construct a tracery panel (*see* page 65):

1. Establish an equilateral triangle, with 60 degree angles.

2. Draw in the altitude line from apex.
3. Bisect ABC to establish its centre.
4. With compass on centre, draw a circle connecting the points of the equilateral.
5. With compass on C and a measured distance of CD as radius draw a part circle that touches the inner circle at two points.
6. With compass point on B and A draw the same size radius part circles.

## TRIANGLES

The isosceles triangle has two sides of equal length, with their two base angles equal. An equi-

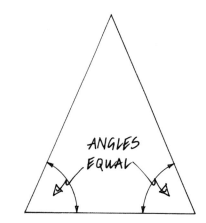

*An isosceles triangle.*

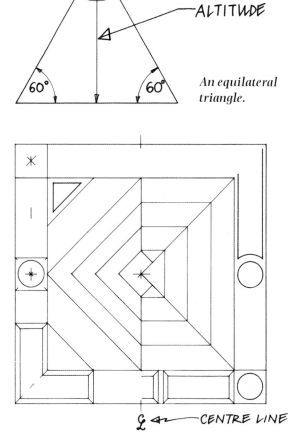

*An equilateral triangle.*

*Subdivision of a square.*

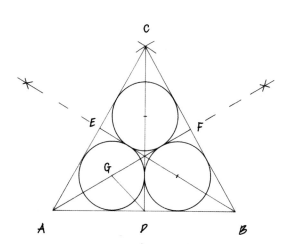

*Inscribed circles within an equilateral triangle.*

lateral triangle has three sides equal and three angles equal, each being 60 degrees. A perpendicular line drawn from the vertex to the base of the triangle is termed the altitude.

To inscribe circles within an equilateral triangle:

1. Establish an equilateral triangle.
2. Bisect sides BAC, ABC and ACB to achieve points D, E and F.
3. Bisect ADC to arrive at G.
4. Using compass or dividers measure off AG and

plot this measurement from B and then from C to establish the centre of the remaining two circles.

A square can be subdivided using diagonals, forming 90 degree angles, which can then be further subdivided.

## PROPORTIONAL DIVISIONS

To divide a distance of any width into an equal number of units, using a rule:

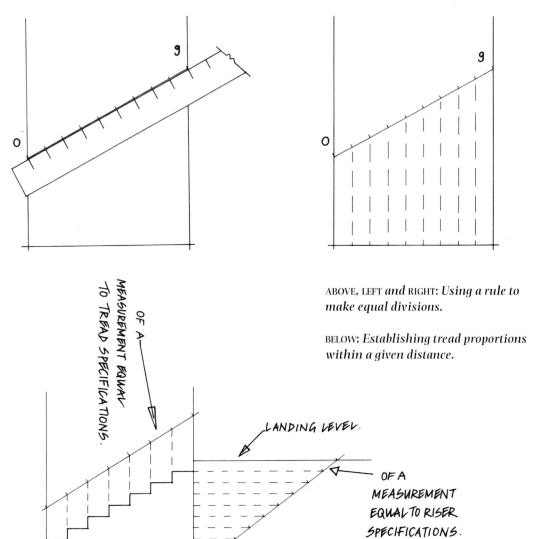

ABOVE, LEFT *and* RIGHT: *Using a rule to make equal divisions.*

BELOW: *Establishing tread proportions within a given distance.*

1. With two parallel lines being the distance to be divided, place a rule diagonally across so that the zero end and its required division connect with the parallel lines.

2. Mark off the divisions as shown.

3. Draw a series of parallel lines as plotted through the divisions.

To establish step tread proportions within a given distance, the same technique applies. The same is

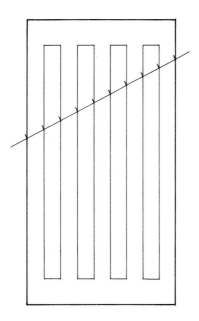

An example of a given distance to be divided into equal parts for establishing regular period panelling.

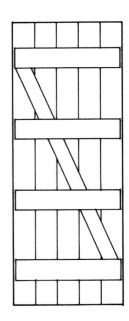

A two stage approach for dividing planking into equal parts on a ledge or batten door.

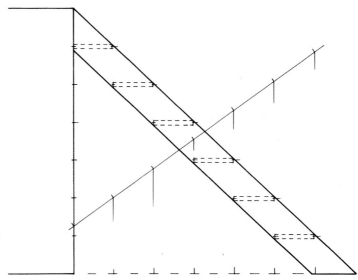

An example of establishing tread proportions of equal units between a given distance for an open stringer staircase.

RIGHT: *An example of establishing tread and riser proportions between two given distances.*

BOTTOM: *Top view establishes the tread depth proportion between a given distance. Elevation view establishes the riser proportion between a given distance.*

BELOW: *Staircase detail depicting pitch, tread (going) dimension and riser (height).*

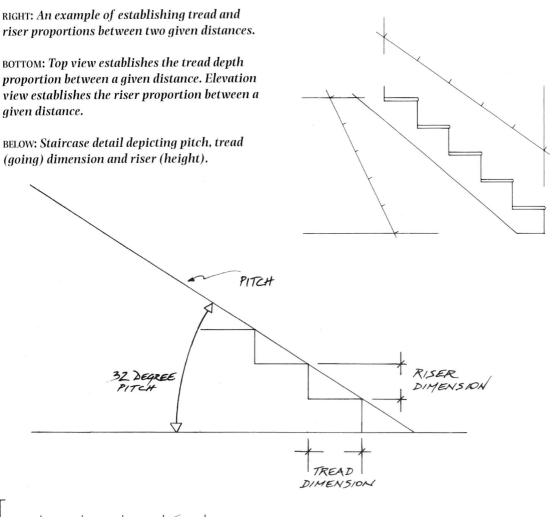

PITCH

32 DEGREE PITCH

RISER DIMENSION

TREAD DIMENSION

ELEVATION.

true for establishing riser proportions between a given distance, from the ground to a landing level, as is illustrated.

## SURFACE DEVELOPMENT

The plan view of a cylinder overleaf shows a quadrant section divided into 15 degree increments as shown in the cone surface development. The elevation view shows the true height and width of the cylinder. The surface development of the cylinder is achieved through marking off twenty-four equal distance arc measurements from the plan onto the development elevation. Alternatively, diameter × 3.141.

69

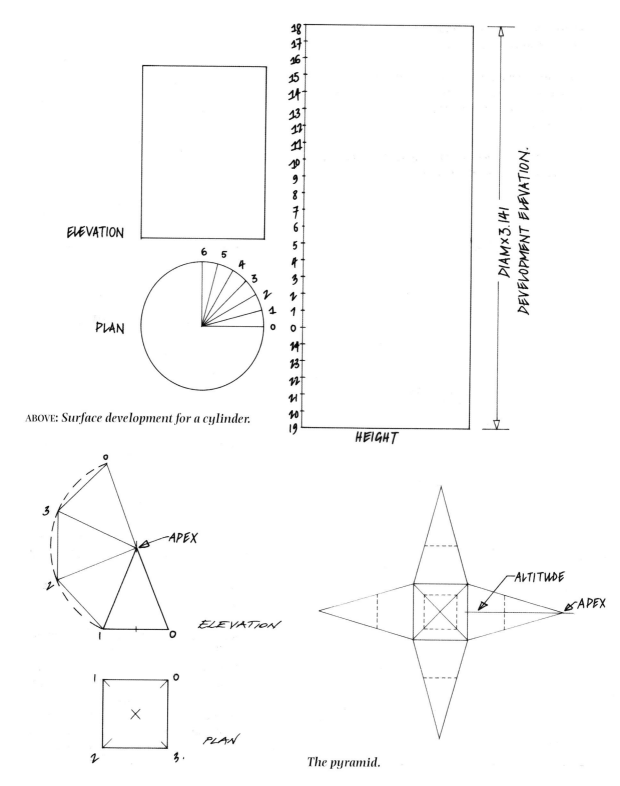

ELEVATION

PLAN

18
17
16
15
14
13
12
11
10
9
8
7
6
5
4
3
2
1
0
14
13
12
11
10
19

DIAM x 3.141
DEVELOPMENT ELEVATION.

HEIGHT

ABOVE: *Surface development for a cylinder.*

0

3

APEX

2

1    0

ELEVATION

1    0

2    3.

PLAN

ALTITUDE

APEX

*The pyramid.*

*Surface development for an octagon.*

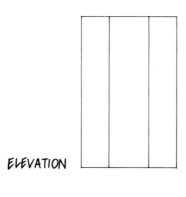

ELEVATION

PLAN

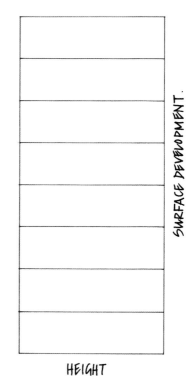

SURFACE DEVELOPMENT.

HEIGHT

BELOW: *Surface development for a cone.*

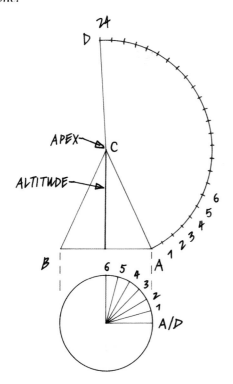

The plan view of an octagon shows proportioning with the elevation above showing true height and width:

1. Measure base side from plan.
2. Transfer to a vertical off the height line within the surface development drawing.
3. Repeat plotting for eight parts to complete the surface development of the column.

The surface area for the pyramid is calculated with each side laid out flat as a plane. The base measurement for one side of the pyramid is taken from plan, and marked off using dividers or a compass along an arc drawn with its centre point as the pyramid apex. Surface planes for each side lie flat, attached to the pyramid base on plan. Each apex is measured up the altitude line from base on each side.

On plan the dash lines indicate where the pyramid will break to become two parts. Therefore plan indicates the true size for the pyramid square base as well the size of the cut plane which become the base plane for the top section.

The plan view of the cone shows the diameter as would occupy space if the cone were sat on the floor (see page 71).

1. Draw within one quadrant of the cone's circumference, 15 degree radials using 45 degree and 30/60 degree set squares in combination.

The elevation is set above plan and shows the true height and width of the cone if seen from the front.

1. On the altitude point C for the apex; place the point of the compass on the apex and draw an arc from A, part way to B.
2. On plan using a small compass or dividers,

measure off one 15 degree increment equal to any 15 degree unit along the circumference.
3. On the elevation mark off this same measurement twenty-four times from point A, as shown.
4. As a quadrant has six segments, there are a total of twenty-four increments within the circumference of the cone. Join number 24 to the apex of the cone. The angle ACD, along with the arc with twenty-four increments, defines the surface area.

To establish the ellipse for a cone:

1. Draw the elevation of a cone, with line for section drawn cutting through as AB.
2. Project the extremities vertically downward to the base horizontal bb.
3. Bisect this distance and draw the semi-circle.

*Orthographic Projection: the cone with its component units – circle, ellipse, parabola and hyperbola. Each is indicated in the elevation view and in freehand.*

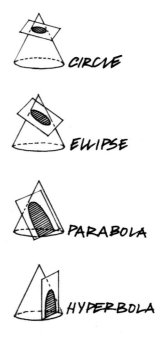

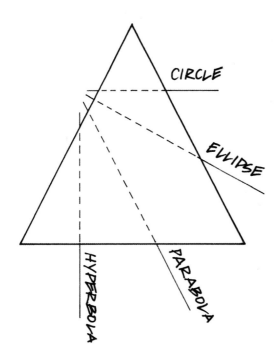

*The ellipse within a cone.*

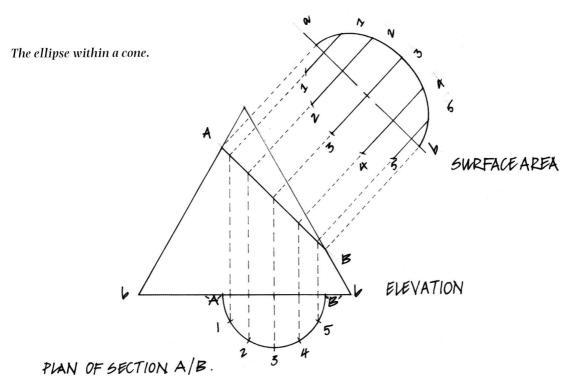

SURFACE AREA

ELEVATION

PLAN OF SECTION A/B.

4. Divide the semi-circle into 6 parts each at 15 degrees, using the 45 and 30/60 degrees set squares. Label them A, 1, 2, 3, 4, 5, B, and then project these points upwards to AB on the cut cone.
5. Project these ordinates at a right angle across the ellipse surface area.
6. Establish a centre line parallel to the cut section AB.
7. Each ordinate left of centre ab and right of centre ab needs marking off with the corresponding measurement found in the semi-circle, which is a plan of section A/B.
8. Draw the outline of the ellipse through these points.

Alternatively, the drawing (to the right) shows the plan of section with an increased number of degree increments on the circumference to achieve a more accurate section view when ordinates are transferred.

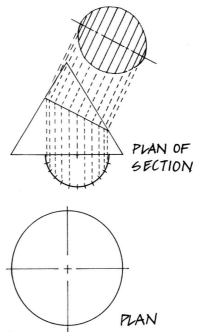

PLAN OF SECTION

PLAN

*Ellipse development with cone.*

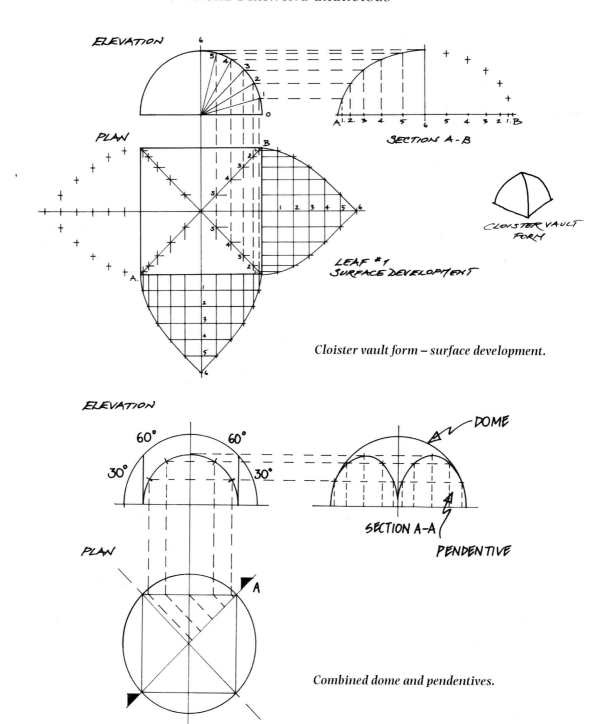

ELEVATION

SECTION A-B

PLAN

CLOISTER VAULT FORM

LEAF #1
SURFACE DEVELOPMENT

*Cloister vault form – surface development.*

ELEVATION

60°    60°

30°    30°

DOME

SECTION A-A

PENDENTIVE

PLAN

A

*Combined dome and pendentives.*

The surface development drawing for the cloister vault form shows three views: plan, elevation, section:

1. Establish plan as square, with diagonals to verify accuracy as well as to aid surface development.
2. Project dimension details above to elevation with diagonal intersection producing the centre for the half circle.
3. In the elevation, mark off within the right quadrant, the 15 degree increments using 45 degree and 30/60 degree set squares; number all increments.
4. Project downwards from the elevation to the plan, the degree increments to intersect with both diagonals.
5. Transfer horizontally all increments along the diagonal to the other diagonal; number all increments as shown.
6. On plan, extend the horizontal axis beyond the plan to begin development for Leaf 1.
7. With a small compass measure one 15 degree increment along the circumference in elevation.
8. On plan, step off 6 such increments along the extended horizontal axis, starting from the edge of the square. Number all increments as shown.
9. Project all numbers along the horizontal vertically to intersect with the same number along the diagonal projected horizontally. The points of intersection form the edge of the surface for each leaf shape.
10. The remaining three leaves can be developed using the same principle as Leaf 1.

The drawing of combined dome and pendentives shows the method to establish views: Plan, Elevations, and Section A-A.

## DRAWING ELLIPSES

There are various methods used to achieve an ellipse. To draw an ellipse using a trammel:

1. Set out the axes AB, CD.
2. On a strip of paper with a straight edge mark off OB equal to OB.
3. Place the trammel vertical with B aligned with D. Mark on the trammel the second 'o'.
4. Place the paper so that O is on the minor axis and O is on the major axis. 'a' is then a point on the curve which is marked.

*Drawing an ellipse by the trammel method, the major and minor axes being given.*

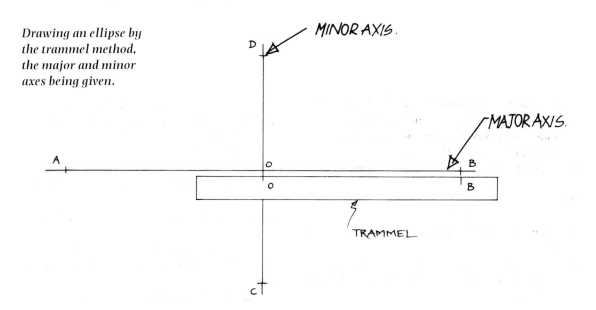

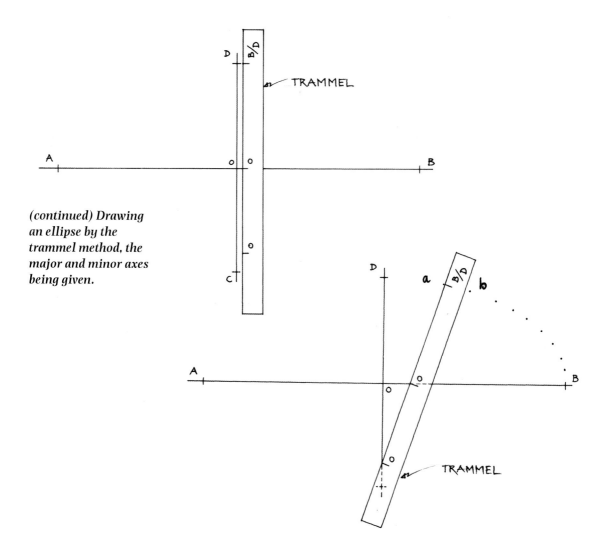

*(continued) Drawing an ellipse by the trammel method, the major and minor axes being given.*

5. Reposition the trammel as per 'b', keeping the left O on the minor axis and the right O on the major axis. Move the trammel to obtain the points. Do not letter the dots.
6. Through these points complete the curve.

To draw an ellipse using intersecting lines:

1. Draw the axis AB, and construct the rectangle EFGH.
2. Divide AE and AO into the same number of equal parts and draw DI, D2, and D3 as shown.

3. 3. Join D to 1, 2, 3 on AE. Join C to 1, 2, 3 on AO. Note: line D1 intersects C1; line D2 intersects C2; line D3 intersects C3.
4. Through the points of intersection draw a quarter of the ellipse and complete the figure by repeating the process for the other quarters.

To construct an ellipse using the string method:

1. Establish the major and minor axis AB and CD, noting E at the centre of AB and at centre of CD.
2. Using the length AE as radius, place the com-

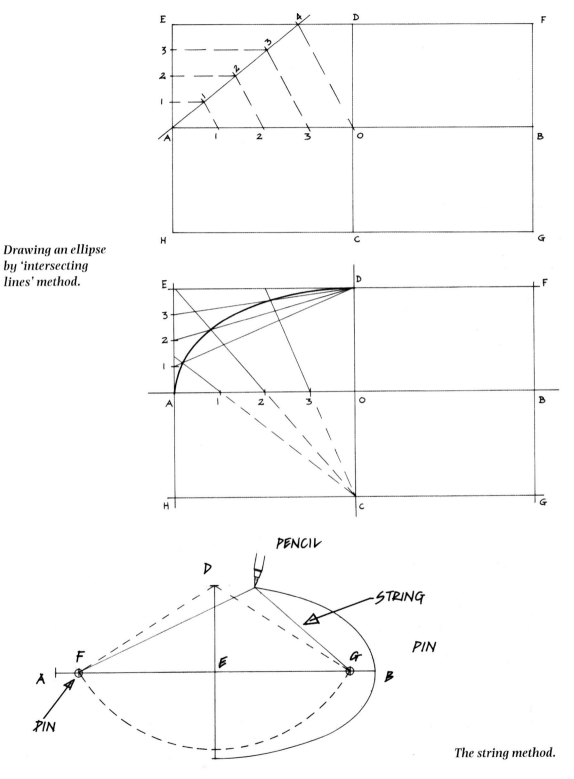

Drawing an ellipse by 'intersecting lines' method.

The string method.

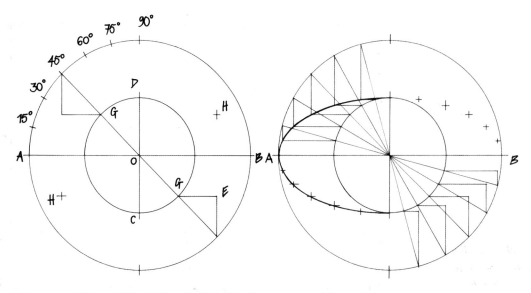

*To construct an ellipse with circle as its foundations.*

pass point on D and draw an arc intersecting AB at F and G.

3. Position nails into board or pins into card at points F and G along AB.
4. Wrap string around the outside of the pins and tie into a loop, with enough length for a pencil to make contact with D, the pencil is placed inside the loop. Keeping the string taut draw the arcs forming an ellipse.

To construct an ellipse with a circle as its foundations:

1. The intersection of major (AB) and minor (CD) axes is centre for both circles.
2. Step off the 15degree increments along the outer circle, in one quadrant only, using the 45 degree and 30/60 degree set squares.
3. Draw lines connecting these points to circle centre and project beyond into the diagonally opposite quadrant.
3. At the point where radials make contact with the inner circle project lines horizontally out to intersect with lines dropped vertically from the degree points along the outer circle's circumference.

4. The points of these intersections are the points through which the ellipse will be drawn.
5. To complete the remaining quadrants project the intersecting points both horizontally and vertically to establish the 'cross' intersections.
6. Complete the ellipse by drawing a line through these intersecting points.

## DRAWING CIRCLES WITHIN SQUARES

### Method one
1. Establish a square of the required size with diagonals.
2. At the point of diagonal intersection draw in the horizontal and vertical axes forming the sub-division of the square into four smaller squares.
3. Plot the diagonals within each of these smaller squares to establish each circle centre.
4. Place the compass point on each centre and inscribe a circle.

### Method two
1. Establish a square of the required size.
2. Draw in the diagonals.
3. Plot the horizontal and vertical axes.

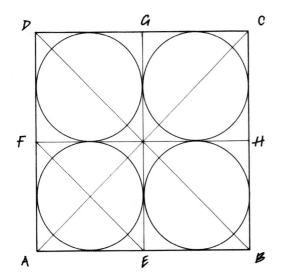

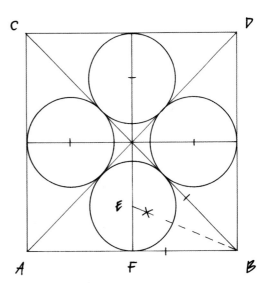

*Inscribing four circles within a given square.*

4. Bisect ABC to establish E intersecting with the vertical at centre.
5. Using the compass, measure off FE and plot these measurements from each edge of the square at the centre of each side.

## DRAWING ARCHES

The carpentry arches illustrated overleaf are (from left to right, top to bottom):

1. The equilateral arched frame: is based upon the equilateral triangle; the radius of the two arcs being equal to each span. Centres are positioned on the 'springing line' at 'a' and 'b'.
2. The lancet is a drawing based on two semi-circles, positioned on the springing line. A radius is equal to half the span. Centres are at 'a' and 'b'. Points 1 and 2 provide the centre for each curve.
3. The drop arch may vary proportionally yet works to the same principle. Draw a triangle plotting the required altitude. Bisect each inclined side of the triangle to produce bisectors to intersect the springing line at points 1 and 2. These points are centres for the arcs.

4. The Tudor arch is drawn by dividing a span on the springing line into four equal parts. Through drawing semicircles equal in radius to the half span, with centre points 1 and 3 the arcs are drawn. To plot the centres of the crown arcs draw quadrants from 'a' and 'b' to intersect the jambs at points 2 and 4. These are required centres for the crown arcs.
5. The four-centred arch: the span is divided into six equal parts.
6. The cyma reversa or wave arch.
7. The ogee arch: used in windows and pavilion roofs.
8. The bell or reversed ogee arch.

### Drawing the Tudor arch
1. Establish AB at the desired width (*see* page 82).
2. Establish CD at the desired height.
3. Set off a desired radius for AF, and establish GB with the same radius.
4. With compass point on F and radius FG draw an arc to intersect with centre vertical at E.
5. Join F with E and project downwards to intersect with a vertical line extended downwards from G to establish H.

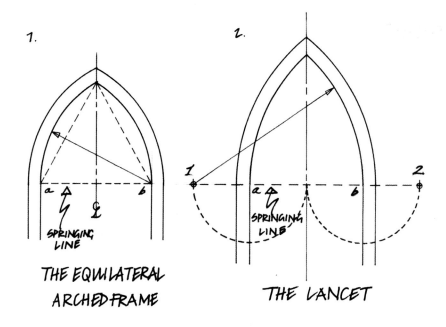

1.

THE EQUILATERAL
ARCHED FRAME

2.

THE LANCET

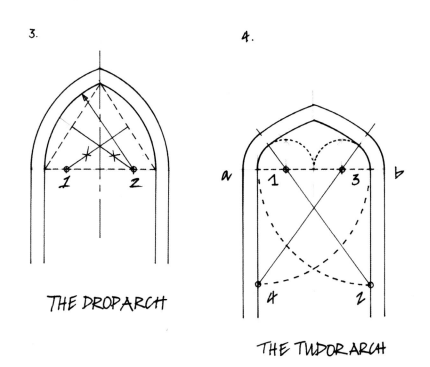

3.

THE DROP ARCH

4.

THE TUDOR ARCH

ALSO OPPOSITE: *Carpentry arches.*

5.

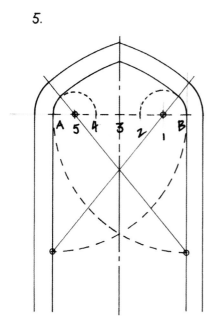

### THE FOUR CENTRED ARCH

6.

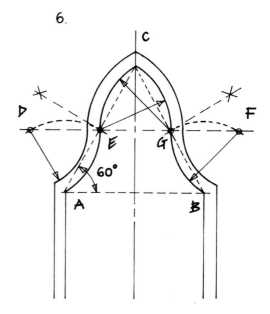

### THE CYMA REVERSA OR WAVE ARCH.

7.

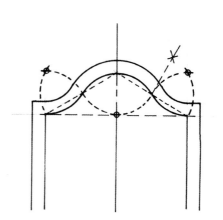

### THE OGEE ARCH

8.

### THE BELL OR REVERSED OGEE ARCH

**RIGHT:** *A semi-ellipse drawn with the five-centre method.*

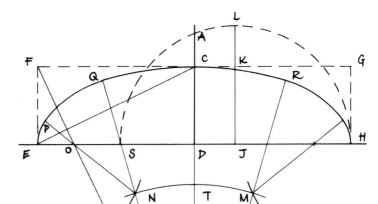

**BELOW:** *Tudor arch or pointed arch.*

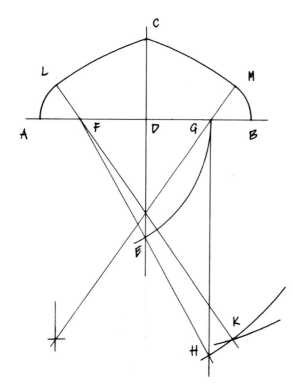

9. Transfer K horizontally across to intersect with a vertical line dropped from L, with the same previous radius draw arc CM and with G as centre and radius FA draw arc BM.

To use the five-centre method to draw a semi-ellipse:

6. With compass point on F and radius FH, draw a short arc, then with C as centre and radius AF plus FH draw a small intersecting arc to establish K.
7. Join KF projecting through to establish L.
8. Placing the compass point on F, and measuring radius AF, draw the arc AL, then with K as centre and radius KL draw the arc LC.

1. With major axis EH and semi-minor axis DC draw in a rectangle forming E, F, G, H.
2. Join EC, and then plot FB perpendicular to EC, intersecting EH at O.
3. Set off DS as equal to DC.
4. Establish centre of SH as J, and with compass on J and radius JS draw a half circle forming SLH.

5. Add the vertical off J to establish K on the rectangle and L on the half circle.
6. Mark off the measurement KL as the same as DT.
7. With compass on B and radius BT draw an arc.
8. Project DC downwards and upwards to establish A and intersection with B.
9. With E and H as centres and radius AD draw intersecting arcs at N and M.
10. Join B to N and project to Q.
11. Join B to M and project to R.
12. With the compass on O and radius OE, draw an arc EP.
13. With the compass on N and radius NP draw an arc PQ.
14. With compass on B and radius BQ draw an arc QCR.
15. The remaining two arcs are to be drawn as a reverse and repeat method numbers 12 and 13.

## PROPORTIONAL DRAWING

Enlarging or reducing a drawing proportionally through squared paper is useful for all freehand enlargements and reductions with scaled proportions calculated in the overall format sizing.

Further divisions of squares may be added internally as is required, where detail increases.

Mouldings can be enlarged or reduced proportionally thus (*see* page 84):

1. Draw the 'given' moulding establishing a base horizontal on which it is to stand. Profile it to scale. Label horizontal OF. Label profile A, B, C.
2. Draw a line connecting OB and projecting beyond. When enlarging, plot a vertical for the 'required' proportion for the moulding width, in this example at 65mm measured vertically in scale. Label it accordingly 'A' and 'B'.
3. Join OC and project beyond. At point 'A' draw a line parallel to OF. Where it intersects is 'C'.
4. Within the profile ABC plot the ordinates and send them vertically to BC. On a curve any number of ordinates may be applied and from each ordinate draw a line upwards to AB.
5. Join O to each ordinate on BC and project these through to 'B' 'C'. Where they connect along BC send them down vertically.
6. Project a line from O through each ordinate along AB, note that profile ordinates have been drawn across horizontally. Each ordinate along 'A' 'B' should be sent across to meet with the corresponding vertical to form right angles at the points of intersection. Draw in the profile line joining each ordinate intersection.

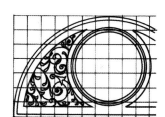
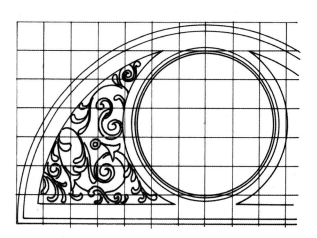

*Enlarging or reducing a drawing proportionally through squared paper.*

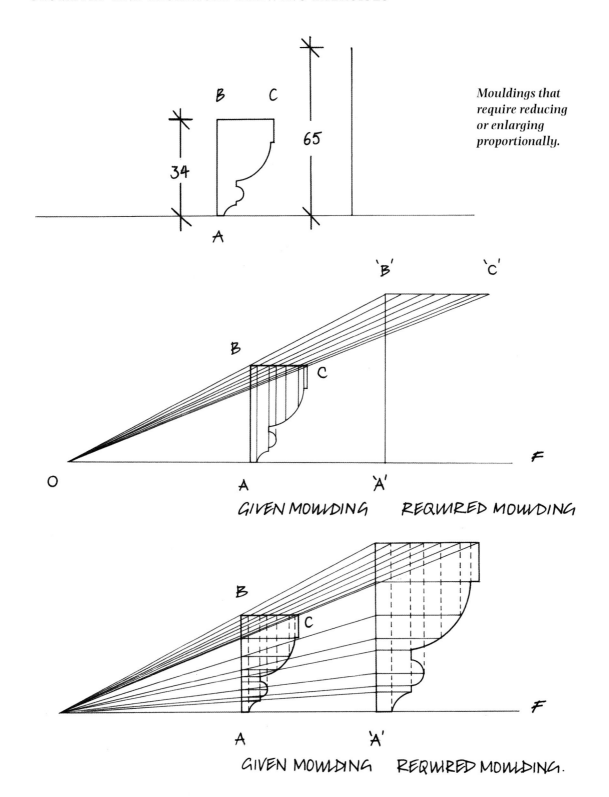

*Mouldings that require reducing or enlarging proportionally.*

GIVEN MOULDING     REQUIRED MOULDING

GIVEN MOULDING     REQUIRED MOULDING.

## The transfer method of drawing

The transfer method can be used to complete fully a drawing where only one side of a symmetrical object is initially drawn:

**Stage a.** Place tracing paper over the original drawing and copy the edges. Indicate radii points as circle centres.

**Stage b.** Flip upside down the copy from stage **a**, and slide it beneath the original tracing paper drawing, aligning both centre lines. Secure with tape.

**Stage c.** Trace over details from the outline below using solid lines for all details viewed. The result is a completed symmetrical drawing.

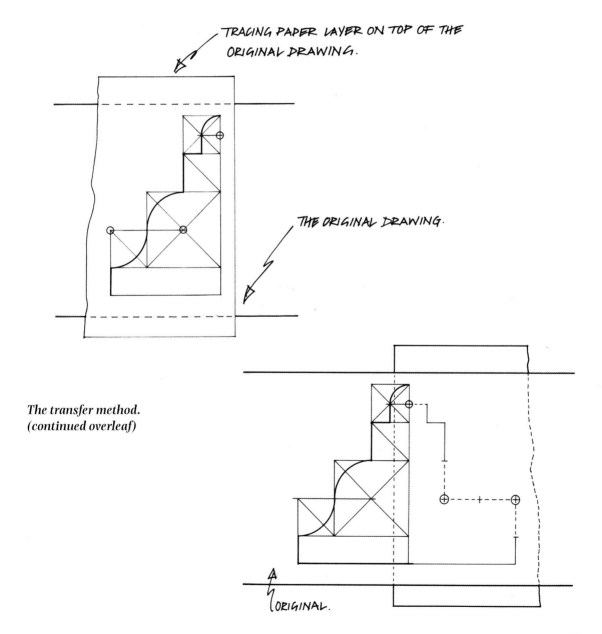

TRACING PAPER LAYER ON TOP OF THE
ORIGINAL DRAWING.

THE ORIGINAL DRAWING.

*The transfer method.*
*(continued overleaf)*

ORIGINAL.

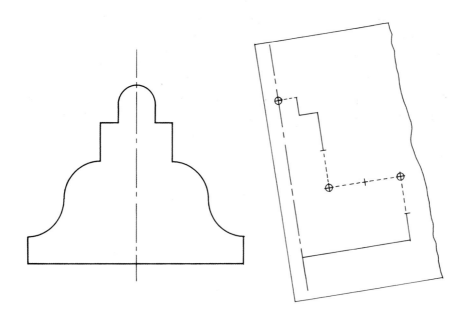

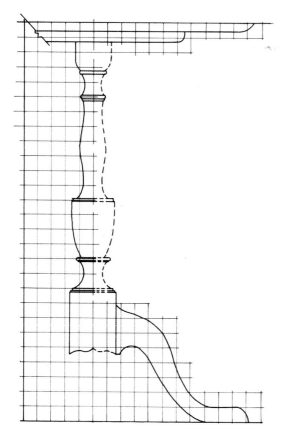

## Using a grid

Using a grid permits construction to scale-up from the drawing. The diagram shows the profile for lathe turning and profile leg cut outs. The turned pedestal is shown as half-drawn, with dashed line contour simply showing the symmetry. With objects having detailed symmetry, half a development with half external contour may be sufficient.

## MOULDINGS

Classical mouldings include straight mouldings, such as 'Fillet' or 'Listel' and 'Fascia' and curved mouldings, such as 'Concave', 'Convex' or 'Compound'. Concave mouldings include 'Cavetto' (a quarter circle), 'Scotia' (a curve of greater rotation than a semi-circle), and 'Conge' (combining straight and curved elements in the same profile). Convex moulding includes 'Ovolo' (equaling or near approximating a quarter circle), 'Torus' (a half round), and a smaller version known as Astragal. Compound moulding includes both con-

*Pedestal leg and table top drawn on a grid.*

RIGHT: *Classical mouldings. Figures left to right, row by row, top left to bottom right.*

1. *Ovolo*
2. *Elliptical Ovolo*
3. *Cavetto*
4. *Torus*
5. *Fillet or Listel*
6. *Conge*
7. *Scotia*
8. *Sunk or raised Fillet*
9. *Bevel or Chamfer*
10. *Quirked Cymas*
11. *Cyma Recta*
12. *Cyma Reversa.*

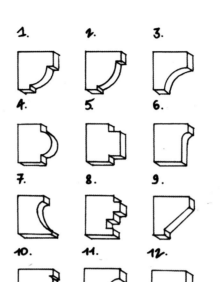

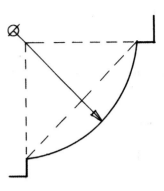

ABOVE: *Cavetto moulding. The projection of the radius curve results in a cord rather than a quarter circle.*

RIGHT: *Scotia moulding. Two gradients of differing radii forming a concave shape.*

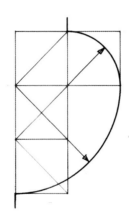

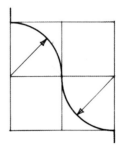

ABOVE: *Ogee or cyma recta moulding set within a square.*

BELOW LEFT: *Scotia moulding in a quarter curve;*
CENTRE: *Nosing with Scotia moulding;*
FAR RIGHT: *Astragal moulding nosing and two Scotia mouldings.*

SCOTIA

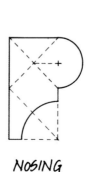

NOSING

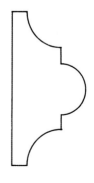

ASTRAGAL

*Fillet moulding, drawing indicating raised fillet, sunken fillet and fascia.*

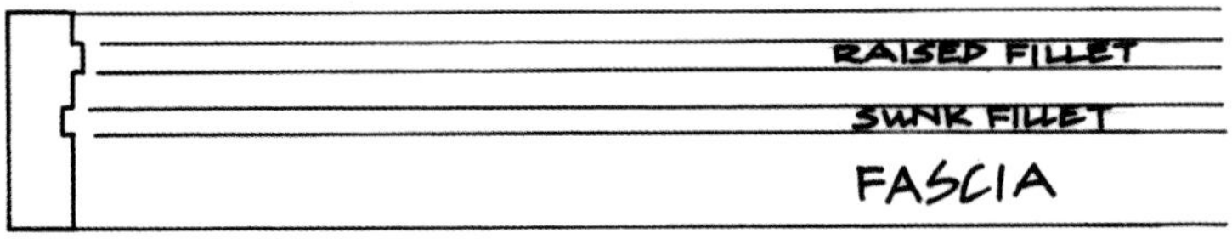

RAISED FILLET

SUNK FILLET

FASCIA

*Toros or Bead moulding.*

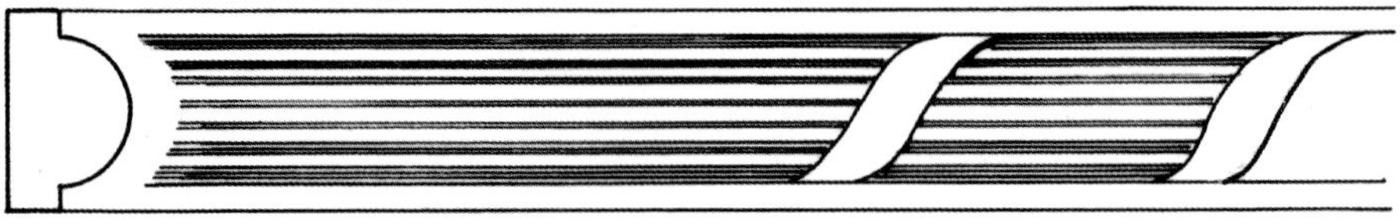

*Ovolo moulding.*

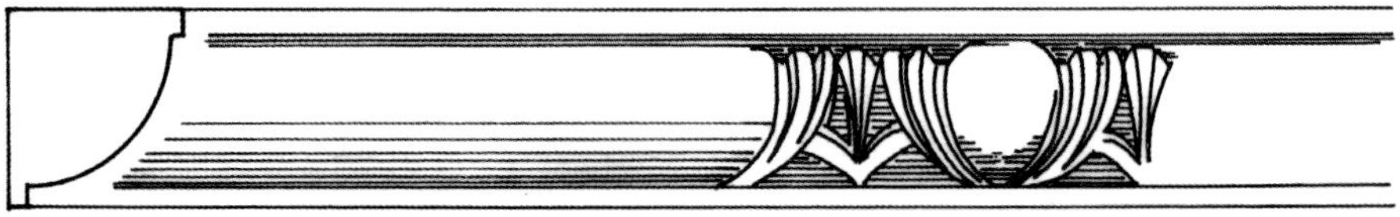

*Cavetto moulding.*

*Scotia moulding.*

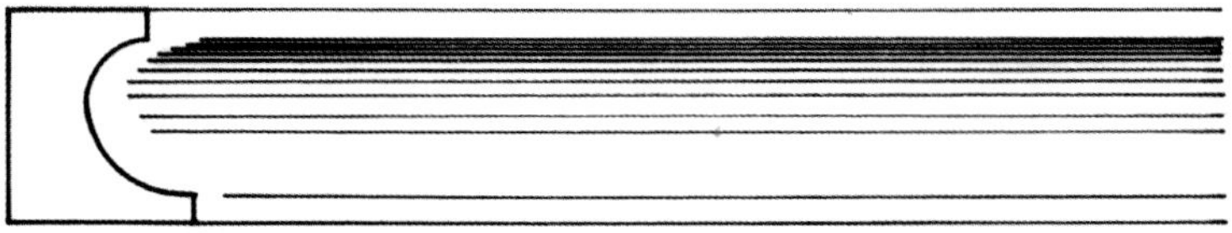

*Ogee or Cyma Recta moulding.*

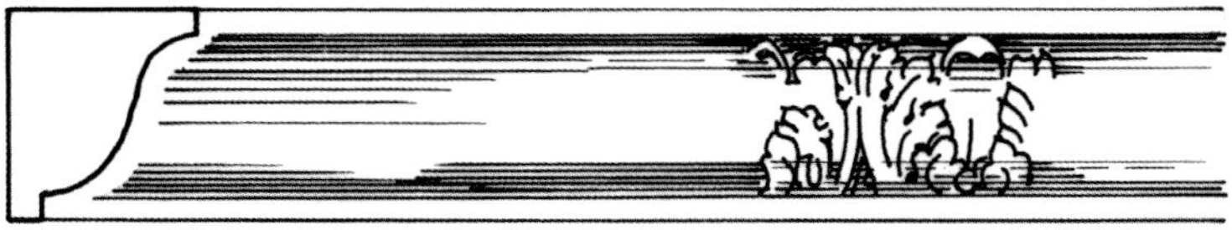

*Cyma Reversa moulding.*

cave and convex, such as 'Cyma Recta' or 'Ogee' (like a wave), concave at the top and convex below, and a reverse version called 'Cyma Reversa'.

'Crowning' moulding is used on non-supportive or non-weight bearing structures and includes 'Cavetto', 'Conge' and 'Cyma Recta'. 'Support' moulding serves the practical function of bearing weight and includes 'Quarter Round', 'Cyma

Reversa' and 'Ovolo'. Profiles that separate and 'punctuate' include 'Fillet' and 'Scotia'. 'Transition' moulding used between vertical and horizontal structures includes 'Inverted Cavetto' and 'Conge Cymas'.

'Compound' mouldings require geometrically aligning to best co-ordinate relationships.

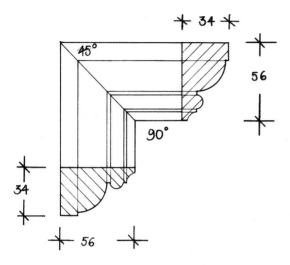

*Mitre moulding of the same size intersecting at an angle of 45 degrees. Both moulding pieces being the same width.*

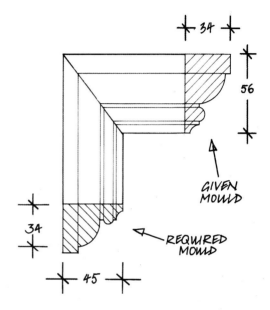

*Reducing the width of mitre mouldings.*

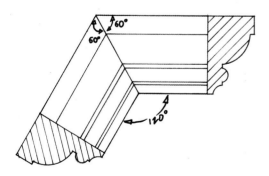

ABOVE: *Mitre mouldings intersecting at an angle of more than 90 degrees, with moulding width being the same in each. Outer and inner lines meet to make a mitre join.*

RIGHT: *Door architrave. Head mould reduced from jamb mould.*

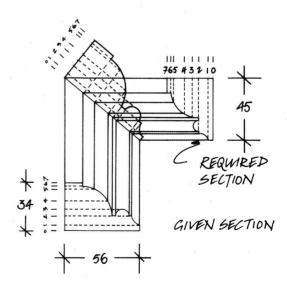

89

In order to reduce the width of mitre mouldings (*see* page 89):

1.  Establish the outline for the given mould, then transfer across the page.
2.  Establish the outline for the required mould and transfer vertically to intersect.
3.  Draw the angled mitre line where inner and outer lines intersect.
4.  Establish the profile for the given moulding attached to the outline then transfer all points for detailing across to the mitre line.
5.  Transfer the intersecting information down to the required moulding.
6.  Draw the profile with the same depth proportions.

For a door architrave, the width may need a reduced head (horizontal) from that in jamb (vertical) due to insufficient height allowance.

To reduce the width:

1.  Draw the jamb given width and profile its features, i.e. 34mm × 56mm (*see* page 89).
2.  Establish width for the required head, i.e. 45mm.
3.  Plot the mitre line where the lines intersect.
4.  From the 'given', project the series of ordinates up to the mitre line.
5.  From the mitre line project intersection points of ordinates across to the 'required', applying the same propositional measurement distances for 0, 1, 2, 3, 4, 5, 6, 7. At right angles they meet to form points along the profile.
6.  Complete the required moulding drawing.
7.  To complete the section view of the mitre join. From intersecting points on the mitre line send each ordinate off at 90 degrees. Measure off proportionally 0, 1, 2, 3, 4, 5, 6, 7 and have both these project across to meet the previous projections at 90 degrees.

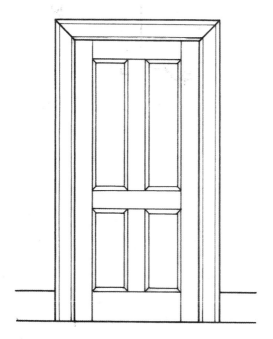

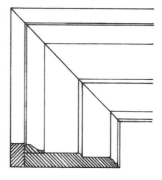

*Four-panel door with architrave. The mitre where jamb and head mouldings intersect will be 45 degrees if the moulding width is the same for jamb and head. Moulding profiles can be effectively done at the scale of 1:1.*

# 7 VENUE DRAWINGS OR THEATRE DRAWINGS

Theatre or venue technical drawings are supplied by the production manager or technical director. The drawings may come in either of two formats: a copy from a hand drawing, or produced through CAD (Computer Aided Design). Hand-drawn are those produced as board drawings by a draughtsman and inked onto draughting film or vellum, drawn at the scale of 1:25 or 1:50 (as indicated on the drawing itself). CAD drawings are those produced using a CAD software program, drawn 1:1 and printed at the scale of 1:25 or 1:50 (as indicated on the printed page). CAD drawings are delivered through the Internet or may be requested as hard copy. To receive a CAD drawing online, the appropriate CAD software is required as well as the recommended format printer capable of producing page size A1 or A0. Alternatively, a professional printing service may accept the document file for printing (with a charge for opening the file along with a charge for the printing). Wherever possible, do request a hard copy of venue drawings.

Venue drawings exist in two formats:

* The ground plan, defining the theatre floor plan including auditorium (classified as Drawing 1).
* The theatre section, defining a side view section taken at centre-stage (classified as Drawing 2).

## GROUND PLAN

The ground plan is a drawing of the theatre floor plan. The plan is not a top view. The plan refers to the actual floor surface, describing through types of line the inter-relationship between architectural feature and floor surface. The venue's depth and width are key features on a plan. However, it is possible to indicate architectural features above stage level. The plotting of such features is through the use of a dash line. Theatres with sub-stage features (those below the surface of the stage, including trap passageways, orchestra pit walls, or structural supports) also need to be included on the plan. Features below the stage are referred to as 'hidden' and the language for hidden lines is a fine dash line. The difference between overhead and hidden is in the size of the dash itself, with hidden being much finer.

Ground plan architectural features include:

* Architecture of the stage area – generally called the acting or performing area, that which is within the majority of sight-lines for the audience.
* Architecture of the off-stage areas, referred to as outside the parameters of the acting area.
* Architecture of the access areas to the stage area (referred to as 'back-stage') – wing space, dock areas, get-in facilities, storage areas, and cross-over.
* Architecture of technical facility – this may include features above stage, features on walls, or built into the floor. These features may include: fly floor, fly bar positions, counterweight cage, flying systems for iron and counterweights, air conditioning units, fire hose reels and extinguisher positions, wall-mounted radiators, tormentors, proscenium opening, sub-stage walls and passageways, orchestra pit area, trap positions and lifts, dressing room access, lighting and sound supply unit positions, iron or safety curtain, doors and opening entrances, and all relevant height clearance measurements.
* Architecture of the auditorium – this includes the audience and the technical facility within

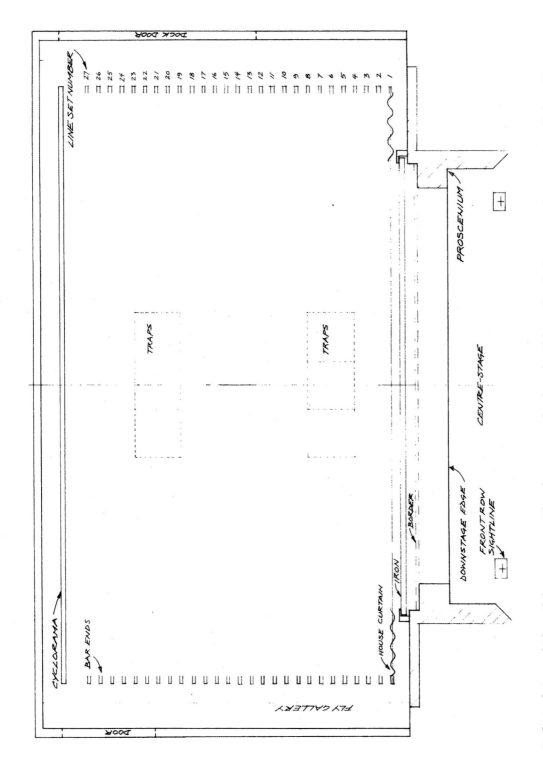

*Technical Ground Plan of theatre venue. Plan depicts true depth and width, and includes proscenium opening, fly bars/line sets, fly floor/gallery, safety curtain/iron, traps to sub-stage, house curtain, header/border within proscenium, front row seating for sight-line.*

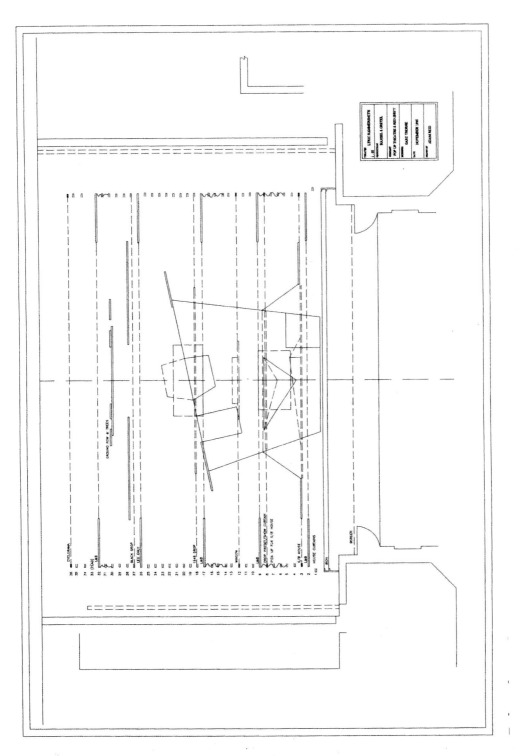

*Technical Ground Plan showing Hansel and Gretel set. Includes: proscenium opening, position for on-stage scenic elements, trap openings, fly bar positions, legs with soft returns and borders, safety curtain/iron.*

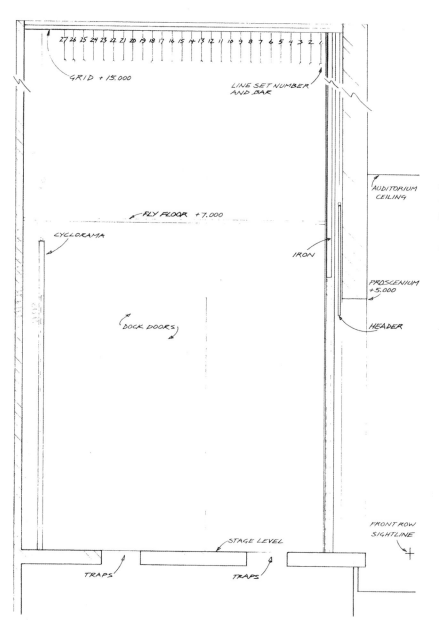

27 26 25 24 23 22 21 20 19 18 17 16 15 14 13 12 11 10 9 8 7 6 5 4 3 2 1

GRID + 15.000

LINE SET NUMBER
AND BAR

AUDITORIUM
CEILING

FLY FLOOR + 7.000

CYCLORAMA

IRON

DOCK DOORS

PROSCENIUM
+5.000

HEADER

FRONT ROW
SIGHTLINE

STAGE LEVEL

TRAPS

TRAPS

*Technical Section View of theatre venue. Section depicts true height and depth and includes: stage level, trap openings to sub-stage, proscenium opening, dock door opening, header/border position, fly floor, safety curtain/iron, grid height (note break line), fly bars/line sets, front row sight-line.*

the area where they are seated. The relationship between auditorium and stage will be the key feature. Auditorium features on the plan depict its depth, width and features above auditorium level which serve performance. Included on the plan will be the seat rows featuring the range of sight-lines as required by the designer, lighting bar positions (those set off from handrails and those suspended), features obstructing audience view (referred to as 'restricted view' seats), audience exits/entrances, and all height clearance measurements.

Typically the plan is provided at scale 1:25. The only exceptions might be where the size of the venue is too large to be scaled appropriately to A1 or A0 paper. Those encountering this issue will scale to 1:50. Generally the Opera Stage is printed out at 1:50 as the size of stage including auditorium makes for too big a drawing to fit the typical drawing board.

## Lines on the plan

The architecture can be depicted in three key ways, each having its own line quality noted by: solid lines, short dash lines, long dash lines, and with CAD the addition of coloured lines. The centre-line, which runs from down-stage through to up-stage, indicating the centre of the stage, is a line type unique to itself and is only ever found elsewhere in the drawing of objects in orthographic where the centre of the object needs to be indicated.

### Solid lines

Solid lines generally refer to where architecture and object make contact with the floor surface, as in a line representing the plane edge of a wall. Consider, as the palm of the hand passes across the surface of the page, the hand in effect is doing the same across the theatre floor surface. Where the hand comes in contact with a solid line, the hand should stop, as the solid line indicates there must be the edge of a solid. Solid lines may have an infill of closely drawn parallel lines that appear shaded in, which indicates a permanent solid form making attachment with the floor. A break within the length of a solid line may indicate access through that wall or plane. A scenic flat with a doorway opening is indicated by the solid line being interrupted, or broken, therefore the shading will also cease where the wall opening exists.

Solid lines represent: the down-stage edge of the stage (setting-line) which runs perpendicular to the centre-line; fixed walls; doors and a shutter or those tracked, trap openings; dimmer traps for lighting electrics; and areas of on-stage floor which lower as a bridge, or have a lift/elevator or revolving drum. Not all CAD drawings include the shading to indicate solids, which makes the reading less obvious initially. It is not until a visit to the venue is undertaken that the position of solids and their parallel planes can be clarified.

The plan will not have dimensions marked for depth or width. Only height measurements are printed as height clearance, referring to the clearance space beneath that object or form. When it is referred to as 'Head Clearance' it makes more sense to the newcomer. Height restrictions include: a fly floor; the underside of a lintel or proscenium opening; dock clearance heights for scenery storage in the wings; and get-in height restrictions for doors and shutter systems. A solid line may also depict the break in a floor where floor lifts exist, or where traps give access to sub-stage.

Protruding or proud features set off a wall will only be a solid where features such as radiators, electric supply units, ducting, or cage surround housing the counterweight system, actually make contact with the floor. If they are suspended off the floor they should appear as dash lines.

### Centre-line on plan

On the ground plan at mid-stage, perhaps equidistant from the opening sides of a proscenium, is the centre-stage position or centre-line, indicated by a unique line type, running up-stage through to down-stage set perpendicular to the down-stage edge of the stage. The line type is a series of long dashes each followed by a very short dash. Its position is usually indicated on the actual stage through some discreet marking. Where a centre-line is included on a studio theatre plan it may be mid-way between side walls, or simply as a point of reference for alignment when plotting seating, and setting symmetrically.

Centre-stage has particular relevance to stage management and the crew. This line, drawn onto the plan, facilitates plotting measurements accurately for the positioning of scenic elements and properties such as furniture, both onto the rehearsal room floor and onto the stage floor. By measuring up-stage from a setting-line (usually the down-stage edge of the stage) and off the centre-line perpendicular to it, points are plotted defining the points where objects make contact with the floor such as the legs or corners for a sofa, the corners of walls for a room, corners of cabinets or free-standing units, and door openings.

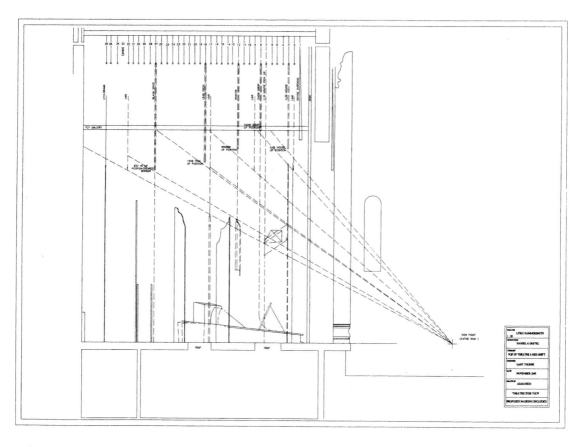

*Section View showing Hansel and Gretel set. Includes: proscenium opening, position of on-stage scenic elements, trap openings, fly bar positions, legs and borders, safety curtain/iron, sight-lines through to Borders.*

*Long dash lines*

Dash lines of a long proportioning indicate that which is overhead or positioned above stage level. A doorway opening set within a wall will appear as a dash line; one in the continuous direction of the wall itself represents that which is above floor level at that point, in this case the door-frame or lintel. Where a CAD drawing does not differentiate over-head lines by a dash line, it may present them as a colour line, specific in colour to the type or category they represent, as for lighting or fly features.

*Hidden lines*

Short dash lines indicate that which is sub-stage, i.e. the things that would naturally be hidden due to the solid nature of the stage floor level. These may include: architectural structural supports for the floor level; walls defining the area for the orchestra pit; passageways through which actors and technicians may pass beneath (either to cross from stage-left [actor left] to stage-right [actor right]); mechanisms supporting or driving lifts; I-beams running beneath the floor plane which frame trap openings; or edge lifts, exit treads or ladders built for exiting stage level to access sub-stage.

## THEATRE SECTION DRAWING

The section is the venue as seen by cutting the venue in half, along its centre-line, with one half

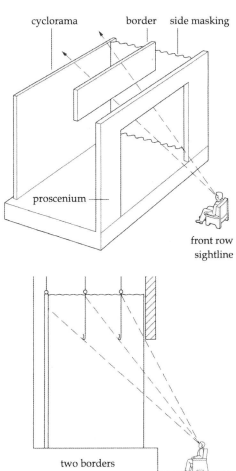

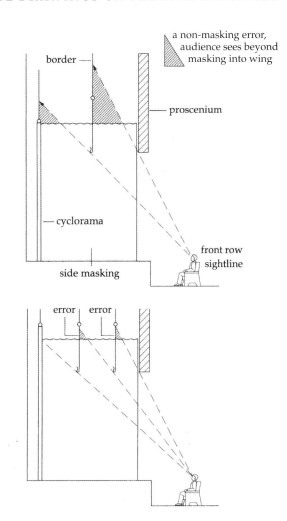

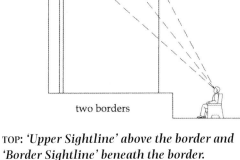

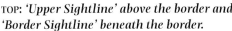

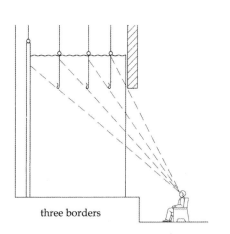

TOP: *'Upper Sightline' above the border and 'Border Sightline' beneath the border.*

TOP RIGHT: *Border and side masking creating an error. The grey area indicates the audience sees beyond into the ceiling or wings.*

ABOVE: *Perfect order, two borders side masking and cyclorama masking in harmony with no grey areas of error.*

ABOVE RIGHT: *The height of cyclorama and side masking are not in-line to mask properly.*

RIGHT: *Three borders enable the height of cyclorama and side masking to be shorter than with two borders.*

## Overhead features

Architectural features above stage level on plan
may include:

✳ Fly floor
✳ Fly bars
✳ Iron or safety curtain
✳ Winch bars
✳ Height clearance for proscenium opening
✳ Overhead height limitations of ceilings in stor-
  age dock areas or off-stage
✳ Lighting bar/truss positions or lighting bridges
✳ Lighting booms and lighting ladders
✳ Heating units or air ducts
✳ Fire hose and extinguishers
✳ Electric plug or power source units

removed and viewing it as if side on. The resulting
view is seen in orthographic projection, in a
cross-section view. The venue's height and depth
dimensioning is 'true'. The section will include
architectural features for depth of stage along
with depth of auditorium (including the seating).
It is typical for the seating to include front and
back rows, stalls, balconies, and higher if appropriate. All information connects to the centre-line
plane, perpendicular to that plane and the line's
depth.

The section drawing details the architectural
features of the stage wall, most typically running
parallel with the centre-line plane, and is therefore
viewed as a 'true' elevation (meaning that it is represented in true height and true depth). Stage level
will be drawn as a solid line to which all features
relate, including those in sub-stage areas.

## Lines on the section drawing

### Solid lines
Solid lines may appear in-filled with the shading as
referred to in ground plans (*see* page 95). That
which is shaded indicates a solid. In this case such
solids have been cut through to establish the sec-

tion view. The up-stage wall of the venue, which
may appear as two vertical lines perpendicular to
the floor level, may well be shown shaded, as having thickness (cut through) – *see* page 168. Yet
many drawings now do not carry this information
unless there is an actor cross-over up-stage of that
wall and this is drawn in as well. Therefore the up-
stage wall may only appear as a line. Solid lines
with no shading, which run parallel to the solid
line of the floor, indicate there is an edge to something, yet it is in the distance. The same applies to a
solid line drawn as a vertical, indicating there is an
edge to something yet it is in the distance.

### Dash lines
Short dash lines indicate something hidden
beyond a feature wall or plane. Beyond a wall may
be corridors with openings or reduced head clearance or height limitations. These constraints will
feature as hidden lines. Beyond apertures or openings in venue side-walls may exist dock areas for
storage, with ceiling height higher than the opening – ceiling height is indicated as a fine dash line
as it is hidden from view. Many such features are of
great interest technically. Restrictions beyond the
venue space affect design, production management, construction and stage crew when it comes
to the smooth running of a show. Productions run

## Section features

Section features include:

✳ height of fly floor and its railing
✳ grid height
✳ all the bar positions at grid level, with cables
  drawn through to the position of the pulley
  above grid level
✳ lighting bar positions and/or bridge positions
✳ lighting booms and ladders, some of which
  may track from down-stage positions to up-
  stage
✳ proscenium opening
✳ dock areas

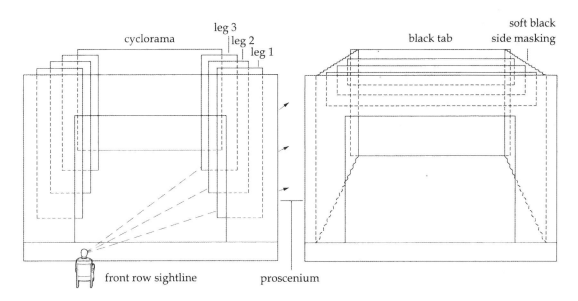

*Side sightlines through the legs to the wings.*

*A Black-Box Theatre created with side masking, borders and up-stage tab.*

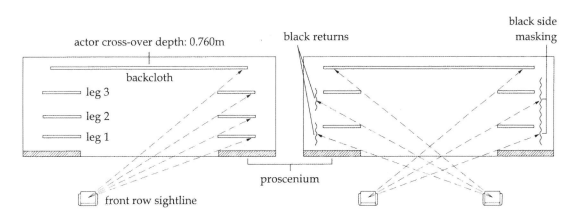

*Three legs perfectly positioned to mask the wings.*

*Two legs with black soft returns or black side markings.*

in repertory need to plot off-stage restrictions to maximize the use of space in the most efficient manner as is technically possible.

## Fly bars

These are noted in their up-stage to down-stage positioning, and are drawn as small circles indicat-

ing the section view of pipe (a pipe cut in half lengthwise and viewed square on to the cut is simply a circle shape). Of key interest technically is the distance from bar centre to bar centre. As the diameter of the bar cannot be drawn accurately, its centre will be a reference point for all alignments. The indication of centre is noted by the attached cable running vertically through to the pulley system.

## Auditorium seating and sight-line

Seating will be depicted as a side view of seats, including those closest to the edge of the stage through to the back rows of stalls, balcony and higher. Sight-line is indicated by a small circle with a cross at its centre, representing the eye of the spectator. Their height above the seat is calculated therein. These sight-lines are of particular importance to design and the production manager, the lighting designer and the director. Sight-lines very much determine decision making in the process of set design development.

## Lighting bars

The section depicts positions of lighting bars within the auditorium. These may be bars attached to balcony handrail structure, those attached to side walls, and those suspended.

## PLOTTING DESIGN ON PLAN AND SECTION

The plotting of the design onto a plan and section involves as much artistic skill as technical skill. Exploiting a venue's constraints is more often about design pushing its limitations to serve the play and its requirements. Understanding the venue constraints allows the draughtsman to push such boundaries.

## The first stage

When drawing plan and section for preliminary and for final drawings the first step is to redraw the original onto tracing paper. This is achieved through simply copying. Place the original on the board, align it to the T-square or parallel-motion arm and secure it down, then place tracing paper over and begin redrawing. During the process of tracing, orientate to architectural features, ask what it is one is tracing. Almost all the information from the original is required on the tracing paper copy, including auditorium detailing. Remember to draw the centre-line. Establish what should be the setting line – either the down-stage edge of the

---

**Below stage level**

Where a venue has a sub-stage the section view will clearly define its depth, and the features within it including:

* structural features such as steel or concrete columns
* beams as they might be cut in section, therefore shaded in as in-fill
* dividing walls
* lifts and mechanically engineered systems
* treads to stage level
* thickness of stage floor

---

stage, if there is one, or add in a line perpendicular to the centre-line which can be easily calculated within the venue space.

NB: Establish where the safety curtain makes contact with the stage floor, with drawing dashed parallel lines, as the iron must make uninterrupted contact with the stage floor or designed floor.

## Line type

The same line type is applied to drawing a design on plan as is used to describe the venue on plan. Solid lines indicate a scenic unit in a fixed position, long dash lines indicate set elements positioned overhead, and where design elements are sub-stage they are drawn as hidden lines.

## Plotting design

Use the setting line and centre-line to plot distance measurements. To establish a point onto the plan, note its required distance from down-stage to up-stage, measure this distance from the setting-line along the centre-line, then measure perpendicular to the centre-line to plot the required distance across (left or right of centre).

Position walls by plotting corners or where planes intersect, and once plotted as dots, join with a solid line indicating a surface plane making contact with the floor surface. Where a

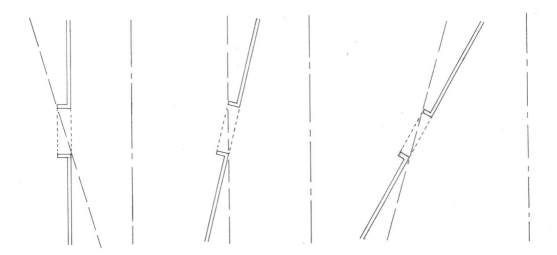

*Calculating one of the two required sight-lines, projected through an opening in a flat. In this instance the flat is positioned in an upstage-downstage direction. The trajectory for sight-line is established through connecting the on-stage door jamb (down-stage) with the off-stage door jamb (up-stage) and extending the line beyond to off-stage. The thickness to a door reveal or window reveal, greatly affects the angle of sight-line and what is viewed beyond. The second sightline for the same opening is determined by a specific audience seat, in this instance the one closest to the stage, on the opposite side of the auditorium; and from that sight-line a line is projected to the onstage door jamb (down-stage) and extended beyond off-stage.*

doorway breaks the run of a wall plane, by being set within it, the solid line representing the wall becomes a fine dash line for the length of the door opening, becoming a solid line thereafter as the wall continues.

Windows within a wall on plan are indicated by overhead dash lines, aligning to reveal width and depth. There is no need to indicate height. Furniture may be indicated as solid lines, if they are fixed throughout the show, yet are often drawn as dash lines depicting overall width and depth.

Levels or platforms above stage are drawn as either solid or dash lines. Stairs are more often drawn as solid lines, although dash lines tell the viewer they are above stage level.

Fly bars are drawn in on plan with only their 'ends' noted with the symbol 'T'. The long stroke of the T is going in the direction of the bar length. There is no need to add in long dash lines for the bar length from stage right to stage left.

A flown scenic unit (or, more specifically, one suspended from a fly bar to be flown) will appear on plan as a dash line and the line will indicate where it will make contact with the floor surface. As it is not fixed in an on-stage position, it appears in dashed line form. Do not draw the bar length; only the scenic unit length is required. This applies to both solid and soft materials that are suspended or flown.

A suspended chandelier will appear as a dashed line, as it is above floor level. A height indicated notes head clearance off stage level, its centre is bar centre, and its diameter needs to make clearance of bars when flown.

On plan, a ramp will appear as having solid lines indicating edges. As with platforms, the edges are drawn as solid lines. A ramp or gradient should have a pointer-line drawn along the 'direction of the rake'. Height may be indicated by H=mm at a point near maximum rise. Step or tread units on plan require height or riser measurement applied to the first tread, with full rise height indicated on the top landing. Both heights '+mm' are placed within a small circle.

Legs are indicated by solid lines; where the leg makes contact with floor. If the leg is flown, it is a dashed line. Pairs of legs are suspended from the same bar – one stage-left, the other stage-right. Leg widths are determined by theatre/venue stock; check venue specification printouts.

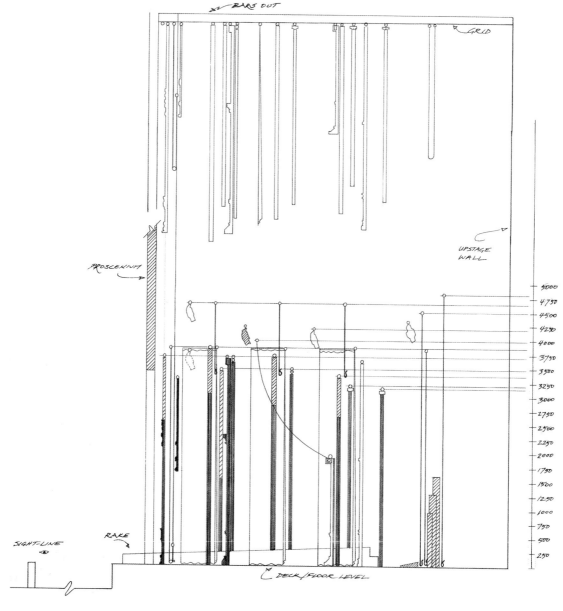

*Theatre Section. Flown scenic elements. View: Centre-stage viewing stage-right (into stage-right wing).*

---

**Example of bar numbering**

BAR 9 – LEGS & BORDER
BAR 8 – ACT II STREET LAMPS
BAR 7 – LX
BAR 6 – LX
BAR 5 – LX
BAR 4 – ACT III BANNERS
BAR 3 – ACT II SHOP SIGN
BAR 2 – LEGS & BORDER
BAR 1 – GAUZE DROP

---

ensions for such units, in terms of hallway walls, off-stage bedroom walls, corridor walls for stair units, and cloths for outside a window, may all be calculated through projecting audience sight-lines.

## The title block on plan and section

The drawing's 'title block' is positioned in its bottom right corner. It appears as a rectangular block lying horizontally, or as a block laid in a vertical position. The scale of the drawing will always be printed within the title block (*see* page 145 for details).

Borders do not need to be drawn in on the plan, yet they are indicated through text within the bar allocation title block; a column with rows (one for each bar) positioned along one side of the drawing page in-line with the bars.

The bar numbers are assigned with bar number one (1) as furthest down-stage. Within the 'bar allocation title block' printed text details what bars are used for. The example above highlights the fact that lighting ('LX') requires a bar for light suspension, as well makes redundant the bars up-stage and down-stage due to the size of lanterns and their shutters.

A flown unit, having depth dimension, requires that the bar-centre be established from where pick-up cables are attached. The thickness of a flown unit will generally be projected down-stage from bar-centre. Pick-up cables are attached to the back of a flat (running vertically down its up-stage plane). Where a flat has considerable thickness, the draughtsman needs to consult the technical/production management.

## Sight-line projection to determine masking wall dimensions

Off-stage wall units viewed by audience, as seen through an on-stage feature wall, require width proportioning calculated through audience sight-lines. Scenic units in the form of walls or cloths in off-stage positions include those seen through a window, arched opening, and doorway. Width dim-

---

**Projecting audience sight-lines:
an example**

1. A door opening is built into a wall. The walls runs perpendicular to the centre-line. Two projected lines are drawn from the widest two seats on the plan, opposite sides of the front row. From one sight-line, connect a rule through to its most distant door jamb, and from the point where the sight-line connects with the jamb draw a line projecting through to off-stage (a long dash line).

2. From the opposite widest sight-line, connect a rule to its most distant jamb opening, and draw a line projecting beyond off-stage (a dash line). These two projecting lines represent the extreme points of view.

3. The hall wall is to be positioned running parallel with the feature wall. Wherever it is positioned, in terms of up-stage, its ends must make contact with these two projected lines. When they connect at either end, this determines the required width for the hallway wall up-stage of the feature wall opening. It is good practice to add 100mm to each end for error.

(To determine the width of masking walls off-stage of feature walls that run in the direction of down-stage to up-stage, *see* the illustration on page 101.)

---

# 8 LETTERING AND PRINTED MATTER

## LETTERING

What is the impact of a drawing with poorly applied lettering? A lack of competence is easily displayed through applying uneven spacing, and inconsistency of proportion and letter formation has the tendency to throw a drawing into doubt. Refinement in applied lettering along with competent calculations in layout delivered in a clear, bold and confident hand produces the overall effect of skilled draughtsmanship. A glance at lettering, labelling, dimensioning, and notes for construction, should communicate competence that casts no shadow of doubt over practical intentions. As is typical, the final stage of a drawing is the application of printed matter after the calculated thinking through of form and the inter-relationship of views has been processed. The final emphasis is on adding information that cannot be drawn and

quality of penmanship and skilled technique enter into the delivery. A noticeable measure of pride resides in a drawing. Excellence is achievable through applied practice, and maintaining principles of good practice through technique.

Precision lettering is important for two reasons: firstly, information is communicated within a drawing in the form of titles, labels and notes, within title blocks, and as dimensioning. Secondly, which is often significant in design, lettering is incorporated into scenic elements, requiring sign-writing skills. Sign writing may take the form of lettering as applied flat or as carved into a surface. Inscriptions, where lettering is carved or where lettering is cast or painted onto surface as ornament, requires reference to original methods and techniques, combined with an understanding of the effect on the eye of the spectator – be it close-up or at some distance. References for period lettering

*Stroke method: vertical and inclined strokes for lettering and numbering.*

enlighten the designer on the artistry of lettering. Script or font type can be referenced through publications on historical alphabets.

## How does consistency come about?

Attractive lettering is achievable through using applied guidelines. Freehand printing is quite different from freehand writing style. Therefore there is no excuse that a poor writing style will get in the way of developing a competent freehand printing technique. Learning the technique of printing capital (upper-case) letters requires an understanding of the basic principles involving the order of strokes that form each letter. Fortunately letters of the alphabet share principles, reducing the number of types of strokes. Guidelines are a foundation for layout and composition. They are concerned with spacing of letters, formation of letters, and adequate space for wording. The emphasis is on developing a competent style with attractive lettering, which is achievable through routine exercises and practice.

## Single stroke method

The ability to maintain consistency in lettering is achieved through the single stroke method, where letter formation is comprised of a combination of strokes, which guarantees uniformity in the shaping of any one letter of the alphabet. Individual letters need to be practised separately, as technique develops through repetition. Thereafter letters are combined into words. Rules on letter spacing and word spacing follow. The technique involved to create the number eight (8) involves four separate strokes, each being a half circle arc. The draughtsman's clear intent should be immediate recognition, to eliminate the chance of one number being mistaken for another.

## Notes about lettering

* Key information needs to be delivered with clarity.
* Finish a drawing before applying printed matter in the form of lettering and dimensions.
* Soft pencil lead for finished quality lines is prone to smudging; to avoid this, place a sheet of A4 tracing paper or copy paper under the hand.

### The stroke method

The stroke method ensures accuracy and consistency. Through practice, the skill for speed and accuracy develops. Define height through drawing faint guidelines in pencil. Practise letters and numbers independently, before attempting to make formation into words. Proceed with care to maintain precision, rather than aiming to achieve quantity. Observe number, order and direction to strokes. Practise with printing between 5mm and 7mm height, as any larger becomes awkward. Do not fix the page to the drawing board, as having a page which can be conveniently adjusted or slightly repositioned allows for more comfort and leads to better accuracy.

* Work through adding printed matter from page left to page right (unless the draughtsperson is left-handed), as smudging is less likely to occur.
* Titles and labels establish what each view is.
* Dimensions clarify exact proportional inter-relationships.
* A title block carries vital information.
* Accompanying notes deliver specific intentions relating to construction and scenic art.
* Letters and numbers positioned upright are called 'vertical printing'.
* Letters and numbers inclined at 65 and/or 70 degrees to the horizontal are called 'inclined printing'.
* Capital letters are used exclusively in technical drawing; never use lower-case lettering.
* Roman script and Roman numerals are standard type in technical printing.
* Dimensioning or measurements are always expressed in millimetres.
* Vertical printing as capitals should be no smaller than 4mm high.
* Average printing height is 5mm and should not exceed 7mm.
* Spacing between lines should be no less than 3mm and no more than 5mm.

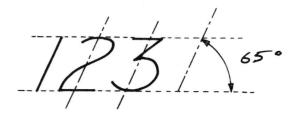

ABOVE: *Vertical printed lettering and numbers with guidelines.*

BELOW: *Vertical printed lettering and numbers, and inclined printed lettering and numbers.*

*Inclined printed numbers at 65 and/or 70 degrees. Establish horizontal guidelines for the printing, then at intervals across the page draw in angled lines at 65 and/or 70 degrees, faintly drawn for guidelines for inclined text.*

ABCDEFGHIJKLMNOPQR
STUVWXYZ 1234567890

ABCDEFGHIJKLMNOPQR
STUVWXYZ 1234567890

* The larger the letter, the more it tends to look weak; as with a narrow lead not complementing the ratio for overall height.
* Aim to perfect 'vertical printing' before moving on to 'inclined printing'.
* Between lengthy sessions of lettering practice, it is a good idea to exercise the hand gently with it extended down the side of the body.

### Inclined capitals
* Proportions for letters and numerals are the same as with vertical lettering.
* The stroke system is the same as for vertical.

* The intended incline is 65 and/or 70 degrees off the horizontal; guidelines drawn at intervals across the page at 65 and/or 70 degrees off the horizontal ensure consistency.
* Letters O, C, Q, G and D are elliptical in shape, with the ellipse leaning to the right.
* Letters V, A, W, X and Y are balanced equally about an imaginary inclined centre line.

## GUIDELINES

Text and numerical notation are printed onto the page only after guidelines are applied. The vertical

## Roman script lettering

'Old Roman' is the name given to both Classical Roman and Renaissance Roman scripts. Until the sixteenth century the letters 'I' and 'J' were not differentiated: in classical inscriptions the letter 'I' is used for 'J'. The curved 'U' is also of a later period as the sharp 'V' was used instead on all Roman inscriptions.

height of lettering may vary and is often determined by what is being said, what is important to draw attention to, and where it is placed in the drawing. These guidelines maintain a consistency for all notations. (For those beginning the practice of lettering, it is recommended all letters and numbers should be 5mm in height.)

Plot guidelines using a standard rule; they should be drawn with a 4H lead and be of a light pencil pressure. Draw horizontal guidelines spaced 5mm apart. Draw in the base and height line first. Estimate the centre vertically between the two parallel lines and define it by making a fine dot. At this point draw a very light horizontal line dividing the parallel lines in half. These three faint guidelines should be visible to the eye close-up, yet be faint enough to not read from an arm's distance; the lighter they are, the less likely they will be to show when professionally copied (dyeline or photocopy). The centre-line registers with the vertical centre of letters A, B, E, F, G, H, K, P, R, X and Y, and numbers 3, 5, 6, 8 and 9. Note alternatively that capital letters look pleasing to the eye when the centre line is placed slightly below centre, as this gives the letter a lower gravity.

### The lettering guide

The most convenient of tools for drawing guidelines is the 'lettering guide', supplied through manufacturers of technical drawing equipment. This tool speeds up the process of drawing guide lines. This clear plastic tool has an inset disc, which can be rotated. Within the disc are drilled a series of equidistant holes just large enough for a pencil point. The series of prescribed holes is set in columns; each column sets a ratio for the height of the letter, and offers the centre for each set of parallel lines. The centre-line guides the printing to space itself proportionally so that the centre of letters and numbers (vertically) falls on the centre-line. The tool facilitates drawing between three and four lines for text. The tool is placed on the page in contact with the arm of the T-square, the pencil lead is inserted and lines are drawn across the page. The tool can also be positioned along the vertical edge of a set-square, to enable dimensions to be aligned to the sides of an object.

## SPACING AND COMPOSITION

Spacing is concerned with applied uniformity, both in the distance between letters and in the distance between the words. As a rule individual letters forming words are not spaced at equal distance from one another; instead, the spaces are to appear uniform by keeping the irregularly shaped backgrounds between them to an approximately equal area. Spacing is therefore dependent on the letter shape preceding it. Thus adjacent letters with straight sides would be spaced further apart than those with curved sides. Where combinations appear such as 'LT' or 'AV' the spacing may actually overlap. Letters should never make contact with one another, as clarity is sacrificed. Letters should never make contact with a solid line – either one found in the title block or those in a drawing – as they should only make contact with guidelines specifically drawn for lettering. Spacing letters the same distance apart results in an uneven nature to spacing. Space established between upright letters ('THE' or 'MEN') appears visually different from spacing of letters with angle ('AWAY' or 'WAVY'). Beginners tend to either space letters too far apart or too close together. The best result is where spacing appears relatively equal, with words easy to read. Critical judgement comes through observing good practice in lettering and trusting the eye to achieve the appearance of equal distance.

Composition is concerned with the best possible arrangement of text; the spacing of words and layout for text labelling and addition of notes. A measure of practical and artistic judgment is required. The plotting in of faint margin lines maintains text alignment, as in bullet-point format. Labelling has its own formatting as appropriate to multi-views of an object. Within the title block and note block centring and aligning text adds clarity.

## Word spacing

The spacing between words should be achieved through imagining one of the wider letters fitting the space ('M' or 'W'). Spacing should generally be not more than the height of the letter.

## Line spacing

The space between one line of lettering and another may vary from a quarter to one-and-a-half times the height of the letter. Initially it is good practice to make the space between lines of lettering the same dimension as the letter height, this being 5mm.

# STARTING UP

### Pencil type and manner of handling

The illustration for Roman script depicts a correct method for single stroke lettering. Set the guidelines, use capital letters only, and proceed using a soft pencil lead, a recommended H or HB on tracing paper size A4. Hold the pencil naturally as when writing, and keep the forearm on the drawing board.

Pencil strokes should be of a bold hand to establish uniformity; lines should have even thickness and carry the same weight. Make all letter beginnings and ends with definite strokes, maintaining firm pressure on the page. Between letters slightly rotate the pencil to avoid a dull lead and at intervals sharpen the lead. Avoid rushing: take time to establish consistency of strokes and a uniformity of letter size and proportion. At intervals sit back to observe the outcome, allowing time for critical judgement. Remember to practise letters and numbers before forming words.

## Study groups

Group the letters of the alphabet to support learning stroke technique.

* Straight stroke letters include I, H, T, L, E and F.
* The vertical is achieved by a downward stroke; the horizontal achieved by a movement to the right.
* Inclined stroke letters include A, K, M, N, V, W, X, Y and Z.
* Begin with the left side of each letter; whether it is a vertical or angled stroke, it is achieved with a downward stroke.
* The horizontal in A is the third stroke, the vertical in Y the third stroke, the right side of the letter W is the fourth stroke and is achieved by drawing downwards.
* The letters O, Q, C and G have circle arcs as their outside curves.
* All curves are similar to the 'O' group, in that their outside curves are circles or circle arcs.
* Letters made up of straight lines and curves include B, D, J, P, R and U.
* The reverse curve within the letter S is a tricky manoeuvre.
* The ampersand '&' is a monogram; an abbreviation for 'et', it is achieved through various stroke forms.
* Roman letters may never be extended wider than their normal proportions of width to height. Roman letters can, however, be made in compressed form if desired.

# NUMERALS

There is good reason to shape numerals with a style of uniformity. Aim to achieve consistency in appearance for all numbers. The circle arcs shaping C, G, O and Q show effective uniformity. Similar uniformity needs be found in number 8, number 3, and the letter S.

For the left-hander there is room for reinvention if necessary, as the methods of strokes need to vary to suit the manner in which the pencil is held, and the preferred most comfortable action suitable to the individual. However, the aim is the same: to produce an outcome similar to that shown in its relationship of parts.

## Notes about numerals

* All numerical values are based on ten basic numerals: 1, 2, 3, 4, 5, 6, 7, 8, 9 and 0.
* All numerals, except number 1, are the same width.
* The number 3 and letter S are based on the shape of the number 8.
* Numeral 8 is made up of a small ellipse centered over a larger ellipse.
* The numerals 6 and 9 are alike but reversed, with both fitting into the elliptical 0 (zero).

## Inclined numerals

Inclined numerals are like vertical numerals, except they lean to the right.

* The stroke system is the same as vertical.
* Horizontal guidelines are drawn in the same manner to the vertical numerals.
* The intended inclined is 65 and/or 70 degrees off the horizontal; guidelines drawn at intervals across the page at 65 and/or 70 degrees off the horizontal assure consistency.
* Numerals 8 and 0 are elliptical in shape, with the ellipse leaning to the right.

## Use of lettering templates

Clear plastic templates are available with the font etched through, offering both capital and lower-case alphabet and numerals. Templates are designed for graphic printing: the larger heights (more than 7mm in height) proving more useful, yet not necessary. It is rare for technical drawing to require such size lettering.

# DIMENSIONS

The view of an object is referred to as a 'projection'. The object view is transferred through projection onto a plane called the 'plane of projection'. Multi-view projection is of various views, informing the viewer through orthographic projection, depicting what an object looks like in its shape and proportioning. The view defines its

---

### The complete picture

For clarity the draughtsman needs to give complete information by means of:

1. *Views:* depicting the object as seen in multi-view projection.
2. *Dimensions:* accurate measurements for each view.
3. *Notes:* text to support the visual information.

---

edges and face features. An object is accurately scaled, and layout describes relationships between views, helping construction to form a mental 3D picture. However, drawing 'for construction' requires additional factual and practical information. Actual measurements defining the dimensions need to be included.

Accompanying the drawing with its dimensions are designer notes. These inform construction on preferred materials, processes of construction, performance demands, and finish requirements. Not always are processes of construction included in great depth, as discussions with Head of Construction determine the best methods and techniques to be applied.

A degree of inaccuracy occurs in all scale drawings, yet measurements are typically well calculated and clearly defined. Slight discrepancies in the drawing do not usually affect the dimensioning, since dimensions are usually accurate calculations. It is, however, essential to avoid a very inaccurate drawing, where proportions are not scaled well. This can mislead construction, and makes comprehension of the actual look of the thing difficult.

Dimension errors can often be corrected by construction staff, as obvious mistakes do become clear when processing for construction. Yet some errors in dimensioning slip through. Miscalculations at scale prove expensive to change when realized. Often the mistake is noticed too late on in the process, making it prohibitive to change. It is critical that a draughtsman reviews the drawing, both at intervals while draughting, and at completion, to safeguard against misrepresentation.

The draughtsman requires a good level of understanding of shop practice. Knowledge of construction methods and materials makes it easier to anticipate issues that may arise. A successful drawing is one in which the instructions relate to the drawing. The drawing facilitates the building of the object; therefore textual information supports accurate interpretation of the drawing. Common sense should always prevail.

## The degree of drawing accuracy

In respect of the degree of accuracy actually possible when plotting dimensions (noting that at a scale of 1:25 the smallest rule increment is equivalent to 2mm, with 1mm being a calculated guess as the centre between increments), it is necessary to calculate measurement divisions on paper mathematically. The scale rule is only a tool, used to apply 'known' dimensions to the page. Measurements are calculated, then applied. As construction will not measure from a drawing, using a scale rule, the emphasis is on dimensions as printed. Inaccuracies found in the drawing should not affect precise calculations. Deliver dimensions as exact as possible.

## Dimensioning methods

Two methods can be applied when dimensioning. Both are commonplace, yet it is not recommended to mix techniques. Use one method or the other, as contradictions make for a confused reading.

### The horizontal or one-directional method

Dimensioning, text, labels, and notes are all placed across the page in a horizontal manner. This sameness makes for easy reading, as the viewer has only to read information laid out in one direction; the point of view is from the bottom of the page. There is no need to rotate the page to read information numbers or text.

### The aligned method

Dimensions and numerals are placed on the page running in the direction of the dimension line.

Therefore, horizontal dimension lines contain dimensions laid in a horizontal manner, vertical dimension lines contain dimensions laid in a vertical manner, and angled dimension lines contain dimensions laid in the same angled manner. The dimension is aligned to the view and is parallel in its direction. To read dimensions clearly and accurately the page must be rotated so measurement information can be viewed accordingly. A drawing featuring a variety of angled planes will demand it being rotated to clarify its dimensions.

## Extension lines

Extension lines are the object's edges projected beyond the object, into the area set aside for dimensioning. The edges of an object are projected beyond the intersecting corners. Internal edges are also projected beyond, into the area set aside for dimensioning. Extension lines run perpendicular to the object's side profile. Avoid extension lines touching the profile of the object; allow for a gap of 5mm (minimum). Do not use a profile line for an object as an extension line.

Avoid extension lines making contact with two views of an object (such as front and side view, or front and top view). Although construction lines are drawn faintly, and may be drawn so one view connects to another view, darkening or inking in extension lines should be done leaving a recommended gap. If construction lines are too darkly drawn then use an eraser and erasing shield to lighten their intensity.

Extension lines may cross one another, and may extend beyond one dimension line through to another dimension line.

A centre-line, registered within an object, may be projected out beyond the profile, and may be used as an extension line. A centre-line may be used like an extension line; it may serve as an intersection for a dimension line. Project a centre line as a solid line from its centre dash; do not interrupt it by breaking its projection.

## Dimension lines

A dimension line runs perpendicular to an extension line. It is drawn parallel to the span or distance being measured. Dimension lines should be drawn nearer the extreme end of the extension line, set further away from the object profile. Leave a gap of at least 5mm between profile and dimension line. Where space permits, make the gap 10mm or more.

Avoid dimension lines crossing one another. Dimension lines for intermediate measurements are drawn first, nearer the profile edge, yet not less than 5mm away. Beyond intermediate measurements, running parallel to these, is an overall dimension. Leave a gap of 10mm between parallel sets of dimension lines. Do not use lines drawn for the object as dimension lines.

Avoid applying dimension lines within the object's profile. Always project beyond the profile into the area set aside to plot dimensions (except for radii points).

*Arrow system*

Dimension lines end with an arrow where they make contact with extension lines. When using arrows, be consistent: avoid using two methods in one drawing. Use either the arrow system or the 45-degree intersection system. The arrows should be small and uniformly applied across a given page.

*45-degree intersection system*

Dimension lines continue beyond the extension line, with the point of intersection indicated by a 45-degree slashed line. Extend dimension lines at either end by a minimum of 5mm. The 45-degree slash crosses through the intersection of the dimension and extension line. This slash should always be drawn with a 45-degree set square. Therefore it is recommended to do these for all the drawing, rather than one at a time as dimensions are added in. The slash is approximately 5mm in length, with its centre on the point of intersection. The 45-degree angle as a 'forward slash' should be consistent across the page.

*Pointer lines*

Where there may not be enough space to include the 45-degree slash (due to the distance being too narrow to add a measurement numerically), place a pencil dot between the lines and draw a line away

into the area set aside for lettering, and print the dimension at the end of the extended line. Use either an inclined line with horizontal tail with the number printed thereafter; or a snake-like line with numerical dimension printed thereafter. The tail horizontal ends up as the centre of numerals, as the tail will continue (lightly drawn) to form a guideline for lettering. The numerals will have an overall height of 5mm.

Where a pointer line is used for text-related information, the same rules will apply. The pointer shaft should be made as short as possible. Avoid a pointer line having the same angle as inclined lines within a drawing, or of 45 degrees. Pointer lines are generally drawn with a straight edge, or ruler. The snake pointer lines are drawn freehand. Freehand pointers may be useful when many lines cross, and an added variation would support clarity. Avoid pointer lines crossing one another.

## The plotting of dimensions

At the centre of a dimension line a numerical measurement is positioned. There are two methods:

1. Print the number above a solid dimension line.
2. Print the number between the lines, with the line interrupted by a space.

With the second method, the line actually continues, yet is faintly drawn for the locating of centre of numbers as a guideline. Above and below the centre line will be guidelines set 5mm apart in parallel.

## Notes about dimensions

* Always draw guidelines for numerical dimensioning.
* Where there is a long dimension line, it may be necessary to allow space between the parallel lines of a dimension line and object profile, for inclusion of intermediate dimensions.
* When dimensions are layered in a parallel manner, with some set beyond the others, avoid alignment of the numerical dimensions; instead, numerical dimensions should be staggered slightly.

* Place a dimension alongside the view which best explains its true characteristic. Look for the most obvious place to plot relevant height, width or depth measurements.
* With views being placed alongside one another, a dimension may relate to both views, therefore include it only once between those two views.
* All dimensions need including which facilitate the viewer comprehending the object. The viewer should not need to calculate dimensions. Avoid duplicating a dimension.

## Expressing numerals in dimensions

All dimensions should consistently be in millimetres (1m is printed as 1000, 10cm is printed as 100, 2cm is printed as 20, 1.5cm is printed as 15). It is not necessary to put 'mm' after a dimension. Do not mix centimetres into the drawing. For measurements larger than 1000mm, print in the same millimetre format (100cm is printed as 1000, 200cm is printed as 2000, 1000cm is printed as 10000). Measurements less than 10mm may have the millimetres included: 9mm, 8mm through to 1mm.

Draughting for theatre construction calls for precision, yet it is not so common to find complex refined dimensions in a drawing (such as 1751mm, 153mm, 27mm) unless a material is of a specific thickness or size known to the draughtsman. However, bench drawings or construction drawings – those prepared by Head of Construction or an engineer – show fine-tuned millimetre dimensioning, appropriate to the materials being used in construction. The designer tends to be mainly concerned with key proportional measurements.

Generally print numerical measurements at 5mm height wherever possible. If they are below 3mm they will be difficult to read. The more effort one has to make to read dimensions, the more likely there will be miscalculations.

Where a dimension is printed alongside a drawing that is not at scale, there should be written alongside the drawing, 'NOT TO SCALE'.

## Dimensions of curved shapes

*Circle*

Depict a circle centre with a cross (a vertical and horizontal line intersecting), using a set-square and the horizontal of the T-square. To add in radii:

1. Draw an inclined straight line as a 'pointer line' from outside the circumference to beyond, and where the pointer touches the circumference draw an arrow. At the other end of the pointer line print the letter 'D' and add in the diameter measurement.
2. From circle-centre draw a straight radial to make contact with the circumference; where it makes contact draw an arrow. Alongside the radial print the letter 'R' and add in the radius measurement.

When plotting the position for a circle contained within a form (such as a square); note the distance from the container's profile edge to the circle centre as a dimension.

*Arch*

Note the centre of the arch with a small cross. At this point of intersection draw an angled line as a straight radial to the circumference; at the end of the radial line draw an arrow. Alongside the radial print the letter 'R' and add in the radius dimension.

# 9 ORTHOGRAPHIC PROJECTION

In orthographic projection the object drawn is presented through a series of views. Each view will represent the individual surface planes, in their true height, depth and width. The spectator's view is at a plane parallel to the object's elevation (such as front view, side view, and top view). Technical information from the object (edges and contour) is projected onto the picture plane through perpendicular projections. The information, once transferred, is joined-up by line to present a view. The view is an elevation often scaled proportionally yet with true dimension applied, in a technical manner. All views deliver the necessary information for construction to process the build, facilitating a three-dimensional impression in the mind.

Multi-views of an object in orthographic projection depict surface as viewed only in two dimensions; it is not represented in three dimensions as may be found in isometric or axonometric projection or perspective drawing. The views are in themselves 'elevations', meaning they give true representation to height, width, and depth measurements. Therefore to successfully represent a three-dimensional object two dimensionally, there is a need to present at least two separate views to describe it. When the object cannot be successfully represented by two views alone, the drawing in

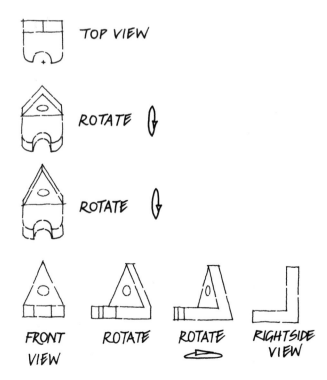

TOP VIEW

ROTATE

ROTATE

FRONT VIEW          ROTATE          ROTATE          RIGHTSIDE VIEW

*The component object shown in various views, as being flipped from top view through to elevation/front view. Then rotated on central axis to arrive at right-side view. Three regular views: top view, elevation and right side view. When observing the elevation, the viewers' right side of the object becomes the right-side view, with the object rotating on an imaginary axis.*

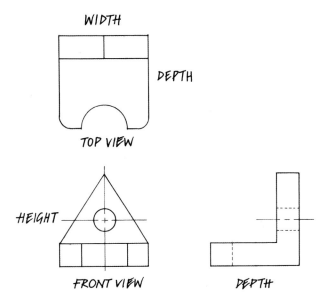

WIDTH

DEPTH

TOP VIEW

HEIGHT

FRONT VIEW

DEPTH

LEFT: *Three regular views of a component unit. Top view showing width and depth; elevation showing width and height; right-side view showing depth and height. Note the right-side view is a rotation of the elevation on a central axis, permitting its right side to be observed.*

RIGHT: *Component unit in four views, showing top view, elevation, plan and right-side view. The plan is not the 'bottom view', instead it is the object sitting on a surface and lines are indicated in a solid where the edges make contact with the floor. Top view: lines include solids, centre-lines, and hidden lines. Visible lines for the edges take precedence over a centre line: the centre line for circle/arc is indicated yet separated from the object sides by short spacing or gaps. Plan: the dash lines indicate the above floor level edges. The centre line through a circular hole is shown as only two short dashes beyond the edges, due to the dash line representing the peak apex to the triangle above the floor.*

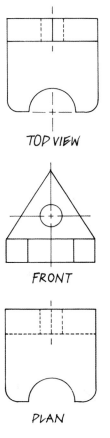

TOP VIEW

FRONT

PLAN

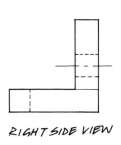

RIGHT SIDE VIEW

*Isometric drawings with orthographic projections in three views: elevation (front view), right-side and plan.*

1. Cube
2. Sphere
3. Cone
4. Pyramid
5. Rectangular Box
6. Cylinder
7. Prism
8. Octagon.

FRONT VIEW     RIGHT SIDE VIEW

PLAN

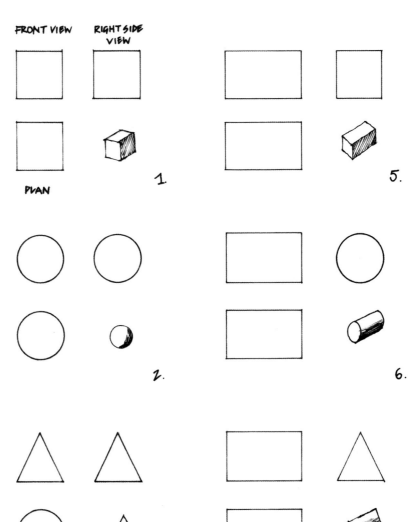

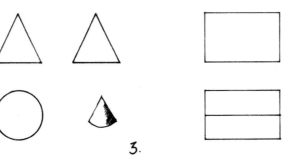

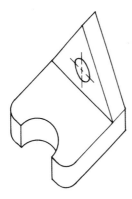

*Object as viewed in axonometric projection set at 45 degrees off the horizontal with measures for height and depth true to the original. No perspective foreshortening.*

**The six views of an object**

Top view
Front view
Bottom view (plan: for theatre practitioners)
Right-side view
Left-side view
Rear view

layout will deliver 'three regular views' or 'multi-views' of an object, or six views of the object are depicted for it to be fully understood. Technical drawing for performance is not as clearly defined with sets of rules, as one scenic element may require only two views, while another may need presenting through multiple views, as it may present a unique problem. The set designer presents unique production demands: with each design arrives a new set of priorities, new ways of looking at things. Clarity of intent is the overall aim when draughting orthographic projection, yet when advice or guidance is needed, support is not far away through consultation with technical or production management, the Head of Construction or with engineers whom one might be fortunate to be working with.

## THE GLASS BOX WITH OBJECT ENCLOSED

Another approach to understanding the relation of views is to imagine a cube of glass encasing the object in question. Through perpendicular projectors off the object's edges and its contours, points of contact with the glass plane are made; the points are joined up to become the view itself. Each view as it appears on the glass plane becomes a

true elevation, forming the six views of an object. Note however that the bottom view is replaced by a plan. By viewing all the drawn multi-views, an understanding of the object's form is established.

## REFERENCE TO LINE TYPE

The meaning of a line has three possibilities. A line can represent:

1. The edge view of a surface.
2. The intersection of two surfaces.
3. The contour view of a curved surface.

When making observation of views of an object, understanding the meaning of line type is important to avoid misunderstanding. For example:

* Where a view shows a contour representing a curved surface, it may be misread as the edge view of a flat surface.
* Where a line is read as an edge, the line may actually be the intersection of an inclined surface making contact with another surface.

### Use of shading to explain contour

Drawings as linear representations do not technically require shading in, as it is time consuming. When shading is introduced, it indicates a contour. The line drawn defining edge to a contour could include within it shading; as the contour recedes from the eye it becomes a darker shade. Shading is taken towards the furthest line curving away from the eye. An adjacent view should show the true contour as defined by a curve or arc.

*Glass box: constructing four views of an object, within the four sides of a cube. Note the distance between object and the glass box planes is immaterial; the distance of side view from front view makes no difference to the drawing. Therefore make it any convenient distance. Begin with the top view and front view elevation by plotting measurements and by projections through from one to the other. The top view is always positioned above the front view. Project relevant height measurements from front view to side views. Depth dimensions within side views are measured and plotted in this method.*

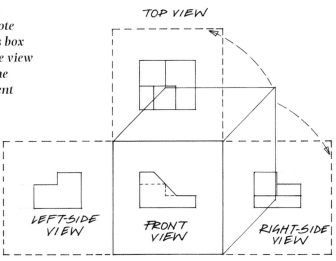

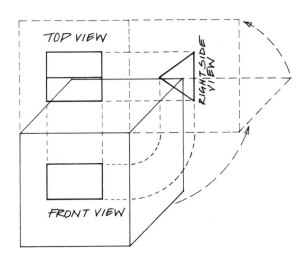

*Glass box: constructing projections from top to side and front view. Right side view's depth and height measurements may be projected across and down, across and up through the cube corners being a centre point for arcs.*

## THREE REGULAR VIEWS OF AN OBJECT

Objects have three dimensions: length, width and height. The two-dimensional nature of orthographic representation requires that views be represented through inter-relationships. The method employed is formatted by principles. The viewer is informed with one established view connecting through to another. The object being viewed is rotated from front to side, as by shifting the object on a central rotational axis. Where line interpretation in one view is not easily articulated or made entirely clear, the inclusion of subsequent views aims to achieve clarity.

Three regular views are comprised of top view, front view and side view.

1. Top view is from above looking down, alike to a bird's eye view.
2. Front view looks straight on, as a face view.
3. Side view looks at one side of the object.

117

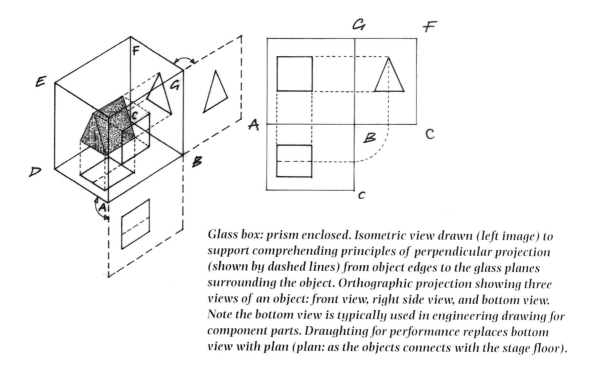

*Glass box: prism enclosed. Isometric view drawn (left image) to support comprehending principles of perpendicular projection (shown by dashed lines) from object edges to the glass planes surrounding the object. Orthographic projection showing three views of an object: front view, right side view, and bottom view. Note the bottom view is typically used in engineering drawing for component parts. Draughting for performance replaces bottom view with plan (plan: as the objects connects with the stage floor).*

Three views presented are often enough to understand the form fully. The image presents how it will look once constructed. The page layout always takes on the same format with views being arranged on the page as follows:

* Top view is positioned at the top of the page.
* Front view is positioned directly beneath, and aligned vertically with the top view.
* Right-side view is positioned to the right of the front view, and aligned horizontally with the front view.

When the right-side view may not inform construction as successfully as the left-side view might, it is considered appropriate to exclude the standard right-side view. The top view is architecturally known as 'top plan', but it is more familiar to performance draughting as 'top view'.

**Transferring dimensions from top view to side view**

As dimensions can be passed from view to view,

through transferring vertical lines up from plan up to front view, and again up to top view, they can also be transferred from side views through to rear view and front view horizontally. However, to transfer depth dimensions from plan or top view through to the side view, another approach is used. Methods used for transferring include the mitre method, the use of dividers, the ticket stub, and the scale rule.

*Mitre method (transferring top view to side view)*

1. Place the object's front view within a box (*see illustration*). Lines drawn as extensions of its external edge form a right-angled intersection, in the upper right-hand corner of the object. A mitre-line is a 45-degree angled line extending from the corner beyond.
2. The depth dimension of the object, in top view, is then transferred horizontally to the 45-degree mitre-line. At the point of intersection a vertical line is drawn downwards to the side view.

The same method is applied to determine depth dimensions for top view when front and side views are established. Depth dimensions are transferred vertically from the side view upwards to the mitre-line; at the point of intersection, a line is drawn horizontally across to the top view.

*Other methods for transferring dimensions*
As it is often difficult to plot with accuracy when drawing an object at 1:25 scale, it is possible to duplicate a measurement from one view to another through using two alternative methods:

1. Use a set of dividers from the compass set. Establish the span between two given points. With care not to alter the distance between the needle points, transfer marking either with a small hole in the page with a needle point or with a fine pencil after locating the distance required.
2. Use a small ticket or stub of paper. Note accurately the distance along one edge, with a sharp pencil. It is helpful to label such points 'AB'. Indicate by making a fine dash on the paper edge, perpendicular to the edge, or mark with a dot; in both cases use a sharp pencil point. Manoeuvre the stub to its second position, and set off the units required. Then transfer the measured dimension across.
3. Use a scale rule, making sure accuracy of measurement is obtained through re-reading carefully. This method is the least accurate.

## SIX VIEWS OF AN OBJECT

Representation through six views offers a designer the possibility to investigate fully an object's formal and structural concerns from all views. Drawings of objects created for performance often need to be drawn up with six views to actually envisage how they will appear. There are but few technical relationships with architecture and interior design, permitting the use of standard templates for drawing up scenic elements. The principles are made different through differing constraints, rules concerning health and safety and the nature of temporary constructions over permanent. Inter-

pretation of historical period requires rethinking form to meet performance requirements. Proportional relationships need typically to conform to architecture/venue constraints, performance demands and material for the build.

Each of the six views represents the elevation planes in true height, depth and width. The same principles apply for six views as for three regular views; each view describes in a two-dimensional form an object's elevations and its plan.

Top, front and side views are explained above (*see* page 114), but rear view and plan are described as follows:

* The plan is positioned below the front view. There is no indication of height.
* The rear view is positioned to the left of the left-side view. There is no indication of the depth.

Note: all the views are elevations, meaning they represent true measurements. The plan object's it is not an elevation of the base otherwise it would be called a bottom view. In drawing for performance a bottom view is seldom called for, as scenic elements and props have their bottom view firmly planted on stage or other surface, rendering it unseen by the audience.

### Rear view
Typically props and small scenic units that are not backed by a flat may require the inclusion of a rear view. This is necessary where the audience views the rear side of an object. This may be during a scene change or if the performance is 'in the round'. Include the rear view to the left of the left-side view.

### The side views explained
The right side of an object is the side to the right when viewing the front view. Rotate the object clockwise, so its right side becomes an elevation (a view of a plane perpendicular to the eye's direction of vision). The back of the object is to the right in this view. If one were to walk to the right of front view, round to the side, the right-side view would indicate true height and true depth. The illustration (*see* page 114) will help explain this further.

The left-side view is the left side of the front view, therefore the object needs to be rotated counter-clockwise until its side becomes a plane viewed as an elevation (meaning the true height and depth are represented). Both right-side and left-side views indicate height and depth, but no width.

## LAYOUT FOR SIX VIEWS OF AN OBJECT

The six views in layout are illustrated though the unfolding or opening out of an imaginary glass box. Simply imagine a cube unhinging. All views/planes are represented: front view, top view, plan, left-side and right-side views (connected or attached to the front view), and rear view (attached/hinged to the left-side view/plane).

Three views are to be positioned vertically. One is placed above the other with the plan at the base of the page, front view above plan, and top view above front view. Four views are positioned horizontally. One is placed to the right of the front view (right-side view), with all others positioned to the left of front view (left-side view to

the left of front view; rear view to the left of left-side view) *see* page 129.

Note: plan view is typically the first view to be drawn onto the page. The designer establishes the plan view for a scenic element upon the ground plan, and thereafter simply copies by tracing this onto the multi-view layout. As is typical, a 3D form is shaped in the sketch model, the information about its positioning is transferred to or plotted on the ground plan; once the ground plan has sorted out sight-line issues and space constraints, the information is transferred to multi-view elevations and then draughted as orthographic projections.

## DEMONSTRATION OF PAGE PLANNING FOR SIX-VIEW LAYOUT

Object to be drawn: a chair.

Chair dimensions: H=1000mm, depth=600mm, width=450mm.

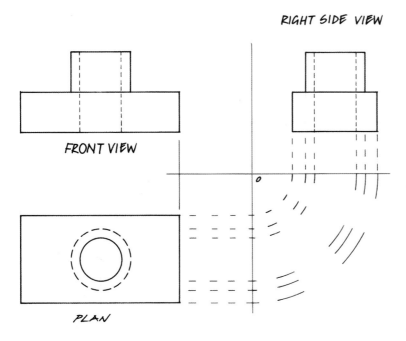

RIGHT SIDE VIEW

FRONT VIEW

PLAN

*Orthographic projection. Object views include front view, plan and side view. Front view and plan are aligned one above the other with information transferred from one to the other. The side view is achieved through both front and plan views transferring proportions across and down and across and up. The right angle at O is formed through adding in vertical and horizontal lines, which gives the intersection for the compass point.*

Each view: top; front; plan; left-side; right-side; rear; to be placed in a geometric box defining its overall dimensions. Rough sketch this out on a sheet of A4.

## Step 1: total vertical page measurement

Vertical layout: top view, front view (elevation), plan. First measure the A3 page vertical height, at scale 1:25; measuring between the top of the page border and top horizontal of title block. This should be 5800mm.

Vertical measurement = 5800mm.

*Total horizontal page measurement*

Horizontal layout: rear view, left-side view, front view, right-side view. Measure the A3 page horizontal distance, at scale 1:25: measurement from border to border. This should be 10000mm.

Horizontal measurement = 10000mm.

## Step 2: calculate object dimensions for vertical layout

Add together (create the sum total) of the three vertical views:

* depth of chair (plan) = 600mm
* height of chair (front) = 1000mm
* depth of chair (top) = 600mm

Answer: 600 + 1000 + 600 = 2200mm.

Total vertical dimension requirements = 2200mm.

Equation: depth + height + depth = dimension requirement.

*Calculate spacing required*

Subtract 2200mm (three views) from 5800mm (page height).

Answer: 5800 – 2200 = 3600mm.

Equation: page height – sum of views = page space remaining.

*Calculate spacing between each view*

Divide 3600mm (page space remaining) by 4 (four spaces required).

Answer: 3600 ÷ 4 = 900mm

Equation: height remaining ÷ 4 = vertical spacing.

## Step 3: calculate object dimensions for horizontal layout

Add together (create the sum total) of the four horizontal views:

* width of chair (rear) = 450mm
* depth of chair (left-side) = 600mm
* width of chair (front) = 450mm
* depth of chair (right-side) = 600mm

Answer: 450 + 600 + 450 + 600 = 2100mm.

Total horizontal dimension requirements = 2100mm.

Equation: width + depth + width + depth = dimension requirement.

*Calculate spacing required*

Subtract 2100mm (four views) from 10000mm (page width).

1000 - 2100 = 7900mm.

Equation: page width – sum of views = page space remaining.

*Calculate spacing between each view*

Divide 7900mm (page space remaining) by 5 (five spaces required)

Answer: 7900 ÷ 5 = 1580mm

Equation: width remaining ÷ 5 = horizontal spacing.

## Step 4: apply dimensioning to page layout.

1. Vertical layout.

Using a sharp 4H pencil, proceed to plot (with fine dots), vertical requirements between page top border and top horizontal of title block. Work from bottom to top; place scale rule (1:25) vertically and measure and plot:

* vertical space 900mm
* depth of chair (plan) 600mm
* vertical space 900mm
* height of chair (front view) 1000mm

* vertical space 900mm
* depth of chair (top view) 600mm
* vertical space 900mm

Result: 900 + 600 + 900 + 1000 + 900 + 600 + 900 = 5800mm (vertical page height).

2.  Horizontal layout

Proceed to plot (with fine dots), horizontal requirements between page border and page border. Work from left to right; place scale rule (1:25) horizontally and measure and plot:

* horizontal space 1580mm
* width of chair (rear view) 450mm
* horizontal space 1580mm
* depth of chair (left-side view) 600mm
* horizontal space 1580mm
* width of chair (front view) 450mm
* horizontal space 1580mm
* depth of chair (right-side view) 600mm
* horizontal space 1580mm

Result: 1580 + 450 + 1580 + 600 + 1580 + 450 + 1580 + 600 + 1580 = 10000mm (total horizontal page width).

## FROM PLAN TO MULTI-VIEWS

### Stage 1

To begin the drawing of multiple views for a scenic element, place a scrap of tracing paper (this can be a thin strip) over the ground plan, positioning it above the specific scenic element or unit that requires development through multi-views. Trace the drawing accurately off the plan with the two taped securely together. Trace in a precise manner using the appropriate tools. Remove the drawing.

### Stage 2

Position a standard-sized page of tracing paper on the board, align it with the T-square arm, and tape it securely in place (*see* page 141). Draw the page border (set in 10mm from edges – *see* page 142) and outline in the title block (*see* pages 142 and 145). Consider the page layout as a rough calculation (*see* the principle outlined on page 120 and

the diagram of four views of an object page 114); planning for only four regular views. Slip beneath the page the tracing paper copy from the plan and align with position for plan. Tape it securely in place.

### Stage 3

With the plan squarely aligned to T-square and set-square, commence with redrawing the plan view. Use a 4H lead pencil. Take care in accuracy and precision. Once completed, remove the drawing beneath, being careful not to lose registration of the top page. Using the same lead, 4H, and a set-square securely attached to the T-square, project lines vertically for the width of the object, including all internal or intermediate widths within the form. The vertical lines should travel the height of the page; use a light pencil pressure. Within the overall width will be established all widths for front view and top view.

### Stage 4

With suitable spacing between the three views, draw a horizontal line across the page establishing the base line for the front view. Measure up vertically above the base line to plot height for the scenic element. Draw a horizontal line across the page at this point, establishing height for the front view and eventually the side view. Above the front view, allowing for a space between, will be drawn the horizontal base line for the top view. Draw the line only between the width (vertical) lines. Measure up vertically, above this base line, the depth. Draw a horizontal defining the position of top view.

Note: between the horizontal lines defining front view height, which span the width of the page, are positioned only two views: front view and right-side view.

### Stage 5

The right-side view is positioned on the page to the right of the front view. Calculate (by estimating) a space between the two views – front view and right-side view – and plot this by a dot upon the horizontal. Measure to the right of this dot the depth measurement for the scenic element. Draw

*Four views of a dresser unit: top view, elevation, right-side view and plan. Minimal hidden lines are added, as they are not required and will be developed on construction drawings. Plan indicates legs make contact with the floor as they are solid lines. The overall contour is dashed, being above ground. There are no drawer knobs indicated in plan.*

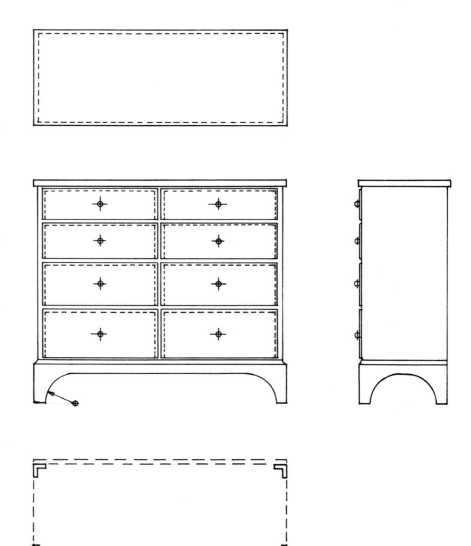

the two vertical lines, within the height lines, which define the dimensions of side view.

The layout should now present the following: four views consisting of plan, front, top, and right-side.

Formulate layout for all views as required at the initial stage. This prevents the likelihood of developing a single view over and above how views inter-relate. Forward planning addresses effective presentation. Once plotted, proceed to draw in construction lines around each view, using a 3H pencil lead. The framing of a view defines that which is the focus of interest. Within each frame intermediate measurements are plotted, defining edges and contours found within a view. As the view develops information can be transferred across to another view. The height of the chair seat can be taken horizontally across the page to be included in other views, through using the arm of the T-square. There is no need to measure its height more than the once. The width of the chair legs, once measure in front view, can be taken vertically down to the plan by using the set-square.

---

### Multi-views of a house

In order to represent the exterior view of a house, six views of the object are required for the best outcome. Each view shows a different elevation (except plan): top view, front view, rear view, left-side view, and right-side view.

1. The front view describes true height and width. Internal dimensioning will describe the front door entrance and living room window. The height of the roof above ground level is a true measurement. There is no indication of depth.

2. Walk round the house to the right to view the right-side view (the draughtsman's right side of the house, when looking at the drawing's front view). In this view the rear of the house will appear on your right. This view shows true height and depth of the house. There is no indication of the house width.

3. Look again at the front view, noting your left side; walk round the house to the left to view the left-side view. In this view the rear of the house will appear to your left. This view shows true height and depth of the house. There is no indication of the width.

4. Proceed round to the back of the house, and view the rear view. This view shows true width and height. There is no indication of depth.

5. View the house from above; look down on the roof construct. It may be the case that some features will appear hidden by the size of the roof. The view describes the width and depth. There is no indication of height.

6. The footprint the house makes on the ground is the plan (this is not an elevation; for an elevation of the house it would be necessary to do a bottom view, looking face on to its base plane). Plan view describes true depth and width. There is no indication of height. Features above ground level could be included in this drawings, yet would appear as dashed lines (overhead lines).

The scale for such a drawing, where the object is too large to fit the page scale 1:25, requires a scale of typically 1:100. Yet it is difficult to provide detailed information as the scale ratio moves above 1:50.

---

The draughtsman's tools do the work after establishing a measurement once. Depth measurements within a side-view have a tendency to need to be measured again, after being plotted in plan or top view.

Two methods are illustrated showing how measurements from top view or plan may be transferred through to side-view using either a compass or a 45-degree angle (*see* page 119).

## HALF VIEWS

The term 'reverse and repeat' is added to a drawing where only half the object is drawn. An object comprised of symmetrical features can be drawn as half view, with the centre-line as one edge and all details within drawn to one side of the centre-line. The other side of the centre-line is the object's silhouette, drawn in as a dashed line. The centre-line is positioned where the object's symmetry divides. For construction the term 'reverse and repeat' indicates that construction should 'build' both sides with proportions and dimensions as indicated in the one side. The intricacy found in a fireplace and over mantle mirror, bed unit, scenic portal units with fretwork, chandelier or wall sconce typically fall into this category. Clearly state 'half view' and include the required 'reverse and repeat' (*see* page 86).

## PARTIAL VIEWS

The inclusion of all hidden lines within side views, as mentioned in 'hidden lines' (*see* page 139) could prove to over-complicate. Partial views eliminate the need to draw an object's hidden lines beyond those immediately near the front surface planes. The correct label is 'right side partial view', or 'left side partial view'.

# DETAIL VIEWS

The detail view is of component parts within an object drawn. The object at scale 1:25 may not make clear intention; a finely lathe-turned finial or decorative carved relief simply will not read. A detail view is enlarged. Page layout needs planning to include a detail view, as it should, wherever possible, be on the same page as the object's regular views.

## Approaching detail views

1. Draw a circle around the object's detail, within one view only, avoiding too small a circle.
2. Position the enlarged view within a larger circle, making sure the same viewpoint is maintained.
3. Within the enlarged circle is noted the new scale.
4. Within the page title block, after 'scale', include within brackets '(unless otherwise shown)'.
5. Dimensions added in the new scale must be made using that enlarged scale.
6. Label the circle as 'detail view'.

# AUXILIARY VIEWS

The inclined surface, often found in an object or scenic element, appears as a foreshortened plane when drawn in three regular views or in multi-view format. None of the multi-views, as previously noted, would permit viewing the inclined plane in elevation.

A foreshortened view of a surface plane is not so unusual within technical drawing. Examples range from scenic units with internal elements set at gradients (such as the raked stage floor), or with designed masking positioned off the perpendicular to set walls. Furniture, such as seating with angled backs, and even small props have inclined surfaces within.

A typical example is the front view of a stage design – not a view always included in the package, yet often necessary. The view is as the audience views the design. It is viewed as a plane, parallel with the proscenium opening or imaginary fourth wall, with all relevant information

regarding edges and contours projected as perpendiculars to that plane.

For example, imagine viewing an interior setting consisting of three on-stage walls. The upstage wall is set perpendicular to the centre line. Yet both side walls are set in a fan, becoming wider in the direction of down-stage. Therefore the front view will depict the upstage wall in true elevation, as it is parallel to the viewing plane, but the side walls are seen in a foreshortened fashion.

The necessity to view an inclined plane as a true elevation is no different from that of viewing all multi-view planes as perpendicular to their surfaces, thus permitting a formal application of true height, width or depth measurements, and allowing internal proportioning to be represented in its true dimension.

To achieve the elevation for an inclined surface, when working in a regular format for views of an

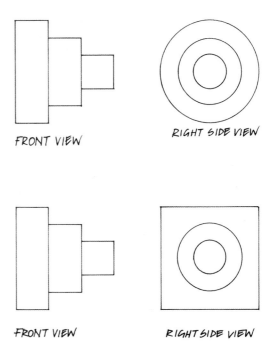

*Component units in two views. In most cases the right-side view is preferred over the left-side view. When showing two views: either the top view and right side view are shown, or the front view and right side view are shown.*

object, involves projecting off the inclined surface, perpendicular to the incline. The elevation for that inclined angle will be a plane positioned parallel to its incline, with all edge and contour information projected as perpendicular (*see* page 134. The page layout for three regular views may permit spacing to include an auxiliary view, thus achieving one extra view beside the top view, front view and side view (*see* page 173). Any dimensions related to the inclined plane should be included in the auxiliary view as true measurements. It is common practice not to include any additional information in an auxiliary view (such as hidden lines) as the auxiliary is there to clarify the oblique plane only. As previously mentioned in views of an object, right- and left-side views do not require hidden line information being included normally. (Page formatting

or view layout should at the initial stages make allowance for this additional auxiliary view with inclusion of appropriate spacing.)

## The folding glass box with auxiliary plane

As with views of an object set within a glass box as previously discussed, the object with inclined plane can also be understood in the same way as connecting to a view by being a plane hinged to the object. As the auxiliary view is set onto a glass plane set parallel to its incline, the glass box must now not be imagined as a cube. Instead the glass box sides now conform to the shape of the object. To understand the logic for how the auxiliary view is seen alongside its other views it is important to note the hinged plane concept.

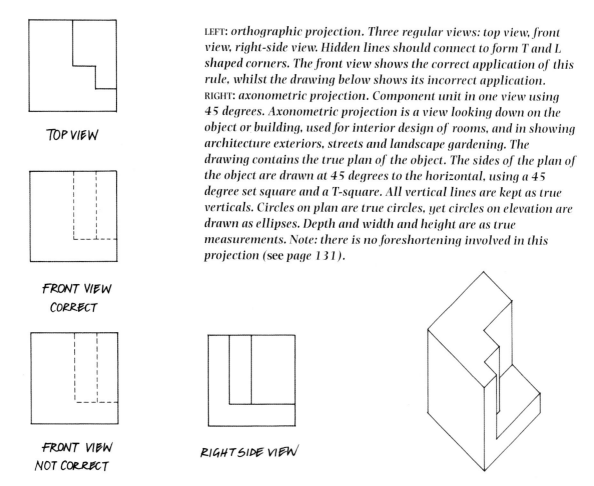

TOP VIEW

FRONT VIEW
CORRECT

FRONT VIEW
NOT CORRECT

RIGHT SIDE VIEW

LEFT: *orthographic projection. Three regular views: top view, front view, right-side view. Hidden lines should connect to form T and L shaped corners. The front view shows the correct application of this rule, whilst the drawing below shows its incorrect application.*
RIGHT: *axonometric projection. Component unit in one view using 45 degrees. Axonometric projection is a view looking down on the object or building, used for interior design of rooms, and in showing architecture exteriors, streets and landscape gardening. The drawing contains the true plan of the object. The sides of the plan of the object are drawn at 45 degrees to the horizontal, using a 45 degree set square and a T-square. All vertical lines are kept as true verticals. Circles on plan are true circles, yet circles on elevation are drawn as ellipses. Depth and width and height are as true measurements. Note: there is no foreshortening involved in this projection (see page 131).*

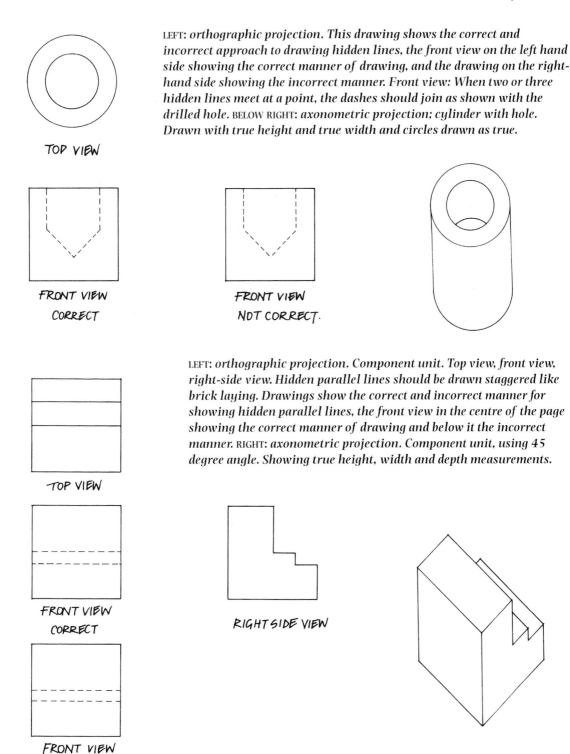

TOP VIEW

LEFT: *orthographic projection. This drawing shows the correct and incorrect approach to drawing hidden lines, the front view on the left hand side showing the correct manner of drawing, and the drawing on the right-hand side showing the incorrect manner. Front view: When two or three hidden lines meet at a point, the dashes should join as shown with the drilled hole.* BELOW RIGHT: *axonometric projection; cylinder with hole. Drawn with true height and true width and circles drawn as true.*

FRONT VIEW
CORRECT

FRONT VIEW
NOT CORRECT.

LEFT: *orthographic projection. Component unit. Top view, front view, right-side view. Hidden parallel lines should be drawn staggered like brick laying. Drawings show the correct and incorrect manner for showing hidden parallel lines, the front view in the centre of the page showing the correct manner of drawing and below it the incorrect manner.* RIGHT: *axonometric projection. Component unit, using 45 degree angle. Showing true height, width and depth measurements.*

TOP VIEW

FRONT VIEW
CORRECT

RIGHT SIDE VIEW

FRONT VIEW
NOT CORRECT

### Reference line approach

A short-cut for drawing an object with inclined plane: eliminate the hinged line and replace it with a reference line, one passing along the object or within it, as in a centre-line. The centre-line is useful where an object's plane has symmetry, permitting the transfer of dimension depth from left to right of centre. Depth measurements, to be set off a reference line positioned along an edge of the object, will require the use of dividers, compass, scale rule or ticket stub.

Where an auxiliary plane has detailed symmetry the use of a centre line allows for development on one half to be finely detailed while on the other half simply defines the main contour or outer edge shape. Such a contour is noted with a fine dashed line. It is not unusual to find such a drawing with the text 'reverse and repeat', indicating the detailed half needs to be built as symmetrical (that is, reverse the detailed drawing, repeat its information and the object will appear as symmetrical).

An auxiliary section is no different from a section view, as it shows the plane and its parts conventionally set out in a cross-section, detailing the orientation of component parts which make up the whole view.

The reference line is also the approach required when making auxiliary views off the ground plan, where set elements are positioned as angled off the horizontal and vertical.

## SECTION VIEW

The orthographic drawing as a section view or cross section represents an object viewed through a cutting plane (*see* pages 146–147). The cutting plane is often taken at centre of the object, yet any position established to cut through an object is at

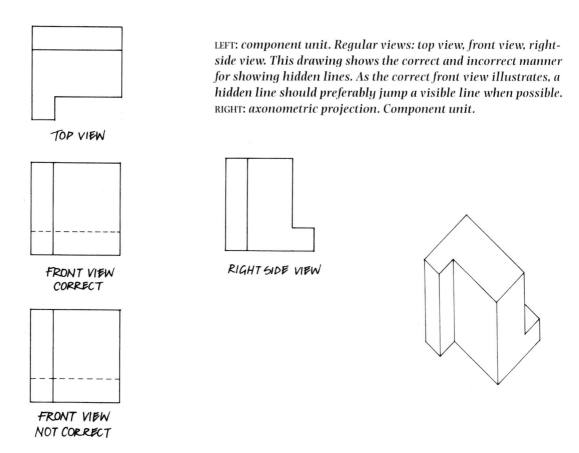

TOP VIEW

FRONT VIEW
CORRECT

FRONT VIEW
NOT CORRECT

RIGHT SIDE VIEW

LEFT: *component unit. Regular views: top view, front view, right-side view. This drawing shows the correct and incorrect manner for showing hidden lines. As the correct front view illustrates, a hidden line should preferably jump a visible line when possible.* RIGHT: *axonometric projection. Component unit.*

RIGHT: *From left: orthographic projection. Component unit; top view, right-side view and elevation. Right: axonometric projection. Component unit.*

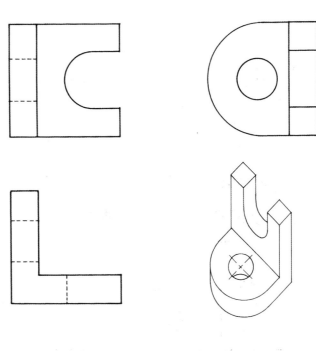

BELOW: *Layout for six views of an object. Views for construction: top view, elevation, plan, left-side view, right-side view, and rear view (shown to the left of the left-side view). Rear view required as object appears different than in other views, so too with the need to include both left and right side views. No dimensioning shown.*

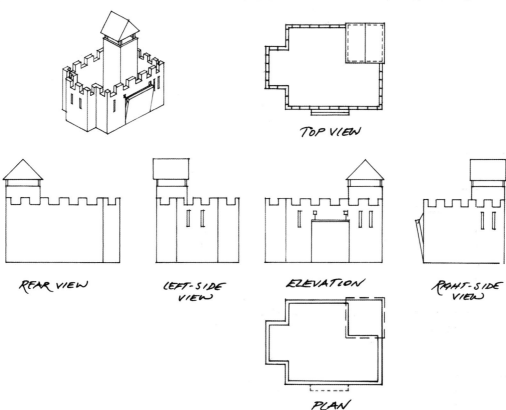

TOP VIEW

REAR VIEW

LEFT-SIDE VIEW

ELEVATION

RIGHT-SIDE VIEW

PLAN

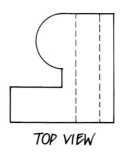

TOP VIEW

LEFT: *orthographic projection. Component unit; top view, elevation, plan and right side view. A hidden line may have three possible meanings:*

1. *The intersection of two surfaces.*
2. *Edge view of a surface.*
3. *Contour view of a curved surface.*

RIGHT: *axonometric projection. Component unit.*

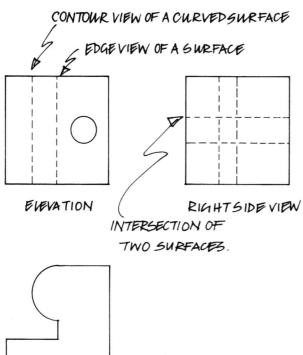

CONTOUR VIEW OF A CURVED SURFACE

EDGE VIEW OF A SURFACE

ELEVATION

RIGHT SIDE VIEW

INTERSECTION OF TWO SURFACES.

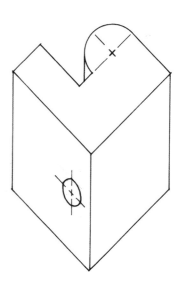

the discretion of the designer. The section view offers representation of internal structuring. Fundamentally an object is cut in half or through at some point: horizontally, vertically or at an inclined angle. One section is removed, and the 'section cut' is then rotated to give a view as a plane defining true measurements. A typical example would be a sash window unit, fireplace, or wall panel. Each of the examples has constructed layers. Through the section, relationships for interconnectivity of parts show how the whole form comes together. Even a stool may require a section

view to describe further how joinery is of a constructed concern. Drawing up a rough section is often essential as a process to assist in better understanding of joinery, the fireplace and sash window being prime examples. The section view may replace one of the side views, as more relevant information may be conveyed through showing its constructed nature. Head of Construction does not require this drawing as a general rule; therefore consider how essential the additional information is when including a section view. In building geometry, plotting a section view for

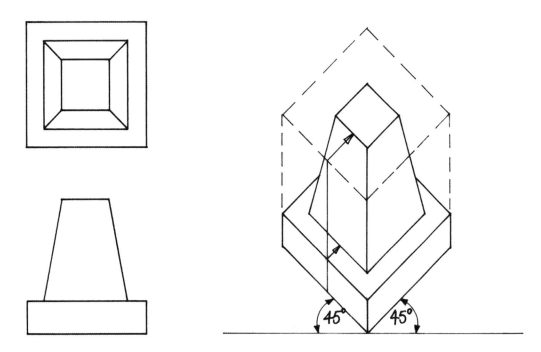

*Axonometric projection. With 45 degree angled lines and vertical lines measured in their 'true' dimensions. Views include: top view, elevation, isometric projection.*

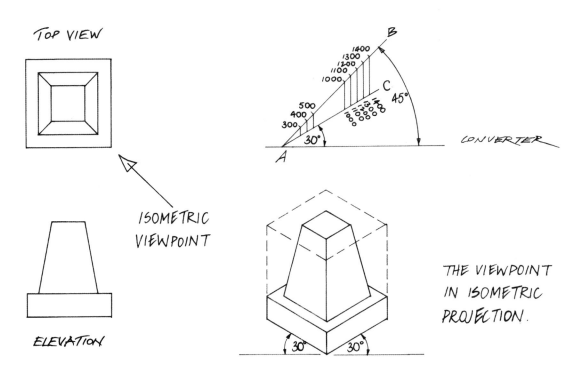

TOP VIEW

ISOMETRIC VIEWPOINT

ELEVATION

CONVERTER

THE VIEWPOINT IN ISOMETRIC PROJECTION.

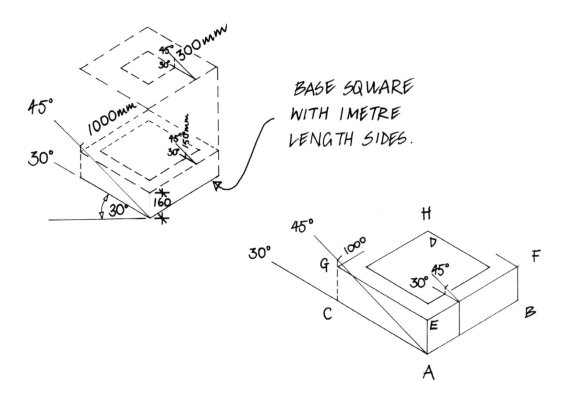

ABOVE: *Isometric projection: this drawing, like the axonometric, depicts three sides of an object in one drawing, thus showing the width, depth and height with a minimum of work and maximum clarity. This drawing contains the plan of the object drawn at 30 degrees to the horizontal, using a 30/60 degree set square and T-square. Circles appear as ellipses in plan and elevation. The bases of the isometric projection are three equally divided radii angles of 120 degrees, the dividing radii giving the isometric axes. Isometric means equal measure, hence the three equal angles. The three directing lines, or three principal axes are drawn first and all lines parallel to them are isometric lines. Measurements are taken from orthographic views with height being true to both, and width and depth calculated through a conversion scale.*

*To construct an isometric scale (see page 131, bottom diagram):*
1. *Draw a line AB at 45 degrees and on it plot width and depth measurements as taken off the plan.*
2. *Draw AC at 30 degrees then drop vertically all points on line AB (the 45 degree line) downwards to line AC.*

*The ratio between the true length and the isometric length is:*
*ISOMETRIC LENGTH = TRUE LENGTH × 0.8165.*

*The drawings illustrate top view, isometric view point and elevation. Drawings show converntion scale set off the 45 degree angle and transferred to the 30 degree angle. Vertical height can be measured as true to its dimension. No foreshortening in all vertical lines, foreshortening only occurs in depth and width.*

building a construct may well help to indicate how an object looks in three dimensions.

## Half front view and section

A section view may accompany a drawing of an object defining its surface detail yet be attached to the given view (front view). A door casing (*see* illustration on page 90) is an example where both views form one drawing. The section uses the lines of the front view in this case to define its width.

Mouldings such as cornice, picture rail, door casing, baseboard or skirting board typically need to be drawn as front view and as section. As the front view gives no suggestion of relief, and the side view depicts only depth and height, the replacement of side view with section offers depth dimensions and the proposed construction layering.

It is not unusual to draw the section view at an enlarged scale, due to the necessary depiction of details pertaining to radii, intersection of arches and flat planes. These larger scales might be in 1:20, 1:10 or 1:5. However, it is typical to find moulding drawn at 1:1, possibly on a page of its own. (*See* Moulding examples on page 90.)

## PRESENTATIONAL DRAWINGS

The refinement from preliminary drawings into

*Plotting an ellipse on isometric projection. The elevation is a true view of the circle set within a square; diameter I-I is divided into eight equal parts, with each division registered as a vertical line connecting with the circle circumference. The isometric projection's right-side plane, shows the same sub-division on line I-I of eight equal parts. Step off with a compass or dividers each measurement from the elevation 1, 2, and 3, onto the isometric plane, as shown. The isometric top view shows the plotting of diagonals, with line A-B divided into 3 equal parts, whose points of division are the centres for drawing arcs. C and D are centres for drawing arcs to complete the isometric foreshortened circle. The isometric top plane is drawn separately to clarify segmenting before dividing A-B into 3 parts.*

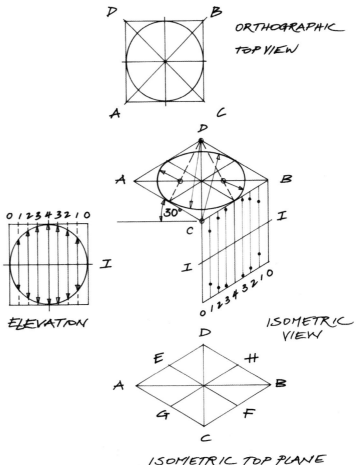

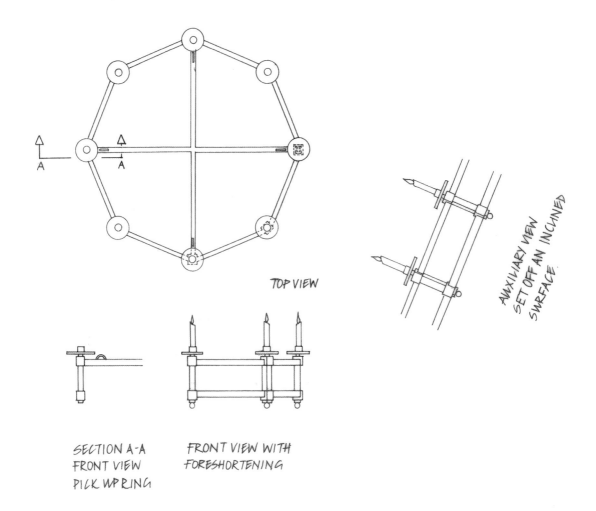

TOP VIEW

SECTION A-A
FRONT VIEW
PICK UP RING

FRONT VIEW WITH
FORESHORTENING

AUXILIARY VIEW
SET OFF AN INCLINED
SURFACE

presentational drawings requires considered decision making both in the model and through drawings. Problem solving reaches a final stage, where the making of the model box facilitates referencing for the build and scenic art department, and the presentational drawings deliver detail as calculated formal dimensioning concerned with formal and structural concerns. The final presentational model communicates precise measurement relating to sight-lines, constraints of theatre venue, material build, and scenic art treatments. The final ground plan and accompanying theatre section complement the exact nature of all scenic element elevations and their detailing. All technical information as a package is delivered knowing the construction drawings can commence.

## NOTES FOR CONSTRUCTION

Designer notes are added in within the 'notes block'. Key information to help construction to make the right decision about material and construction processes is to be included. Knowledge of scenic art treatments to be applied to surface enables construction to propose proper foundations. The practical nature of the build can be influenced through knowing how actors will interact with scenic elements. Anticipating the demands made on scenery and props by the performance encourages effective construction methods. Designer notes are looked upon as essential, being based on practical points of view that encourage cost-effective decision-making.

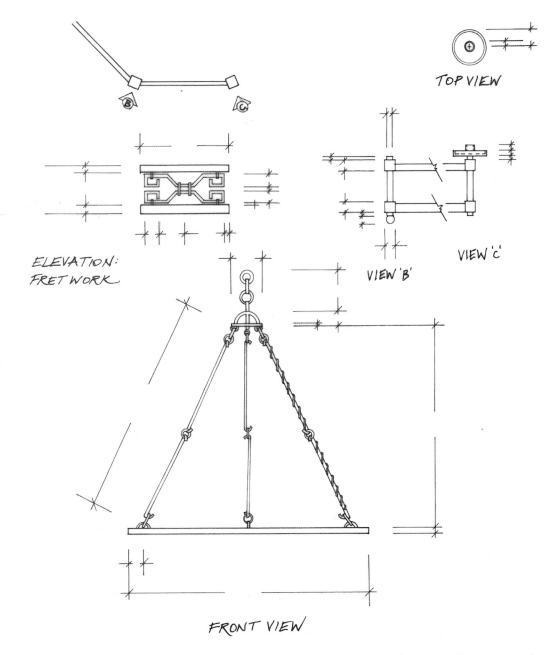

TOP VIEW

ELEVATION:
FRET WORK

VIEW 'B'

VIEW 'C'

FRONT VIEW

ABOVE AND OPPOSITE: *Chandelier: metal work. Views: top view; section A-A; front view (foreshortened). Top view depicts radials from centre and octagonal shape with position for candle holders at junctions. Section A-A depicts the cross bar radial with pick-up ring. Front view depicts visual effect with candles implanted, with auxiliary view depicting same. Dimensions to be applied.*

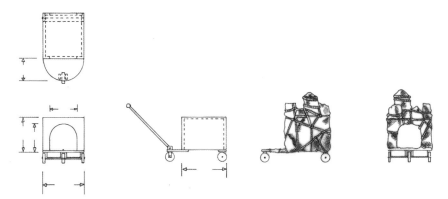

*Dog kennel truck unit. Top view, elevation (front view), side view and finished views. In addition to the drawing including dimensions, it may include notes for Construction; to clarify intentions in support of the build, its finish and use.*

*Notes:*

1. *Light plywood construction.*
2. *Wheels wood discs with dowel axle.*
3. *Pull handle controls front wheel pivotal steering (not indicated).*
4. *Kennel openings at front and rear gives access to interior.*
5. *Exterior dressed with polystyrene, canvas/hessian and rope.*
6. *To contain puppet of dog; operated through rear opening by actor.*

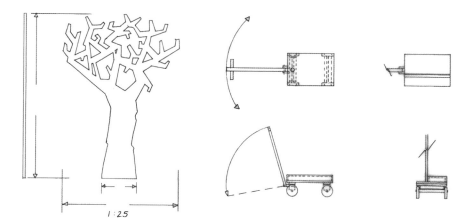

*Turnable truck with tree. Views: tree left side view and front view, truck top view with hidden details and top view (shown to the right), front view and right side view. The addition of designer notes informs construction of two parts for assembly and demands made by performance. Notes:*

*Notes:*

1. *Wood truck unit requires plywood tree being fixed permanently (off-centre).*
2. *Strongly built to support weight of tree and actor stood behind tree.*
3. *Truck base houses weights to maintain balance.*
4. *Pull handle as 'T' shape.*
5. *Pivoting front wheels.*
6. *Wood disc wheels at 150mm diameter.*

# 10 LINE CHARACTERISTICS AND DRAWING UP

The different stages in drawing require consideration of variation in line density and type. Plotting page layout for the positioning of views and drawing guidelines (upon which printed matter will sit) require a hard lead 4H pencil with thinner lines and light pencil pressure. These are the lightest quality lines on the page, and will appear faint enough to not require erasing at a later stage before printing, as they tend not to show once the drawing is copied. Lightly drawn lines make allowance for error, where mistakes do not affect further work in drawing up. It is recommended as good practice to always work with a light hand using a hard lead pencil until the drawing is nearly complete. As a drawing reaches completion finished line quality is applied, with emphasis on what is of specific importance.

All lines except construction lines, page layout lines, and guidelines for text and measurements, should be dense. Avoid producing a grey, dim or indefinite line, as they will not reproduce clearly in the copying/printing process. The centre-line should be dark and visibly of a finished line nature. The characteristic of line is in the thickness and in the degree of blackness.

## Pencil types

There are three pencil types:

* H and HB should be used for the thicker lines.
* 2H should be used for the thinner lines.
* 4H should be used for the light thin lines (layout and text guidelines).

There are three distinct thicknesses to line:

1. Thick: used for page border, for the visible or finished lines, as cutting-plane lines and short break lines, and object lines.
2. Medium: used for hidden lines, text, measurements, and centre-line.
3. Thin: used for long break lines, section lines, centre-line, dimension lines, extension lines, phantom lines, and overhead lines.

## TERMS

### Border lines
These dense thick lines with HB pencil frame the page with a border; plotted 1–2cm inside the page edge.

### Page layout
These thin light construction lines made with a 4H pencil establish object layout and spacing, maintain a light pressure. Lines should not be visible at an arm's distance away.

### Construction lines
These thin lines made with 3H pencil block in the object views, their outline and internal details, and are used after the page layout is achieved. If correct, when the drawing is finished some will become thick, some medium and some thin lines.

### Finished/object/visible lines
These thick lines with HB pencil finish the drawing and emphasis the object's outline or object shape defining its elevation proportions.

### Outlines
These thick lines, made with HB pencil, define

137

## Type of lines

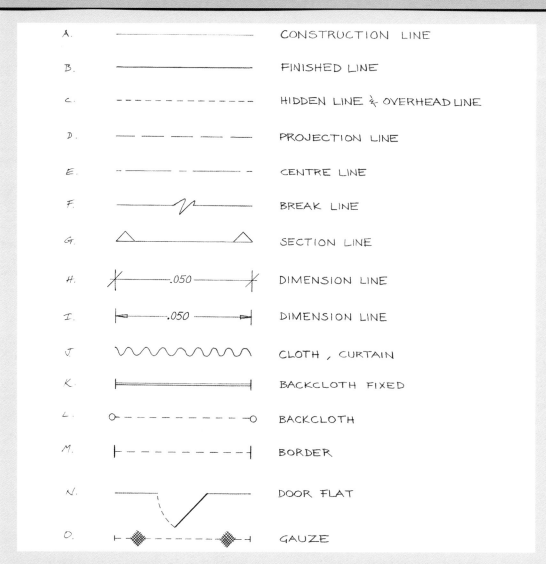

A. Construction Line in all views to determine layout and plotting

B. Finished Visible Lines of Objects and edges in development

C. Hidden Lines (in objects in all views) and Overhead Lines on Ground Plan

D. Projection Line

E. Centre Line and Axes Line

F. Break Line

G. Section Line or Cutting Plane Line

H. Intersecting Dimension Line

I. Pointer Dimension Line

J. Cloth, Curtain

K. Fixed Cloth and Legs

L. Flown Cloth

M. Border or Flown Leg

N. Door Flat

O. Gauze

the ground plan and theatre section main wall features, including shading.

## Dash lines

These indicate either hidden or over-head, and are made with 2H pencil using firm pressure. They include sight-line and projection lines. The centre-line (a dashed line of sorts) is made with a medium-line H pencil.

*Hidden lines*

A line of fine dashes represents an edge not in view, generally included to represent clearly how one unit aligns with another. A hidden line typically resides behind a surface plane. They are very short dashes with very short spacing between (approximately 3mm for each dash with 1mm spacing). The lines are of medium thickness. Use a hard pencil lead '2H' and make a firm start and finish stroke to each dash.

Views of an object in side view do not tend to require extensive hidden line information; drawings with an excess of hidden lines may deliver more information than is necessary. Avoid repeating hidden lines from one side-view to another side-view. A 'cross section' or section view of an object may prove a likely view to include hidden lines.

Key rules for drawing hidden lines (*see* pages 126–130):

1. Where a visible line is to continue but becomes hidden, leave a gap between the continuous line and the first hidden line dash. This applies with straight lines and curvilinear lines.
2. Where there is a 'T' or 'L' intersection formed by the meeting of visible and hidden lines, always have them join up.
3. Where a hidden line crosses over a visible line, place the 'gap' between dashes so the visible line passes through it without making contact.
4. Where a straight line runs parallel to another and both are hidden, stagger the dashes. The exception can be if the total number of dashes (for one line) is four or fewer.
5. Where hidden lines cross one another or meet, have them intersect with one another.
6. When drawing a circle where centre lines or quadrant radiants are included, have the dash connect with these lines but not pass through and beyond them; for the curve to continue thereafter leave the necessary 'gap' and begin again.

*Sight-lines*

A ray comprised of long dashes separated by small spacing. When drawing a sight-line to plot the proportional span for off-stage scenic units: use a straight edge to join the audience sight-line position (audience seat) to, say a doorway opening. Use a rule (2H thin line) long enough to connect both points and continue in the direction of off-stage. From the point where a sight line makes contact with (in this case) the door jamb, draw a dash line continuing to off-stage. Avoid drawing the sight-line from the seat to the object, as enough information is in drawing it from the point of contact with the scenery. (*See* Plotting traditional legs and borders, pages 97 and 99).

*Projection lines*

These are found on elevations and plan, made up of medium-length dashes (5mm) with small spacing. They depict projection of information for edges and contours from one view through to another. Use 4H, thin line.

*Overhead lines*

These dashes are long (ranging from 10mm to 20mm) with short spacing. The weight of line is thin and dark. They are found on the ground plan indicating that which is above stage floor level. Many venue features do not make contact with the floor surface, such as the edge of the fly floor, the fly bars, heating ducts and so on. Object edges above stage are represented with an overhead line. The proscenium beam above stage level is indicated by an overhead line. Use 2H, thin line.

*Centre-line*

Found on the ground plan, a thin dark line in

pencil lead 2H, the centre-line consists of a long dash (between 50mm and 80mm in length) with a small space. This defines centre stage of the theatre.

## Section lines
This is a medium thickness (pencil lead H), finished line, which depicts the point where a section or cross-section view takes place. The cutting of an object along a section line facilitates revealing the cut plane in true measurement. The section-line has arrows attached at both ends, pointing the direction for the desired view.

## Break lines
A short break line is a dark line (pencil lead H) of medium thickness. It defines where a desired break will take place, to remove a segment of an object and shorten the full length, to allow it to fit a page requirement. Removing the segment from its length is understood to not alter the real nature of the form. For example, a classical column of 20 metres in length has a segment of its middle shaft removed. A break line indicates where the segment was removed. The dimension calculated and delivered in such a drawing will, however, be for the true length of 20 metres. A long break line is thin, and drawn with 2H.

## Dimension lines
These are fine lines using pencil lead H. They are drawn making intersection with extension lines (*see* Dimensions, page 109). Dimension lines define true measurements of height, width, and depth; they can either be interrupted with a numerical measurement or drawn as a solid line with the numerical measure above or below the line.

## Text lettering and numerical guidelines
The guidelines for lettering and measurements should be with pencil lead 4H. Use H for lettering.

These faintly drawn thin lines are for printing upon. Lettering guidelines should be 5mm high (minimum), which allows for clearly readable text. All text and numerical printing is placed on guidelines (*see* Chapter 8: Lettering and printed matter).

# THE DRAWING OF LINES
## Drawing horizontal lines
If right-handed: position the T-square head firmly onto the drawing board at the left-side vertical edge, with the T-square arm flat against the page in a horizontal position. Draw the line from left to right. Lean the pencil towards a 60-degree angle, in the direction of the line. Maintain a perpendicular position between page plane and pencil.

If left-handed: position the T-square head firmly onto the drawing board at the right-side vertical edge, with the T-square arm flat against the page in a horizontal position. Draw the line from right to left. Lean the pencil towards a 60-degree angle, in the direction of the line. Maintain a perpendicular position between page plane and pencil.

While drawing a line, slowly rotate the pencil to produce a line that is uniform in width.

## Drawing vertical lines
Use a 30/60-degree triangular set-square, as it offers the greater length edge. Draw the line upward, rotating the pencil. The pencil needs to be at 60 degrees to the paper. Always assure contact between set-square and T-square, as alignment is essential for accuracy.

## Drawing angled and inclined lines
Angled lines are all drawn using a set-square or adjustable set-square. Note that one edge of the set-square must always be in contact with the T-square arm.

Using only the 30/60-degree set-square, draw the following angles: 30, 60, and 90 degrees. Use both the 45-degree and the 30/60-degree set-squares interconnecting together to achieve 15 degrees, 45 degrees and 75 degrees off the horizontal. An entire 360-degree span of a circle can be divided into 24 sectors of 15 degrees using these two set-square triangles (*see* pages 50–51). For any other angles, use the adjustable 45-degree set-square.

Note: maintaining secure contact between T-square arm and the set-square requires practice. It is good practice to place the pencil point on the point of reference, before moving the set-square into position.

## Drawing parallel lines

*Horizontal and parallel*
The T-square arm produces a true horizontal; therefore, moving the arm up the page produces parallel horizontal lines.

*Vertical and parallel*
To produce parallel lines to a vertical line, establish the vertical first with the set-square then slide the set-square across the arm from left to right to produce parallels to this.

*Inclined and parallel*
Use the set-squares or the adjustable 45-degree set-square to produce all parallel lines to an established inclined line, by first establishing the intended angle; then slide the set-square left and right along the T-square arm to produce parallels to it.

*Using the adjustable 45-degree set-square*
Maintain contact between T-square and the set-square at all times. Make adjustment to the set-square by loosening the metal threaded nut; turn by a half turn only, to avoid losing it. The adjustable set-square slides open for a required angle. Tighten the thread knob and slide the set-square along the T-square to draw in parallel lines if required.

## Drawing Perpendicular Lines
Perpendicular lines are those at a right angle (90 degrees) to a given line. The set-square is used to draw perpendiculars to the horizontal. The adjustable set-square offers perpendiculars to any inclined line. Establish an angle but before drawing it, tighten the nut. Draw the inclined line. Make by observation an estimate for the 90 degrees off the given angle. Rotate the adjustable set-square to acquire this desired angle, noting that the set-square must not be re-adjusted. Once located, with set-square firmly on the T-square, draw the line. The set-square will always serve up the required right angle. Locating it requires simply rotating the instrument, placing it on the arm, and drawing it.

### Reminder: use of the eraser shield

The eraser is for editing out mistakes. Maintaining light pencil pressure until completion of a drawing helps avoid errors that are difficult to erase. Avoid spoiling a drawing by making use of the eraser shield: this facilitates the removal of specific lines whilst avoiding erasing other information, within a selected area.

Note: a 30-degree angled line to the horizontal will have its perpendicular in the 60-degree angle of the same set-square.

Note: a 45-degree angled line to the horizontal will have its perpendicular in the 45-degree of the same set-square.

When using the adjustable set-square, an inclined line drawn to the horizontal has its perpendicular established within the set-square. Simply rotate the adjustable set-square on the T-square to establish the perpendicular.

## PAPER ALIGNMENT

1. Place the T-square on the drawing board, with its arm lying horizontally across the board.
2. Position the arm at the base of the board, being sure it sits securely.
3. Double check that the T-square head is secure squarely with the board's side vertical.
4. Place cartridge paper on the board in landscape format.
5. Place the page base horizontal along the upper edge of the arm, aligning both.
6. The paper's vertical edge nearest the T-square head should be positioned approximately 20mm in from the board edge.
7. Place 50mm strips of masking tape diagonally across each of the four corners. Press firmly. Avoid any folds or creases, or untidy edges to the tape, as they will become loosened by the constant shifting across of equipment.

8. Place tracing paper over the cartridge paper, align squarely and tape securely all four corners.

9. A small strip of tape placed at the top centre and base centre along the horizontals will protect the page from being torn by the T-square arm sliding upwards and downwards.

## PAGE BORDER

Tracing paper requires a border, squarely framing the drawing aligned to T-square and set-square.

1. A border is drawn along all four edges of the page. Position these lines approximately 10mm to 20mm in from the page edge. Use H pencil lead, drawing the horizontal lines (with firm pressure) to the taped corners. Follow on with drawing the vertical lines, using the set-square firmly positioned on the T-square arm. The junction of border lines, where vertical and horizontal meet, form true 90-degree angles.

## TITLE BLOCK

This rectangular block is positioned in the bottom right of the page. It contains descriptive text. The particulars are to include:

* First line: name of show; name of theatre/venue; date of opening.
* Second line: drawing description; scale.
* Third line: designer; director; lighting designer (full names are required).
* Fourth line: name of draughtsman (full name or initials); date drawn.
* In the numerical block (far right corner of the title block): drawing number.

### Step 1
Measure 45mm vertically up from the base border horizontal and make a dot with an H pencil. Draw a horizontal line through this point from the right-side border vertical to approximately the centre of the page (A2). At the centre of the page draw a vertical line down to connect with the base border horizontal (*see* page 145).

### Step 2
To plot a numerical block within title block, position the T-square arm below the border base horizontal. Set a small 45-degree set-square on the T-square arm. Place the pencil point on the bottom right hand corner of the title block. Draw a 45-degree line (very faintly) upwards to intersect with the top horizontal of the title block. At this point of intersection, position the pencil tip and draw a vertical line downwards. This forms the square called the 'numerical block', within which the drawing number will be placed.

### Step 3
Along the vertical side at page centre, measure off and mark with a dot increments of 5mm using a metric ruler scale 1:1. With T-square arm and pencil lead 4H (no pencil pressure), draw horizontal lines within the title block (not into the numerical block). This series of 5mm-high parallel lines are guidelines for lettering.

### Step 4
Print the text in Roman script (capitals only). Text is placed on every second set of parallel lines (*see* Lettering, page 106), and never makes contact with the lines of the title block. Draw a vertical margin line (4H with light pressure) within the title block parallel to the left vertical. Set it 5mm in from the left. The first line of text will be positioned 5mm below the title block top horizontal. (Note: the title block has four sets of parallel lines for text.) The final set of parallel guidelines, at the bottom of the title block, will need drawing through into the numerical box.

## NUMERICAL BLOCK

The numerical block has printed the word 'drawing' on the set of parallel lines. 5mm above the word 'drawing', draw a horizontal line, to divide the block into two parts, with the word 'drawing' now isolated in a rectangle of its own. The space above is for the numerical block drawing number. Drawing numbers start with #1 (ground plan), #2 (theatre section). Numbers 3, 4, 5, and so on are for elevations and multi-views of scenic elements.

**Title block details: guidelines set within the title block horizontals**

_____ (top horizontal of title block)

Space (5mm high)

_____ (guideline #1)

NAME OF SHOW (text 5mm high); NAME OF THEATRE; OPENING DATE

_____ (guideline #2)

Space (5mm high)

_____ (guideline #3)

DRAWING DESCRIPTION (text 5mm high); SCALE

_____ (guideline #4)

Space (5mm high)

_____ (guideline #5)

DESIGNER: (text 5mm high); DIRECTOR; LX DESIGNER

_____ (guideline #6)

Space (5mm high)

_____ (guideline #7)

DRAWN BY: (text 5mm high); DATE DRAWN

_____ (guideline #8)

Space (5mm high)

_____ (base horizontal of title block)

Note: the distance between the top and base horizontals of the title block is 45mm.
All lettering is printed in CAPITALS.

## DRAWING UP

### View selection

1. Choose views that best represent the object.
2. Use the least number of views to clarify intentions. Often a top, front, and side view will be enough.
3. With an object of a complex nature use more views to represent it, such as left- and right-side view, rear view, and where necessary include 'cross section' and 'detail drawings', which may be included at a differing scale to the original. (*See* Detail drawings, page 125.)
4. Prop drawings often require more explanation through multiple views.
5. Scenic flats and platforms with exit steps generally require plan, front view, top view and side view.

### From ground plan to elevation (multi-views)

1. The plan is obtained from tracing over the unit as described on the ground plan, found in drawing #1. The emphasis is therefore on establishing correct relationships for scenic elements on the ground plan first.
2. Where scenic elements have the addition of complex features (such as window, fireplace, or where stairs join a wall), additional drawings, often in detail, are featured.
3. With ground plan plotted, even as a rough drawing, the development of elevations can commence. Square the ground plan (tracing paper drawing) to the drawing board drawing

143

arm, and secure with masking tape. Place a scrap or small page of tracing paper (A3 or A4) over the plan with interest on one scenic unit (one flat). Use detail paper at 53gsm or tracing paper at 60gsm. Tape securely. The top page of tracing paper is simply used to copy scenic flat details, as they appear on the plan.

4. Trace carefully all information for that scenic unit, using T-square and set-square, or adjustable set-square if required.

5. Remove the top tracing paper and ground plan from the drawing board.

6. Position a clean page of A2, 63gsm tracing paper, positioned squarely on the board. Tape securely on the two top edges only.

7. Slide the 'copy' or tracing of scenic flats beneath this, aligning it to where it should be plotted on the page. The position at the base of the page allows for the projection of information upwards to develop elevations for front view and, above that, top view. Calculate appropriate spacing to achieve proper layout. Align the T-square with the drawing, making sure it is squarely positioned. Tape securely both drawing pages down.

8. If a particular unit is set off at an angle to the horizontal or vertical, it will require squaring to the horizontal before drawing as plan in multi-view.

9. As plan depicts true width and depth, it is necessary to transfer the width upwards to the front view, and then measure above the base line to establish height. (Front view shows true height and width.)

10. With overall height and width dimensions established, internal or intermediate height and width measurements can be applied. Details may include the height and width of a door opening, and the height of a window and its position across the width. Additional detail such as mouldings, picture rail, chair rail, cornice and door casing may be added.

11. With internal proportioning calculated, this information may be transferred across horizontally to the side views and rear view (if required).

## FROM ELEVATIONS TO MAKING THE MODEL

Hand in hand with the development of the ground plan goes the positioning of constructed form into the model box. Problem solving processes on plan helps to solve practical problems with the model. Typical issues with working on the ground plan are sight-lines, on-stage to off-stage areas, flown scenic elements, and designed masking.

It is good working practice to follow this suggested approach:

1. From sketch model plot information as a rough on ground plan.

2. Make adjustments as necessary and further develop sketch model.

3. From sketch model plot more accurately ground plan intentions, then develop elevation for scenic elements.

4. With elevation photocopied, glue to card, and assemble into a preliminary design.

The above example supports a process through which design evolves. The skills involved in creative and practical problem solving are complementary. The ground plan tends to be the first technical reference when working with architectural constraints, once things begin to shape themselves in 3D.

### Rough drawings (scale 1:25) are copied to make the sketch model

Once a rough drawing depicting the elevations or views of a scenic element is complete, it can then be copied, either using the dye-line method, or by photocopying. The resulting copy is attached (using a spray-on glue) to 'mount board', the recommended card for model making. Attach firmly, then carefully cut out each view using a fine scalpel blade cutting tool. The views are assembled by gluing with strong wood glue (PVA).

Note: There may be need of slight adjustment to measurements of card width, depth and height, to allow for card thickness when gluing together. Several copies of a view may be required, as elevations often depict layered detailing.

For example, the front view of an upright piano depicts the keyboard's vertical supports (legs) in front of the piano's face plane. The face framework that houses the keyboard will also feature as proud, or in the foreground. As details are easy to define in rough drawings, such details feature as a linear drawing once the sketch model is glued together. Lines drawn may represent positions for wall mouldings such as cornice, picture rail, chair rail, skirting board, door casing, and even door panelling. The rough drawings actually serve to highlight the intention of proud features, to be applied, rather than applied as relief in sketch model.

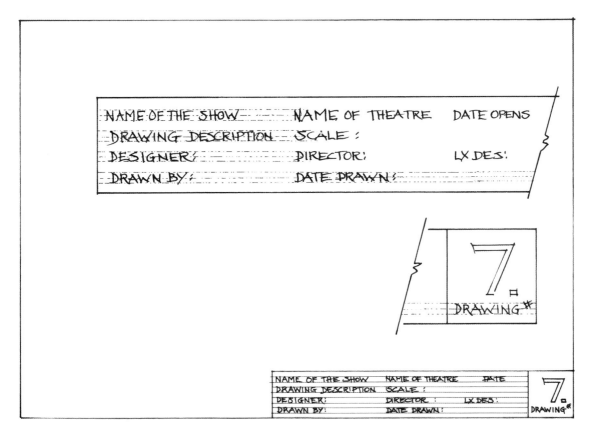

*Title block. The title block is positioned in the bottom right corner of the page, 4.5cm/45mm high above the border and ending at the centre of the page. Text guidelines and spacing are drawn at 5mm distances. The drawing number is then placed in a true square in the bottom right hand corner of the page, and printed as illustrated.*

# 11 SCENIC ELEMENTS AND TERMS

## THE SCENIC FLAT

A scenic flat consists of a frame supporting the application of a hard plywood surface or soft canvas surface, upon which construction detailing such as architectural moulding may be applied, or upon which scenic art treatments are applied. Flattage is typically of a lightweight nature to enable easy handling, flying, or transporting. A hard material surface is termed 'clad'. Frames with only a canvas surface are similar to stretched canvas frames traditionally used by artists and painters. The frame consists of wood rails (horizontals) and stiles (verticals) assembled in the traditional manner using mortice and tenon joinery methods. Flats may be built as a wall for interior setting, as a portal to create openings such as a proscenium arch, or as legs and borders. Clad flattage enables application of 3D and relief including applied texture as well as paint, whereas canvas-covered frames more typically have only 2D paint applications. Flattage may be constructed for a ceiling within a set, and within wall flattage are commonly featured doors, windows, fireplace,

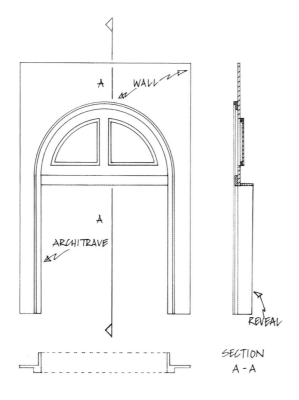

*Door arch. Views: elevation, plan, section A-A, as cross-section. Where features are proud of one another, a cross section cut through vertically facilitates comprehending the layering effect for features. Door reveal gives the impression the wall has thickness, yet is only planking on-end forming a frame on the offstage side.*

RIGHT: *Wall book case unit insert. Three regular views: top view, elevation, right-side view. The base panel section is drawn showing no depth other than thickness of wood itself, to allow for recess paneling. Shelves being practical have sides, top and backing.*
*Dimensions to be inserted.*

BELOW: *Four-panel solid door: one elevation with three variables (shown in section views).*

*Section 1. Stiles, rails and muntins with 'inlay' or 'planted' moulding running flush with door proud surface.*

*Section 2. Stiles, rails, muntins with 'inlay' or 'planted' moulding set back from door proud surface.*

*Section 3. Solid moulded door with mouldings worked on the stiles, rails and muntins.*

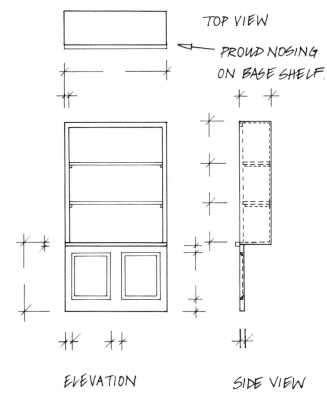

TOP VIEW

PROUD NOSING ON BASE SHELF.

ELEVATION

SIDE VIEW

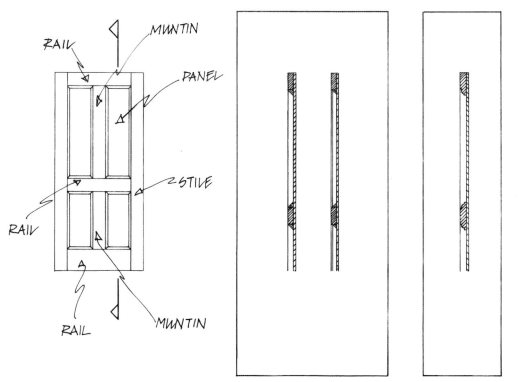

RAIL

MUNTIN

PANEL

STILE

RAIL

MUNTIN

RAIL

147

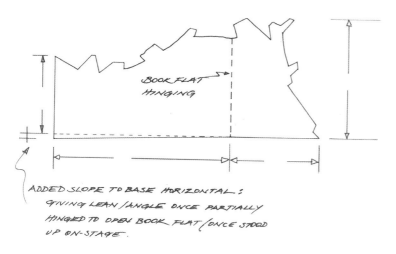

BOOK FLAT
HINGING

A

ADDED SLOPE TO BASE HORIZONTAL:
GIVING LEAN / ANGLE ONCE PARTIALLY
HINGED TO OPEN BOOK FLAT / ONCE STOOD
UP ON-STAGE.

*Elevation of profile flat: base construction. Cut out edging, with overall dimension lines. A grid would be required to facilitate drawing on wood sheeting or canvas for scaling up a drawing. Shading indicates the base profile flat, with applied fretwork design. A grid would be required for scaling up the fretwork onto wood or canvas.*

PROFILE BASE

arch openings and recesses. A frame clad in plywood may also have canvas stretched and glued upon it, offering a preferred surface for scenic art treatment.

## Flown flats

Flattage constructed to withstand suspension for the purpose of being flown requires specific construction methods and specialist hardware. Not all suspended scenic elements are required to fly; cabling to a fly bar may only serve as an additional form of bracing. Scenic cloths, even those that are framed, may remain as fixed throughout a performance, yet are suspended from bars. For the draughtsman to plot suspended and flown scenic elements successfully on the Theatre Section,

careful calculation is required to avoid an unworkable proposal. Flown scenery must avoid coming into contact with adjacent lighting, soft or hard borders, and other scenic elements. There is demand when drawing-up to understand venue limitations, the fly system, technical capabilities in terms of stagecraft, and the construction methods likely to be employed. How a show will run in performance and whether there are repertory restrictions (as another show may also have scenery suspended) requires preliminary research through making inquiry. Elements flown or suspended include: hard scenery; lighting; borders and legs; cloths of various types; gauze; leaf or snow drops; possibly props; and occasionally actors in prop costumes.

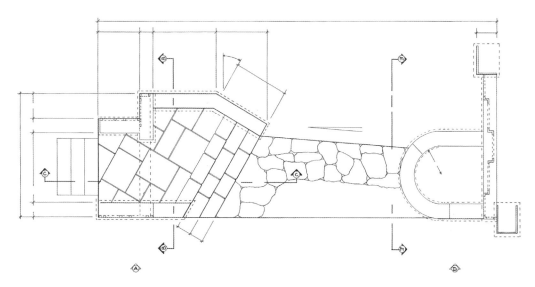

*Garden unit ground plan (mid-stage section only). View: plan with landscaped surface of various type stone; brick walls; arch trellis opening (S.R.); semi-circular pond with walled trellis (S.L.). Cutting planes indicate sections to be drawn for B-B, C-C, and E-E. Elevation views to be drawn for view A and view D. Each section/view produces an elevation showing true measurements. Dimensioning to be added to drawing.*

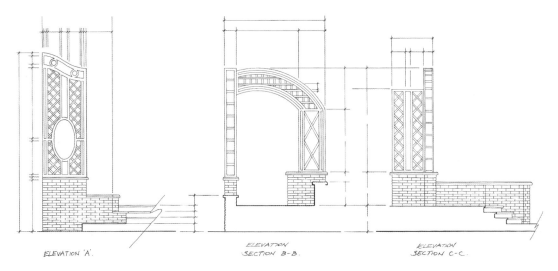

*Garden unit elevation views and elevation of sections. Views include: three elevations, positioned along the same base horizontal (theatre deck/floor level). Elevation A showing height and width. This feature face elevation includes a brick wall with trellis woodwork. A break-line indicates the floor section extends beyond (see plan). Elevation Section B-B showing height and depth. This feature face elevation depicts brick wall with trellis arch opening in woodwork. Elevation Section C-C showing height and width. This feature face elevation depicts brick wall and trellis woodwork. Dimensioning to be added to this drawing.*

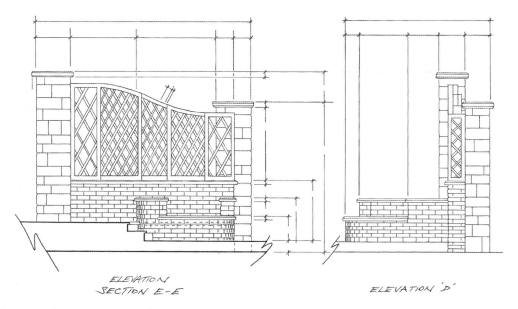

ELEVATION
SECTION E-E

ELEVATION 'D'

*Garden unit elevation views and cutting plane section views. Elevation E-E showing height and depth, depicting the face feature with brick wall semi-circular surround for pond, stone clad pillars up-stage and down-stage, and trellis woodwork. Break-line indicates design continues up-stage and down-stage (see plan). Elevation D showing height and width depicts the face features with brick pond surround, stone pillars, and trellis woodwork. Dimensioning to be added to this drawing.*

## Notes about flats

1. Flat hardware: wood frame flats require 'iron-mongery' in the form of 'flying irons' bolted to the base rail to which cables are attached, and flying-line attachments ('grommets') running down the back of a flat through which the cables are threaded. The fly line length, extended beyond the flat through to the pickup attached to a fly bar (which to an audience is out of sight) is called the 'drift'.

2. Flattage constructed from metal will have more strength than if made with a wood frame. Therefore a metal flat will only require ironmongery bolted to the top vertical of the frame for attachment of cable pick-up.

3. Flattage constructed with mortice and tenon will have its rails and stiles positioned 'side-on', therefore it will have as its depth only the 21mm of the wood used. The flat depth will increase by cladding in wood sheets, typically of 4mm ply.

4. Flattage constructed with 'end on' batten framing will be 70mm thick. Timber battens are applied with their narrow to the back of the flat. The flat depth will increase by cladding with a wood sheet by a minimum of 4mm thickness.

5. To strengthen a frame, end-on battens may be added. Frames with battens added 'end on' require less overall stiffening as this is a strong structure.

6. Flying cables and their attachments are secured onto the back of a flat. The draughts-man needs to compensate (in 'section view') for the reveal (thickness), to allow it to fly uninterrupted. To achieve 'plumb' is of priority to avoid a scenic element making contact with other elements on fly bars down-stage and up-stage. When calculating proportions, it is necessary to consider all proud features that are applied.

7. The exact measurement from bar centre to bar centre is crucial to the draughtsman. When a venue technical drawing appears doubtful, a recce is essential to clarify distances.

8. The 'reveal' is an addition of thickness to the outer edges of a flat. The reveal gives the impression a flat has real thickness. Constructing a flat with real thickness is an unnecessary expense, and theatre is particularly successful at creating illusion with economy. A reveal may be added to a window frame opening or onto a door opening, requiring the draughtsman to consider depth issues when such scenic elements are flown.

9. The package of technical drawings needs to clarify architectural details to be applied as surface embellishment to flats. All features applied to the surface of a flat, such as mouldings, require timber rails (horizontals) built within the frame to support them. Applied features may include shelves, animal head trophies, pictures and wall sconces for lighting.

10. Where protruding features look structurally weak without the addition of supports, consider inclusion of designed or period brackets, such as corbels. Where the protruding feature is weight bearing, brackets or corbels may need metalwork engineered within.

11. Touring productions make particular demand on design to plan flat breaks, and effective design disguises such breaks through adding architectural features to mask vertical and horizontal material breaks. Breaks are determined largely by given sizes of material used by construction, as well by the transport constraints. Note that ply sheeting typically is offered as 1220mm x 2440mm. Additional concerns for the draughtsman are the get-in doors – their size and position and access, and limitations by available manpower, along with turn-around time.

12. Flattage constructed in a curve or arc on plan, when concave, raises concern for relief surface as applied. When they have a single radius, mouldings require a fine series of vertical scorings on the back (partial cutting through) to facilitate bending without breaking.

13. Flattage constructed in a curve or arc on plan, when convex, raises more of a question when moulding is to be applied, as front scoring is not possible. Moulding may have to be of a flexible nature.

14. Where curved flattage has more than one radius (two radii intersecting to produce a curve) particular attention is needed to achieve a fluid transition from one arc to another. A draughtsperson needs to apply principles of building geometry, for the effect on the eye of two arcs meeting can result in an uneven transition, resulting in an irregular blemish running vertically.

## THE FIREPLACE

A central feature to the home historically, the fireplace's changing nature owes much to both technology and engineering as to period fashion and its interior proportioning. Period style and decorative detail highlights or celebrates period craftsmanship. The principle of a successful fireplace is to generate heat in an outwards direction while maintaining a safe draw of gas or smoke upwards. Heat is thrown out by radiation, reflection and by movement of heated air. Receding fireplace walls that angle or slope as they extend back reflect heat outwards. Fireplace sidewalls extending straight back do not reflect. A sloping back wall (generally found to be part straight then part sloping) enables heat to be further reflected back into a room. The fireplace features in many a play, with good reason – it contributes visually to context by type, helped often by the very fuel being burned, or through its magnitude of presence. Often it is not the real fire itself that makes for a convincing fireplace on-stage; it is more what it evokes.

### Notes about fireplaces

1. With the development of chimney systems the fireplace moved from the centre of the room to become attached to walls.

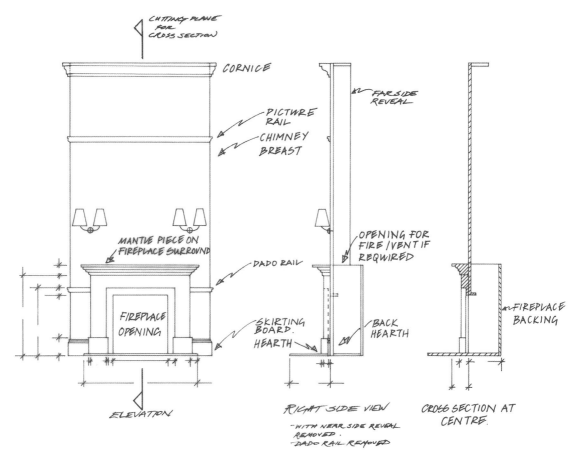

*Fireplace. Views include: front/elevation; right-side view; cross-section. Elevation depicts chimney breast, mantlepiece and hearth. Mouldings include: cornice, picture rail, dado rail, skirting board. Lighting requirements shown as wall sconces. Right-side view depicted with near-side reveal, cornice and dado rail removed. Dimensions to be added.*

2. The floor immediately beneath a fire needs to be protected from the heat of a fire by a hearth.

3. For a wood- or coal-fuelled fire to burn successfully, sufficient flow of air beneath the grate is required.

4. Ash needs to fall beneath a grate to prevent the fire from becoming choked.

5. Air vents supply a fire with sufficient cross airflow; vents may be set in the floor in front of the fireplace, or set within the chimney breast wall strategically placed on either side at floor level. Adjustment of the vent permits control of the desired draught.

6. Historically, fireplaces not only supplied heat to the home but also provided light.

7. With wood becoming historically less easy to obtain and manufacture of coal on the increase, the fireplace evolved to become a smaller opening.

8. Real flame is achievable on-stage yet rarely introduced, as it is a complex health and safety problem to solve.

9. A little haze and moving light effect within a fireplace is highly evocative.
10. The designer considers architectural layout for a chimney breast and its flue within a house because observation of period exteriors highlights appropriate positions for flue and vent.
11. Ground-floor fireplaces are typically fitted central to the chimney breast.
12. Bedroom fireplaces are seen to be fitted off-centre; this is the result of several different flues rising up inside the same chimney breast.

## Terms

* Andiron (sometimes called a 'dog', 'dog-iron', or 'firedog'): a horizontal iron, a bar upon which logs are laid for burning. Usually supplied in pairs, within older periods they were used as a rest for a roasting spit. Andirons allow for a draught of air to pass beneath and around the burning fire, to minimize smoke. Designed with legs and typically connected to an upright guard, it ensures that wood logs and coal remain in the fireplace as burning occurs.
* Back hearth: the area of the fireplace level with the hearth. The depth of a wood-burning fireplace needs to be approximately 460mm.
* Brick: a block of ceramic material used in masonry construction.
* Brick or stone enclosure: that which forms the wall or chimney breast, the foundation of the fireplace forming its opening.
* Chimney: a structure for venting hot flue gases or smoke, designed to provide flow of gas and smoke from a boiler, stove, furnace or fireplace to the outside atmosphere, typically vertical or as near as possible to vertical.
* Chimney breast: of brick or stone, travels the height of the house emerging with an opening that forms the flue.
* Concrete: a construction material composed of cement as well as other materials such as fly ash and slag cement, construction aggregate, water, and chemical admixtures.
* Damper: an adjustable metal plate, allowing flow of smoke upwards.

* Dog grate: used in the back hearth area, holding burning wood or coal.
* Fire irons: a set of tools made of iron designed to manage fire preparation and its maintenance during and after burning. Tools include shovel, poker, tongs and brush.
* Fireback: a cast-iron backing to fireplaces protecting the brick backing from damage, often richly decorated with relief.
* Firebox or firepit: the part of the fireplace where fuel is combusted.
* Fireplace opening: the opening with arch or lintel supporting the chimney breast.
* Flue: the passage between the chimney opening and smoke chamber.
* Gather: typically the fan shape to the chimney breast which funnels the smoke through to the flue and beyond.
* Hearth: usually flush with the floor, of stone, marble or tiled concrete, projecting outwards into the room to protect floor surfaces from embers. It is supported by being fitted into the floor joists, or with stone set upon a trimmer arch of wood, which has been fastened to floor joists.
* Jambs: these support the lintel, which carries the mantelpiece, and may be carved or cast, as applied detail, making historical reference to architecture trends.
* Lintel: an arch or horizontal supporting the stone or brick chimney above, or a heavy metal strap supporting the arc above which is stone or brick; or a heavy oak beam protected by angle iron. The lintel or frieze may feature the same design of the jamb or be of a plain nature.
* Mantlepiece: the decorative fireplace surround, made from stone, marble, slate, wood or cast iron, historically of an ornamental nature. Comprised of jambs supporting the lintel; the lintel may be a continuation of the jamb design in detail or of a plain nature.
* Marble: a rock resulting from the metamorphosis of limestone composed mostly of calcite.
* Masonry: individual units laid in and bound together by mortar (masonry). The most common material of masonry construction is brick.

153

* Mortar: a paste formed by mixing cement, water and fine aggregate masonry; used to bind construction blocks together and fill the gaps between them.
* Overmantle: the upper section of the mantle, typically mirrored in late 1700s and throughout the Victorian period.
* Register grate: a fitted grate, typically cast iron, which houses the fireplace opening. It comprises an iron frame surround with aperture opening and 'register' panel, which opens and closes to allow smoke to draw through to the flue.
* Smoke chamber: below the flue and above the patent damper, with the smoke shelf set back from the throat.
* Tile: a manufactured piece of hardwearing material such as ceramic or rock.
* Walls: The stone or fireplace brick walls lining a fireplace hearth, of sufficient thickness (100mm minimum) to prevent the heat from penetrating through to other construction materials.
* Wrought iron: commercially pure iron, with a very low carbon content. It is a fibrous material due to the inclusion of slag.

# WINDOWS

When drawing a window for construction first make close observation of a period reference. Study carefully the external view noting the practical nature of the window, its relationship to the architectural surround, and how through being layered it forms a composite form. Observe the interior in the same way. The image as it is architecturally observed is often the designer's aim when making a facsimile, although methods for construction will understandably vary from the original. The effect a window has on the eye of the spectator gives the impression of it looking real, yet it is only a facsimile on one side. The illusion of reality may be further disguised by lace, net, drapes or blinds, and perhaps scenic treatment of grime, breakdown or decay. Productions on occasion make demand for a practical sash, enabling actors to interact physically, with construction solutions often veering from an authentic mechanism of weights, cords and pulleys towards much simpler solutions. A degree of authenticity is delivered when adding depth (reveal) to the window opening, suggesting the wall has external thickness; this is especially the case when walls run at

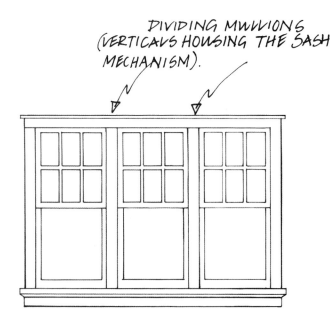

DIVIDING MULLIONS
(VERTICALS HOUSING THE SASH MECHANISM).

*Victorian sash window: view of exterior face. Victorian sash arrangement showing glazing bars in upper sash only. The mullions separate the sash windows and house the sash mechanism of weights and cording.*

*Victorian and Edwardian sash window: view of interior facing. Views include: elevation, cross section, plan and right-side view. Cross-section depicts component parts in depth relationship (glazing not shown) Shaded areas indicate that which is cut through along section line (see elevation view). Variations include: four panes over four panes; two panes over two panes, one pane over one pane (as drawn). The window sill shown in the cross-section drawing is likely to be a solid plane going front to back. It is not broken by a wall as shown in the drawing. The dashed line shown in the right-side view indicates the sill hidden by the end of the side wall and window reveal. Measurements calculated for construction need be kept to a minimum, providing the main measurements where necessary. Construction calculate fine detailing in their bench drawings with key dimensions provided by the designer.*

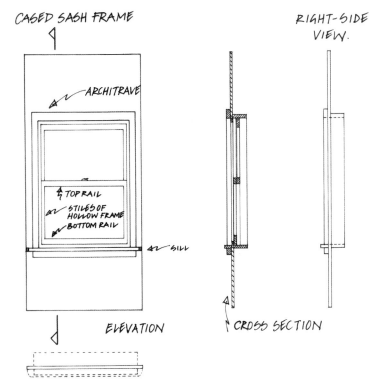

CASED SASH FRAME

RIGHT-SIDE VIEW.

ARCHITRAVE

TOP RAIL
STILES OF HOLLOW FRAME
BOTTOM RAIL

SILL

ELEVATION

CROSS SECTION

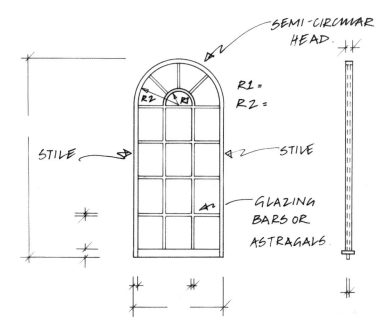

SEMI-CIRCULAR HEAD.

R1 =
R2 =

STILE

STILE

GLAZING BARS OR ASTRAGALS.

*Late Georgian window with semi-circular head. Cross bars or astragals for glazing became decreased in number with the fashion for larger panes. This same window design also exists as a sash. The stiles and base rail have more depth than the cross bars, as is discernable in the right-side view. Dimensions to be inserted.*

155

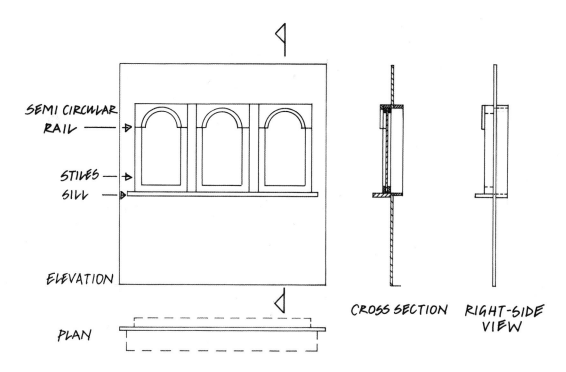

SEMI CIRCULAR
RAIL

STILES

SILL

ELEVATION

PLAN

CROSS SECTION

RIGHT-SIDE
VIEW

*Casement window. Views: elevation, plan, cross-section, right-side view. An early form of window with many period variables, including bay windows, French windows, leaded panes (tracery of cames), in square or diamond shape, produced in metal or wood. Within a bay or feature window, casement windows as inset may hinge open.*

an oblique angle (up-stage to down-stage) to the audience. Dimension thickness to wall features when viewed 'end-on' is much harder to determine; in many cases less depth is required.

To better understand proposed relationships between component parts, it is first advisable to do rough drawings of front, side and cross section. It is informative to draw a cross section view through a cutting plane made horizontally through wall and window. These three views help establish the construct's 3D form as well as providing research to refer to. Research reveals that stiles run vertically from top to bottom, offering a smooth edge against the sash side support; it also offers period proportions for plate glass, stiles and rail count, drawing attention to architectural and manufacturing developments.

Wood may be a substitute for metal, as scenic art may treat it to replicate material finish as desired. Production meetings assist in the discussion of appropriate material, processes for construction, joinery methods, materials and finish, such as paint effect.

Note: due to health and safety, glass is avoided in theatre set construction. Although production costs may increase using polycarbonate or clear PVC, conditions for health and safety may lead decision-making. Alternative materials include: clear film applied and stretched; vacu-formed clear PVC panes; and gauze.

When drawing a window, bear in mind the audience point of view, taking into consideration sight-line angles, and aim for design intention to complement what is visibly on show. Con-

*Georgian style window. Window and semi-circular head. Views include: elevation and cross-section; detail elevation of cross bar and moulding implanting; and cross section.*

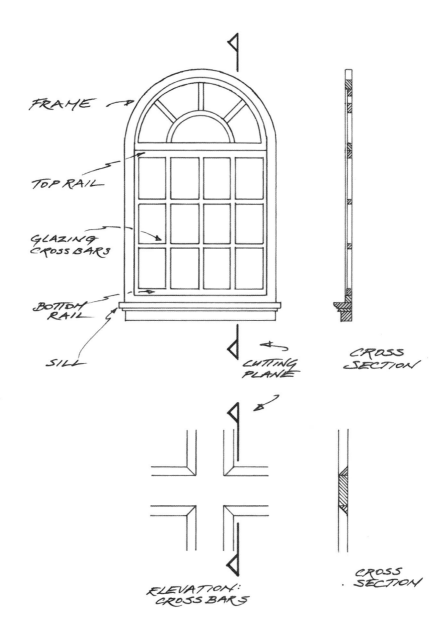

sider that a casement opening may prove effective without glazing material spanning its area; instead various types of blind could be fitted, serving as masking to encourage the eye of the spectator to stop short in looking beyond.

In terms of practicalities, the decision that an actor will handle a vertical sliding sash involves production discussion regarding the height, and mechanism to allow a window to remain open.

When an actor may crawl through a window sash, issues of weight-bearing points, the nature of sash mechanics and its ability to remain open are to be discussed.

### Terms

* Architrave: a general term that is used to describe the various parts that surround a window or door, such as a lintel, jamb and mouldings.

* Astragal: the bars that divide each sash into its paned parts. The astragal supports a glass pane, and features moulding detail, which helps to define the period: the moulded detail and number of cross bars is particular to period.
* Awning window: a window that swings outward.
* Bay window: comprised of three windows, set in a curve or bow, yet may be square. The angles typically used on the inside corners are 90, 135 and 150 degrees. Projecting from the building at obtuse angles, extending to the ground forming a bay within the room, most typically the bedroom and living room/parlour.
* Bow window: also known as a 'compass' or 'radial' bay, comprised of a curved window projecting from a wall in the shape of an arc. A composite of four or more windows; typically windows are joined at obtuse angles.
* Cames: lead glazing bars typically forming a lattice of small diamond-shaped or square-shaped panes of glass.
* Casement window: a window unit that swings open on the side, as in a door, to the right or left. The side-hung casement is hinged on the vertical side, opening outwards as is commonly seen in the UK. French windows are a form of casement window, yet they serve as doors. Casement windows comprise of two vertical stiles, the horizontal top rail, and horizontal bottom rail. With more than one casement, a vertical mullion is positioned between any two. Two casements set one above the other have a horizontal 'transom' dividing them. Early casements had glazing bars made of a lattice of lead 'cames' with diamond-shaped panes.
* Casing: the moulding applied to a window frame, or doorframe. A feature frame or decorated moulding is typically applied proud of the wall surface, attached to the frame jamb and head.
* Circlehead: referring to any window unit with one or more curved frame members, positioned over a window or door.
* Dormer: a constructed space protruding from the roof of a house, typically housing one or more windows.

* Double-hung window: *see* 'Sash window'
* Fixed window: non-venting or non-operable window (also known as 'picture window').
* Frame: the fixed frame of a window that holds the casement or sash, which fits within the masonry opening.
* French sliding door: a sliding door that has wider panel members around the glass, giving the appearance of a French hinged door.
* French window: also known as a French door, this term is used to describe two casement windows in one frame, hinged on the sides to open in the middle. The sash extends to the floor and serves as a door to a terrace or porch.
* Glazing: the glass member of a door or window, of single glaze or for more energy efficiency double-glazed.
* Glazing bead: a strip typically of wood, applied to the window sash around the perimeter of each glass plane.
* Head: the horizontal member that forms the top of a window.
* Header: a horizontal framing member or lintel, positioned above the window opening to support the weight of wall resting upon the window frame. The header transfers the wall weight above the window to the supporting wall structure on each side. The term 'header' generally refers to a wooden beam, whereas a steel beam is normally known as a 'lintel'.
* Hinged window: a window that has an operating sash hinged to one side.
* Jalousie window: a window that consists of narrow overlapping horizontal glass louvres. By either cranking a handle or pulling a lever the louvres pivot to open.
* Jamb: a vertical member at the sides of a window frame (side jamb).
* Lintel: the supporting horizontal beam or member above a window opening that transfers the building weight above the window to the supporting wall structure on either side. The term is generally used in reference to a steel beam, whereas a wooden beam is normally known as a header.
* Main frame: a term referring to the composite of head, sill and jambs of a window.

✳ Masonry opening: the space designed into a masonry (stone or brick) wall, left open for windows or door.

✳ Meeting rail: the rails positioned at the base of the upper sash and the top of the bottom sash; on a double-hung sash where rails meet a mounted lock is introduced.

✳ Mortice and tenon: the top rail of the upper sash and the bottom rail of the bottom sash are joined to the stiles by a mortice and tenon joint. Meeting rails are joined to stiles with dovetail bridal joints. Mortice and tenon is a strong wood joint made by fitting together a mortice in one board and a matching projecting member (tenon) in the other.

✳ Mullion: typically a wooden member positioned vertically and used structurally to join two window or door units, of notable structural importance.

✳ Muntin: a bar positioned vertically or horizontally, used to separate panels and panes.

✳ Pane: (1) a piece of glass in a window; (2) one of the compartments of a window or door consisting of a single sheet of glass in a frame; (3) the separate panel or panels in a wooden wall, or door frame.

✳ Parting stop: in a double-hung window, a strip of wood applied to the jamb to separate the sash.

✳ Pelmet: a framework constructed above a window, used to hide the curtain top where it joins the rail mechanism (similar to a valence).

✳ Picture window: a non-operable window used as a feature window (also known as a 'fixed window'.

✳ Rail: the top and bottom horizontal members of the framework of a window sash.

✳ Rough opening: the framed opening in a wall into which a window or door unit is to be installed.

✳ Sash: a single assembly of stiles and rails made into a frame for holding glass.

✳ Sash balance: a system of weights, cords, pulleys and or coiled springs, which assist in raising double-hung sash windows. The system keeps the sash in any one position when moved vertically up or down.

✳ Sash lift handle: a protruding plate handle typically of brass fixed to the inside bottom rail of the lower sash on a double-hung window.

✳ Sash window: a window formed in two parts which overlap one another. The two parts slide up and down within a frame called the 'case' and are separated by parting beads. They operate through a counterbalanced system with weights, on cords, and run through pulleys. A sash window comprises two vertical side stiles, a 'top rail', a 'bottom rail' and the 'meeting rails' where the sash rails overlap to oppose one another when both are closed.

✳ Sill: the base horizontal part of the window frame, which is angled downwards to ensure that rain flows away from the sash.

✳ Single-hung: a double-hung window with the top sash fixed or impractical for opening.

✳ Stile: the upright or vertical edges of a sash or door.

✳ Stop: a moulding used to separate window parts.

✳ Tenon: A rectangular projection cut out of a piece of wood for insertion into a mortice.

✳ Transom: a small window positioned over a door or window for additional light.

✳ Transom bar: a horizontal member that separates one window from another above, or separates a door from a window panel above the door.

✳ Unison lock: a casement lock that secures windows at locking points through the turning of a handle.

✳ Weatherstripping: a material applied to seal openings and gaps on windows to prevent flow of water or draught.

✳ Window: (1) a glazed opening in an external wall of a building; (2) an entire unit consisting of a frame sash and glazing, and any operable elements.

✳ Window frame: the frame within which is housed the sliding sash, comprised of two vertical 'jambs', at the top a 'header' and at base a 'sill'.

✳ Window seat: a flat wooden board fitted within the arc or box bay window and installed beneath the sill, providing a seat.

## STAIRCASES

Types of stair include: the closed stair where the steps are built in between walls; the open flight of stair, which may have a balustrade on one side and a wall on the other, or balustrades on both sides; open tread stairs with no solid riser; practical and non-practical stairs; audience stairs and actor stairs.

A few rules should be observed when draughting staircases or stair units: define the difference between audience and actor stairs; obtain the most comfort for any rise; and meet practical health and safety standards – all staircases present a form of hazard. The horizontal plane called the 'tread', the part that is stood upon, needs to be of sufficient 'going' (depth) for the safe positioning of an average length foot. The vertical plane is called the 'riser', which is the step-up and should be of a comfortable step height. The total distance from one level to the other level is called the 'rise' (the distance between one floor and the next), and is equal to the sum of the heights of all the risers. The horizontal distance from the face of the first step to the face of the top riser is called the 'run' and is equal to the sum of all the treads.

The dimension for riser and depth of tread needs careful proportioning. In respect of what a character requires, actor staircases may vary in proportion, as a grand proportion may reflect the

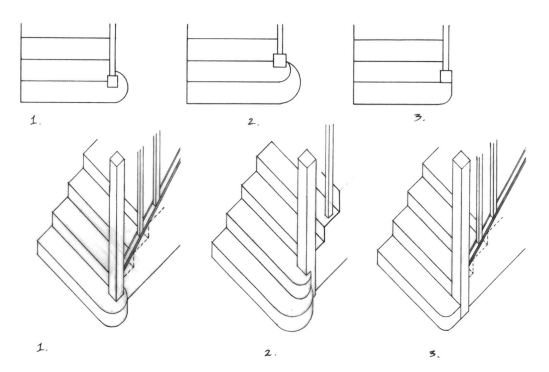

*Three staircase entry configurations.*
1. *First step: Curtail. A half round edge giving breadth to entry. Not ideal for narrow halls. Balusters/ spindles set into base-rail running up stair pitch.*
2. *First two steps: Double curtail. Two half round edges giving more breadth to entry. Not ideal for narrow halls. Balusters/spindles set into tread.*
3. *First step: Bull nose. A quarter round edge ideal for where hall is narrow, gives some breadth to the look. Balusters/spindles set into base rail running along stair pitch.*

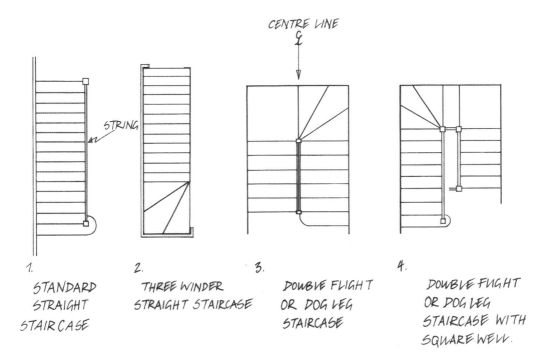

CENTRE LINE

STRING

1. STANDARD STRAIGHT STAIRCASE

2. THREE WINDER STRAIGHT STAIRCASE

3. DOUBLE FLIGHT OR DOG LEG STAIRCASE

4. DOUBLE FLIGHT OR DOG LEG STAIRCASE WITH SQUARE WELL.

1. *Standard straight staircase with newel post at base and on top landing. Handrail as indicated in drawing. Staircase featuring a curtail first step.*
2. *Three winder straight staircase. Staircase is walled in, with no indication of handrail.*
3. *Double flight or dog leg staircase: straight staircase with three winders and quarter landing. In some cases the strings are in the same plane from one continuation to another continuation, as one is exactly over another in plan. Here there is a small space either side of the centre line, so each string plane would miss one another. The double handrail indicates a space between. Staircase featuring a bull nose first step design.*
4. *Double flight or dog leg with square well. Newel posts positioned at right angle junctions. With upper landing having 'guarding' or balustrading along its length (not shown). Staircase featuring a curtail first step design.*

character's status. The opportunity to design proportions as is required is typical. However, when designing staircases of any kind for an audience, the rules are very different, as defined by standard health and safety rules.

Generally speaking for actors, a comfortable ratio for a riser is no more than 180mm and for the thread the going should be no less than 250mm. The nature of the play's context for character is not the only factor when determining stairs, as there may be a necessity to compromise due to a theatre's architectural constraints or sight-line restrictions. Once the actor is out of sight-line, change occurs but never in the ratio of riser from top to bottom. Any change in height of riser on a staircase introduces a stumbling place and becomes a safety risk.

### A turn in direction

Within a staircase is frequently introduced a turn of 90 degrees (a quarter turn) or a turn of 180 degrees (a half turn). To alter direction a landing

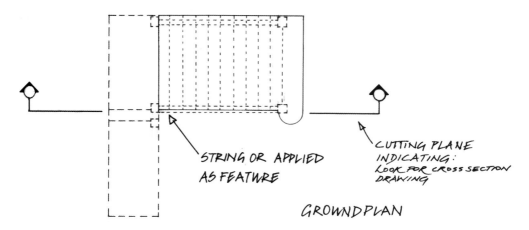

STRING OR APPLIED AS FEATURE

CUTTING PLANE INDICATING: LOOK FOR CROSS SECTION DRAWING

GROWNDPLAN

*Staircase unit: ground plan, showing upper level as dashed (overhead), to permit actor access below. Tread and riser unit connected to theatre floor; solid lines define edges making floor contact. Curtail feature on first tread. Newel posts positioned within first and second step, on first landing and within twelfth and thirteenth step; and within thirteenth step and upper landing. Cutting plane indicates there will be a cross section drawing (see below). String feature clarified in an elevation drawing.*

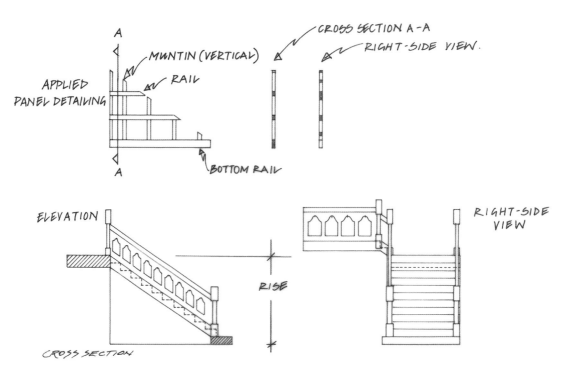

MUNTIN (VERTICAL)

RAIL

APPLIED PANEL DETAILING

CROSS SECTION A-A

RIGHT-SIDE VIEW.

BOTTOM RAIL

ELEVATION

RISE

RIGHT-SIDE VIEW

CROSS SECTION

*Staircase views: front elevation as cross section; applied panel detailing, its right side view and cross section; staircase right-side view.*

*Elevation/front view: shown as cross-section, due to cutting plane in ground plan (see above). True height and depth measurements to be added. Depiction of closed string on main rise, staircase with applied stringer, and fretwork balustrade panel, hand-rail and newel posts.*

*Right-side view: detailing landing guard, which is a continuation of the staircase balustrade as viewed in elevation view, and additional newel post.*

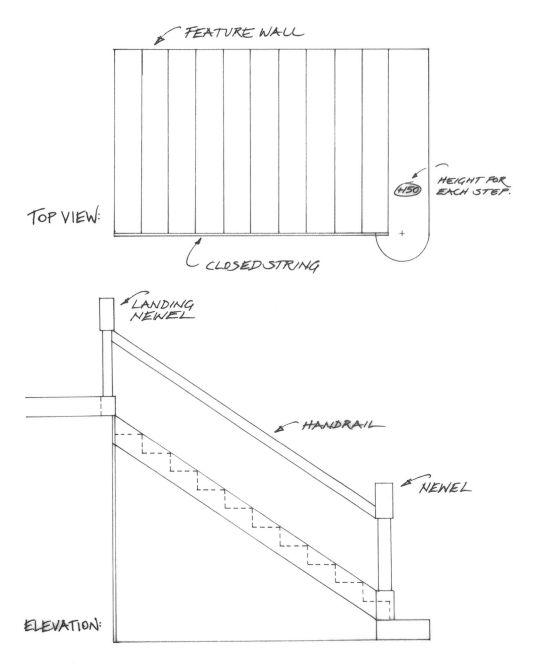

TOP VIEW:

FEATURE WALL

150  HEIGHT FOR EACH STEP.

CLOSED STRING

ELEVATION:

LANDING NEWEL

HANDRAIL

NEWEL

*Views include: top view and elevation. The emphasis is on overall proportions; depth, width and height with internal tread and riser configuration, handrail and newel posts. Closed string and solid wall to side of staircase indicated. No dimension lines drawn yet. Top view measurements transfer downwards to the elevation for tread positions. Riser height indicated on first tread at 150mm above deck/floor level.*

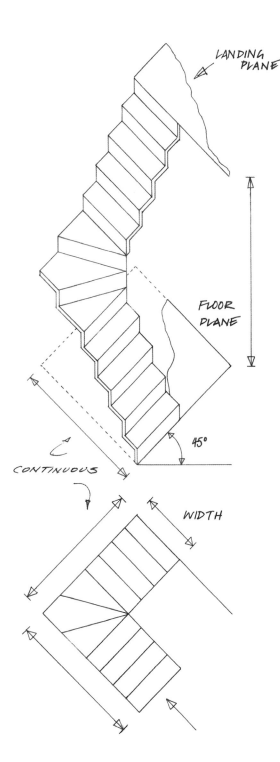

*Axonometric projection: 45 degree staircase with three winders through to landing. Rise: true distance (height) between ground floor plane and landing level. Continuous: the depth measurements on plan for each straight section of stair. Width: refers to width of stairs which have no required dimension other than designer specified. Axonometric view developed to facilitate making an observation of the unit prior to developing the final design for 3D model development.*

would serve, yet where space is at a premium the use of 'winders' is typical – the advantage being that by using tapered treads a 90-degree turn can introduce three treads. When winders occur within a stairway with straight steps, the size of a winder should be the same size width as the tread width; to plot this dimension on the winder it is necessary to measure along the walking line, at the centre of tread width.

The dog-leg is a half turn stair, with balustrade below running in the same plane as the one above. The open-well staircase is also a half-turn staircase, yet has a space between balustrade below and above. Geometrical stairs are those with a turn in direction yet have a continuous uninterrupted direction: the winding staircase with string and balustrade having a continuous curve; the spiral staircase with central post and winding treads; and the helical spiral staircase with an open space between the continuous curve of balustrade and string.

## Handrails

Handrails on a 'straight continuous' staircase should have a 'newel' post at commencement and at the end. Within a residential home the starting newel is securely bolted through to the floor joists, with the landing newel secured through the landing similarly. Where the handrail changes direction a newel post is required. The centre-line of the handrail should align with the centre of the newel. Note that traditional reference depicts the stair

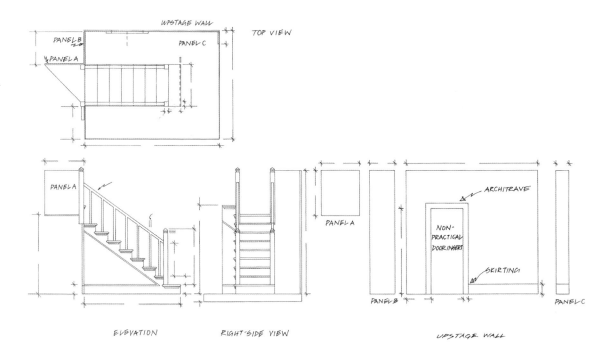

Hallway and staircase unit views include: top view; elevation; right-side view; elevation of panels A, B, and C; elevation up-stage wall with non-practical door. This hallway unit was positioned up-stage of a fixed flat with door opening. The door into the apartment is not shown in this drawing. The audience sight-lines determined the size of the unit. The hallway entrance has a staircase running through it to the floor above, across the hall is the neighbour's front door to their flat. The staircase was non-practical, meaning actors did not walk up the treads. The staircase is on a platform to raise it to room level. Handrails are positioned with spindles on both sides. The flats are drawn with the thinnest set of parallel lines, as they did not require any reveals or depth dimensioning. Dimensions in the drawing are to be added. The views included are only those which support it being built. Notes for construction and scenic art need be added and may include:

1. Stairs non-practical.
2. All woodwork to be painted off-white, including mouldings.
3. Walls to be painted as per the model.
4. Carpet runner positioned up as continuous.
5. Platform unit 180mm high, to make level with entrance doorway and room interior.
6. Hall platform painted hardwood; painted as noise of shoes is essential (text requirement).
7. Tread nosing as half round.
8. Newel posts hollow.
9. Applied moulding on closed stringer.
10. Door insert see drawing number.
11. Door architrave, see drawing number.

riser external edge intersecting with the newel along its centre-line. As a rule draw both handrails, as there is information that may well differ between the handrail on the outside and the inner (against the wall).

## Headroom

Headroom on a stairway should be consistent and run at no less than 2000mm, allowing sufficient safe clearance while walking up a stairway. Drawing the section view through the stairway including the newel, balusters and handrail gives construction a clearer idea of practical heights.

## Landings

Landings may introduce a turn of 90 degrees, meaning they involve a quarter turn of 90 degrees when travelling up. Landings may have a turn of 180 degrees off the landing, meaning they involve a half turn of 180 degrees when travelling up. It is recommended not to include a riser step in such a landing, as this becomes a trip hazard.

## Drawing up

The plan, elevations and top view are drawn in scale as per the model box, 1:25, although detail is difficult. With mouldings, newel, rail, and balusters these can be redrawn as detail drawings at a larger scale, 1:10. Plot the risers and the treads, using the scale rule, as described in principles of dividing a line into equidistant parts, to assist in quickly formulating the number of units per rise and run. When risers are to be numbered, to facilitate easy reading, number them from the bottom step. Stairs present innumerable problems for the draughtsman, mostly to do with aspects of theatre versus reality. Health and safety issues guide the decision making, as technical specification may enter the equation. Materials for construction and the processes for construction largely depend on performance demands. Rules often embrace common sense; when in doubt follow up through production management, a technical director or the local authority in charge of public building safety standards.

## Notes about staircases

1.  Maintain a consistent dimension to the riser across a full rise. Do not vary any riser proportion within a staircase unit.
2.  Maintain a consistent dimension to tread going throughout all treads within a staircase unit, unless landings are introduced which interrupt direction.
3.  Different rules apply for the public and the actor.
4.  Where details such as mouldings/nosing are applied to a tread edge, all treads on a stair unit must have them. The nosing will make the climbing of stairs easier as the riser is further from the toe.
5.  An open flight of stairs with no risers requires an overlap of tread; the front of a tread needs to overhang the back of the tread below by 25mm.
6.  A public raked handrail needs to be between 840mm and 1000mm in height above tread nosing.
7.  Balustrade (vertical supports to a handrail) spacing, in domestic regulations, must not allow for a 100mm-diameter ball to pass through.
8.  A handrail can end with a vertical post; otherwise it must end either by joining another handrail or attaching itself to a wall.
9.  The width of landing should be the same as the tread width.
10. Headroom is calculated by measuring at 90 degrees off the rake pitch; headroom is 1900mm. Alternatively headroom is calculated through measuring a plumb vertical off the tread; headroom on a plumb line is 2000mm (minimum).

## Terms

* Baluster/spindle: the vertical member, fixed at base to the upper part of the string or tread, of plain or decorative carved detailing, serving as in-fill between the handrail and base rail or tread.
* Balustrading: the formal name for unit assembly comprised of: handrail, base rails, newels, spindles and caps.

* Bullnose step: usually the bottom step or the final two, where one or both ends of the tread end in a quarter circle design.
* Closed string: (*see* String) treads and risers are constructed within the string. The profile of the tread and riser cannot be viewed when looking at an elevation of the staircase.
* Continuous handrail: using straight lengths of handrail, found connected to handrail fittings and where there are ramps. The handrail runs over the tops of newel posts forming a continuous handrail.
* Curtail step: a decorative shaped end to the tread on the first step.
* Cut or open string: has notches cut into its upper edge to accommodate the tread being placed onto its cut-away horizontal notch. Cut also to accommodate risers, so that the profile of tread and riser is a visible feature.
* Going: 1. the horizontal distance between the face of the first and last risers. 2. The individual going of a step is measured from face of riser to face of riser and for domestic use should be a minimum of 220mm.
* Newel: at base and top of rise, and every turn in direction, a vertical post into which is fixed a handrail.
* Nosing: the edge of a tread, as applied moulding projecting beyond the face of the riser and applied to the face of a cut string, therefore proud of the string surface.

* Pitch: the angle between the pitch line and the horizontal.
* Pitch line: in elevation a line drawn connecting the nosing of all treads in a flight of stairs.
* Rake: the pitch of the stairs.
* Rise: the rise is the vertical measure between the floor and landing or floor above, connected by a flight of steps.
* Riser: the board or plank that forms the face of the step, giving it height.
* Staircase: the entire structure of a stair comprising of treads, risers, strings, balustrade, and landings.
* Stairway or stairwell: the space or void provided for the provision of stairs.
* Step: the tread and riser combined.
* String: the ends of treads and risers meet with the solid wood string or stringer, a raked plank of wood serving as an end support to tread and riser. Two types exist: (1) the closed string that has two parallel sides raked in the direction of the run within which treads and risers are attached; (2) the cut string that has notches cut into its upper edge, which accommodates the tread being placed onto the cut horizontal notch.
* Tread: the top or horizontal surface of a step.
* Wall string: the string of a staircase fixed flush with a wall.
* Winders: radiating steps narrower at one end that are used to change the direction of a staircase through 90 or 180 degrees.

**Rake ratio PLAN DEPTH/RUN measurement = 2500mm (2.5 metre)**

OA 1:20 HEIGHT=125MM
OB 1:15 HEIGHT=166MM
OC 1:10 HEIGHT=250MM

[OA] 1 in 20 (1:20) Depth 2500mm Equation : Distance ÷ ratio = height (125mm).
[OB] 1 in 15 (1:15) Depth 2500mm Equation : Distance ÷ ratio = height (166mm).
[OC] 1 in 10 (1:10) Depth 2500mm Equation : Distance ÷ ratio = height (250mm)

## THE RAKED STAGE

The raked stage is a performance surface that has gradient or inclination to its plane. To propose designing a rake into performance, design needs to consider standardized guidelines, which may be in place for health and safety or technical reasons. A surface with gradient or raked ratio may need regulating depending upon the type of production, for example musical, drama, or dance. Production concerns centre on hazard and the well-being of performers. Construction concerns centre on the

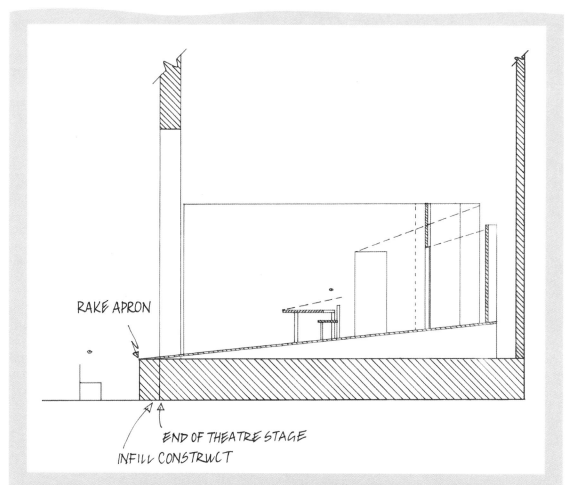

RAKE APRON

END OF THEATRE STAGE

INFILL CONSTRUCT

Section view: raked stage with box set. Section at 300mm stage-left (SL) of centre-line. (*See* ground plan.) View includes: theatre floor/deck level, back wall, proscenium opening, raked surface, stage-right show wall, upstage face wall, masking units. Depth dimensions transferred across from ground plan to section. Section view is customary at centre-line, instead this section view as indicated (above) is 300mm stage left (SL) of the centre-line. View is into stage right wing. Form that is shaded indicates being cut-through; a solid at the point of the cutting plane. Shading includes: theatre sub-stage, apron supporting the rake, raked floor surface, proscenium opening, the centre stage wall above the door opening, masking flat upstage centre, table and chair positioned on the section line. Solid lines indicate both vertical and horizontal edges of objects as viewed in the distance; beyond (further stage right) of the section line.

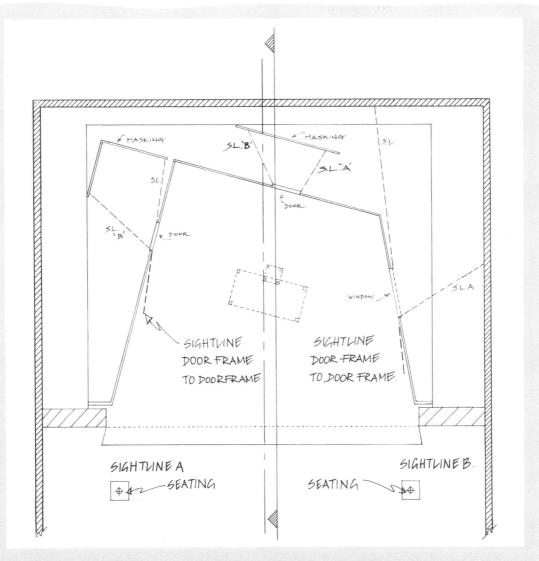

MASKING    S.L. 'B'    MASKING    S.L.

S.L.'A'

S.L.

DOOR

S.L. 'B'

DOOR

WINDOW

S.L.A

SIGHTLINE
DOOR FRAME
TO DOORFRAME

SIGHTLINE
DOOR FRAME
TO DOOR FRAME.

SIGHTLINE A
SEATING

SEATING    SIGHTLINE B.

*Ground Plan. Box set on-stage: Raked platform (showing depth/run and width), rake extension breaks proscenium opening; S.R. (stage-right) wall with door to adjoining room; U.S.C. (up-stage-centre) wall with door to hallway; S.L. (stage-left) wall with window to outside; Table and chair position.*

Note: 1. Rake platform does not fill the stage depth or width. 2. Design shows features connected/perpendicular to floor level showing true depth and width proportioning. 2. Rake proportions determined by masking requirements (U.S.C. and S.R.). 3. Flattage indicated by finely-drawn parallel lines (of minimal distance apart). 4. Hallway masking U.S.C. – sight-lines from seats A and B (widest seats in front row) connect to their opposite door jamb vertical, and project beyond as dashed lines, indicating widest possible audience sight-line. Hall wall is positioned parallel to feature wall. Increase of between 100–200mm at each end allows for on-stage adjustment. 5. S.R. wall masking in adjoining room: Seat B sight-line joined to down-stage door jamb vertical, and projected beyond as dashed line. Sight-line connected from door jamb to door jamb and projected beyond as dashed line (*see* page 105). Masking positioned. Increase of 100mm to wall ends allows for on-stage adjustment. 6. S.L. window masking to be resolved, after considering whether window is see-through; outside is nature or architecture, made of hard or soft masking; glazing is semi-transparent due to blinds, curtains, lace, net or grime; window is translucent requiring a light-box effect; glazing is poly carbonate, film, gauze or to remain empty.

needs of the performance – the nature of the build, and the material, taking into account factors such as touring or repertory. Raked ratio is the degree of gradient.

## Rake structure

The structure supporting the raked surface may include: manufactured (trademark) steel truss units with plywood sheeting of 18mm applied; manufactured steel bar framework, assembled by being slotted together, with plywood sheeting of 18mm applied; wood batten rostra gate or folding-gate units with 18mm plywood sheeting applied. The type of structure used is dependent on production practicality: cost, weight-bearing issues, portability, and soundproofing. Where the production tours, a folding-gate rostra system may prove most appropriate. Soundproofing prevents the surface from becoming like a percussion instrument. Performance demands should be discussed as part of the preliminary production meeting. Further considerations may include get-in requirements, sub-rake construction allowing for sub-stage access (traps and lifts), and most importantly how actors will manage physically over the period of the run.

## Ramps and audience

Where set design is integrated with audience, resulting in their coming into contact with ramped areas through entrance and exit, it is essential that design be authorized in proposal state to meet the strict rules governing health and safety. Such authorization generally comes through making an application to local authority officers. Standards for health and safety regarding the audience fall within legal obligations. Initially approach the venue contractor, building manager, and the council officer for public buildings, otherwise the technical director or production manager for the theatre or venue. Safety specifications relating to rakes/ramps, treads and riser proportions, handrails, seat/aisle and row spacing, audience capacity and the number of exits to be provided within the venue are of legal significance. Take no risks with audience safety: follow the rules.

## Rake and actors

Guidelines for the raked stage in terms of performers requires research through relevant unions or associations such as British Equity. Guidelines defined by Equity UK clearly show recommendations for risk assessment on all rake ratios. Management will be required to initiate a proposed risk assessment. The well-being of performers – actors, dancers and singers – is of professional importance. Health and safety issues include suitability of access, suitability of movement, footwear, clothing/costume, provision of exercise/rest, suitability of surface, as well as construction requirements relating to supporting the weight.

## Notes about the raked stage

1. The distance between two points A-B (one (A) established down-stage, the other (B) established up-stage), both plotted along the centreline, or equidistant from that centre-line, represents the true depth dimension on plan (run). This is the measurement for the flat surface area that will be occupied by a raked stage unit. There is no indication of a raked surface on a plan other than (1) an arrow pointing in the direction of the increase in rake (pointing to up-stage); or (2) a numerical measurement denoting height (+mm) above stage level at its highest.

2. The raked inclination, as it travels up-stage, increases in slope reaching its full height at point B. The raked surface or 'distance of slope' between A and B will be a longer measurement than for its run as viewed as A-B on plan. With a change in rake ratio (an increase in the degree of slope) point B becomes higher. The higher the rake above B on plan, the longer the distance of slope.

3. The distance of slope between two points A-B on section will be longer than the run of A-B as viewed on plan.

4. The raked stage in 'section view' or 'side view' (a view set parallel to the direction of the rake) represents the true rake inclination (its true angle or degree). The angle is set off the horizontal plane of the venue deck or floor (which is 0 degrees). In section the raked

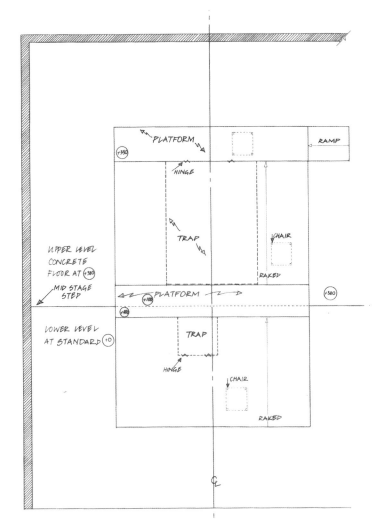

LEFT: *Ground Plan (plan rotated 90 degrees to align with section). View shows: mid-stage theatre divide with rise (increase) of 380mm; designed raked platforms and mid-stage level platform; up-stage level platform joining onto exit ramp; trap position in both rakes showing hinging; chair positions; centre-line position and 'direction of rake' set parallel to centre-line; theatre right-side and up-stage walls (shaded). Rake ratio in accordance with platform heights.*

BELOW: *Section (positioned to align with ground plan). The section is a view taken from centre-stage along centre-line looking into stage-left wing. The view shows: mid-stage theatre divide with rise (increase) of 380mm; designed raked platforms and mid-stage level platform; up-stage level platform; sub-stage access to down-stage rake; traps in opened position; chair positions (down-stage chair counter-raked); theatre up-stage wall (shaded). All features projected downwards to floor level (perpendicular to stage floor), then transferred (projected) upwards through to ground plan.*

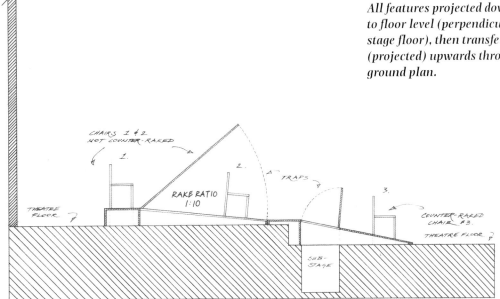

stage can be critically observed and measured to define its true distance of slope. If the run dimension on plan is known, a rake ratio can be calculated to determine its height at point B.

---

## Calculating rake ratios

In this example, the direction of the rake is parallel to the venue centre-line.

A rake ratio of 1:10 implies an increase of 1 unit (in height) for every 10 in distance ('run') measured across the flat surface of a stage; that is, an increase of 1cm in height for every 10cm in 'run' (in the direction of the proposed rake).

First, place the venue plan on the drawing board, aligning the centre-line squarely to the T-square or set-square. Plot the down-stage edge of the proposed rake (set as a line running perpendicular to the centre-line). Calculate the intended run that the raked stage should occupy in depth. This distance is measured from down-stage to up-stage. Remember to plot at the same scale as the venue drawing. This depth measurement is how much space the rake will occupy on plan. It will differ from the measurements calculated for the distance of slope or the depth of the raked surface.

## Percentage incline for a raked stage

A gradient may be discussed by 'grade'. This describes the inclination as a percentage. Road signs for gradients are presented by grade.

An equation for formulating grade:
Rake 1:10
Height ÷ run = grade.
Example: 250mm ÷ 2500mm = 0.1 grade.
To convert to a percentage, multiply by 100.
Grade x 100 = per cent incline.
Example: 0.1 x 100 = 10 per cent incline.

---

*Calculating a rake ratio at 1:10*
*(5.7 degrees, 10 per cent incline)*
1. Take the measurement for run as calculated off the ground plan. The illustration shows a run of 2500mm (*see* page 167).
2. To plot ratio 1:10; divide the run (2500mm) by 10.
3. The rake height up-stage is 250mm above deck. First plot the run on section, then plot a vertical off the horizontal, and measure upwards 250mm.

Answer: 2500mm ÷ 10 = 250mm.
Equation: run ÷ ratio = height.

*Calculating a rake ratio at 1:15*
*(3.7 degrees, 6.6 per cent incline)*
1. Take the measurement for run as calculated off the ground plan. The illustration shows a run of 2500mm.
2. To plot a ratio at 1:15, divide the run (2500mm) by 15.
3. The rake height up-stage is 166mm above deck. First plot the run on section, then plot a vertical off the horizontal, and measure upwards 166mm.

Answer: 2500mm ÷ 15 = 166mm
Equation: run ÷ ratio = height.

*Calculating a rake ratio at 1:20*
*(2.8 degrees, 5 per cent incline)*
1. Take the measurement for run as calculated off the ground plan. The illustration shows a run of 2500mm.
2. To plot a ratio at 1:20, divide the run (2500mm) by 20.
3. The rake height up-stage is 125mm above deck. First plot the run on section, then plot a vertical off the horizontal and measure upwards 125mm.

Answer: 2500mm ÷ 20 = 125mm.
Equation: run ÷ ratio = height.

## Guidelines for treads and ramps to a raked stage

Get-on treads and ramps offer access to a raked stage. It is generally considered a ramp is preferable to a tread (or step unit). Where a tread unit is employed, best practice veers towards making the tread plane level with the theatre floor plane, and that a landing or larger step as top step is factored in. This offers actors/performers an area for adjustment, serving as transition between one surface and another.

In respect of visibility for actors/performers, both the edge of a rake and the step edge require appropriate markings to highlight the hazard, and where low levels of light may affect performers' vision it is necessary to highlight steps with a luminous product to denote edges.

## To draw a raked stage

To draw the rake, both the theatre plan and section are required. For learning purposes, it is advisable to approach a local theatre with a flat stage, asking for a copy of ground plan and theatre section, preferably both in the same scale and in hard-copy format. A studio theatre/venue will also be suitable.

Note: the ground plan (see Chapter 6) depicts depth and width measurements. This will allow for plotting the ground area, as occupied by a raked unit in depth and width. The theatre section depicts depth and height measurements. This will allow plotting the actual gradient or angle for the raked surface, in true depth and in true height.

*The plan*

Work in the same scale as the technical drawing. Typically, plan and section for a small to medium-sized venue will be at scale 1:25. Plot a point down-stage where the rake commences. With a rake running in the direction of the centre-line, draw a mark along the centre-line down-stage (point A). Measure through to up-stage from point A the depth measurement as desired and make a mark on the centre-line (point B). Draw two lines (perpendicular to the centre-line) defining the down-stage edge of the rake and the up-stage edge of the rake.

Calculate the rake proportion as width. Measure left then right of the centre-line the calculated distances forming the rake width. Draw two lines running parallel to the centre-line which connect, by intersecting, the previously drawn lines. The intersection forms the four corners of the raked stage; its area is defined within these parameters.

Write down the numerical depth dimension between down-stage and up-stage. It is recommended to measure along the centre-line as this is in the direction of the rake and is a visible line already established on plan.

*Transferring to section view*

The down-stage edge of the rake, point A, needs plotting on section first. If the down-stage edge of the rake (the line set perpendicular to the centre-line) does not align itself with any architectural feature such as proscenium opening or down-stage edge of the raised stage, it will be necessary to then establish point A at a true distance from some other feature in the venue (such as front row of fixed seating, or the distance between the up-stage wall of the venue and point A). Once plotted accurately, the rake depth and rake height can be calculated, measured and plotted.

Position the plan alongside the section drawing, aiming to align both in such a way that the up-stage wall in each drawing registers and a down-stage feature aligns itself. The centre-line on plan will need to be set parallel to the stage floor on section. Other architectural features will also appear aligned, such as proscenium opening, front row of seats, any traps to sub-stage, and fly bar positions if the venue has them.

The depth dimension of the rake, (A-B on plan), needs to be measured and plotted on the section drawing. Take the measurement from point A to up-stage point B. Avoid errors that may occur through plotting B as a measurement from the up-stage wall, or other architectural point of reference. Note that this dimension is a distance along the surface of the venue floor or deck and is a true measurement for depth (run).

*Establishing the height of a rake*

At point B, draw a vertical line, perpendicular to the theatre floor, in the direction of the height to be established. Upon this vertical line is measured the height for the rake ratio as calculated through the procedures mentioned above (*see* page 172), and a fine dot marks the height. With a straight rule a line is drawn joining A to the height above B. The resulting gradient line, drawn as a solid in H pencil, is the actual angled rake in section.

*How to calculate a rake ratio from a drawn gradient*

1. Measure on plan the distance from down-stage (point A) to the up-stage edge of the rake (point B), calling this the run.
2. Plot on the Section drawing points A and B. Draw the height required (purely as a visual calculation) above B (perpendicular to the venue floor/deck). Join point A to the height above B, as wished.
3. Measure the height of the rake at point B, calling this the height.

Equation: distance ÷ height = ratio/percentage.

*To draw an elevation for the raked surface*

The elevation of any floor design is its true view showing actual width and depth as a surface plane. Through projecting off the angled rake at 90 degrees onto a surface plane running parallel with it, the elevation view is draughted. Perpendiculars off edges and their intersecting points produce dimension for depth.

For construction of rostra folding-gate units, the raked floor surface sheeting is laid on supports whose lengths run in the direction of the rake (down-stage to up-stage if the rake direction is the same as the centre-line). To be included in the elevation is the separation of sheeting with a depth for each sheet being 2440mm and a width of 1220mm. It is of interest that this information be added to the section view (although it will appear as a finely drawn line). Breaks between ply sheets are drawn between each sheet, at 90 degrees to the surface plane. Use the adjustable set-square to establish and fix the angle of the rake as required (in section view). Rotate the set-square until the required 90 degrees to the established angle is found – do not readjust the degree setting. Transfer the ply sheet breaks across onto the elevation. On the elevation plot the width for each ply sheet (1220mm) making allowance for the 18mm overhang for the side fascia stage left and right.

## Determining height at any point within the raked area

To determine the height of any point on a rake (which has only one 'direction of the rake') follow these steps:

1. Determine a point on the plan within the raked area.
2. With set-square transfer this point across to the line 'in the direction of the rake' (typically the centre-line), being sure to transfer at 90 degrees off the 'direction of the rake'.
3. Transfer this point to the section view: align section and plan, as mentioned previously; using a set-square transfer this across to the section view, plotting it on the venue floor/deck. With set-square perpendicular to the venue floor at this point, draw a vertical line upwards to connect with the rake. With scale rule measure the distance from stage level to rake surface.
4. On section, calculate the distance from the down-stage point A to the required point up-stage, applying the following, if known: distance ÷ ratio = height.

## Develop a design on plan then section

1. Establish on plan positions for scenic elements such as flattage and positions for furniture, drawing in as is normally done for a level stage.
2. Align the two drawings (plan and section) with the centre-line of plan set parallel with the stage level floor on section and fix to the board.
3. Using a set-square find the perpendicular to the centre-line on plan, then transfer all depth dimensions across to section, through to where they register with the floor/deck level.
4. Transfer scenic elements attached to fly bars in the same way.
5. Remove the plan drawing from the board.

6. Using a set-square, transfer vertically these points, from floor level upwards to intersect with the rake.

7. Proceed to establish vertical heights for flattage, being sure walls are plumb.

8. Where furniture is to be transferred, draw lines vertically off venue floor level, to intersect with the rake. Lines drawn above the rake, noting the furniture's form, need to be plotted as perpendicular to the raked surface, using the adjustable set-square, as typically most furniture is unaltered to sit upon the rake.

9. Where furniture is to be counter-raked (that is, it will stand plumb – true vertical – with back legs shorter and front legs longer), all lines noting its form, above the raked surface, need to be drawn as true vertical.

## Develop a design on section then on plan

Where plotting is done on the section first – noting positions of depth for scenic elements and drawing furniture onto the raked surface – it is advisable to transfer all the plotted points vertically downwards to floor level. The distance from point A (downstage edge of the rake) measured up-stage through each point is calculated and then re-plotted directly onto the plan using measurements alone. Note: it is essential that points on the raked surface in section register as perpendicular to floor level.

## Notes about 'true view' elevation

1. A 'true view' elevation depicts actual built dimensions for a floor surface.

2. It is a separate technical drawing, to be included in the package of technical drawings for a show.

3. It enables production to propose materials, processes of construction, and costs for construction purposes.

4. Accompanying notes should include: type of effects intended or materials as preferred (painted wood grain or stained wood planking, for example); break or join details for surface ply; demand made by performers, such as dancing, fighting, or physical activity; and proposed weight endurance.

5. It indicates where specific floor treatments change; within the overall rake area, floor detailing may vary due to interior, adjoining rooms, and exterior.

6. The elevation conveys dimensioning of floor surface for material size (as in applied tiles, stone, or marble slabs), and describes through labelling where applied texture or paint treatment will be.

7. Scenic art costs materials and paint expense from the elevation.

8. Scenic art and construction scale up from the elevation, where detailing is dimensioned.

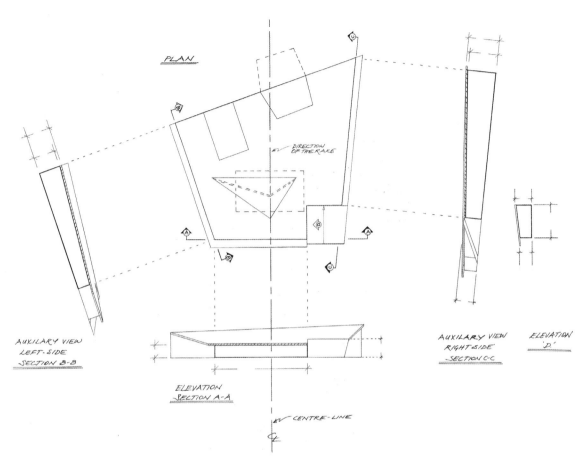

*Raked platform. Views include:*

1. *Plan showing sub-stage trap as dashed, triangular trap opening, position for scenic units on rake, ramp exit down-stage, section views to be drawn A-A, B-B, C-C, Elevation D.*
2. *Elevation Section A-A (auxiliary view – parallel to the rostrum/platform face) shows true width and true height of facing (through cutting-plane A-A). Shading indicates platform surface (wood sheeting) cut-through. Some key dimension lines included.*
3. *Elevation Section B-B (auxiliary view – parallel to the rostrum/platform face) shows true depth and height of facing (through cutting-plane B-B). Shading indicates platform surface (wood sheeting) cut-through. Some key dimension lines included.*
4. *Elevation Section C-C (auxiliary view – parallel to the edge of the platform) shows true depth and height of rostrum/platform facing (through cutting-plane C-C). Shading indicates platform surface (wood sheeting) cut-through. Some key dimension lines included.*
5. *Elevation D shows true depth and height of rostrum right-side face (down-stage) where ramp cuts into its proportions. Some key dimension lines included.*

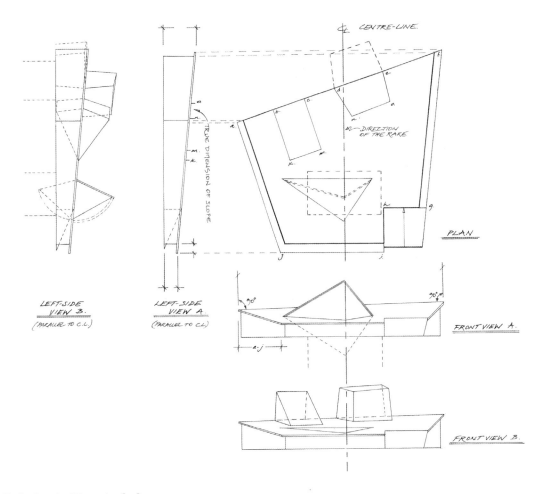

PLAN

LEFT-SIDE VIEW B. (PARALLEL TO C.L.)

LEFT-SIDE VIEW A. (PARALLEL TO C.L.)

FRONT VIEW A.

FRONT VIEW B.

*Raked unit. Views include:*

1. *Plan has thick lines indicating rostrum facing meeting stage floor, with lighter lines beyond these indicating rake edging above stage level. Dash lines indicate trap opening;*
2. *left-side view A drawn parallel to centre-line (direction of the rake), rake shown at true rake ratio, with distance of slope as a true measurement;*
3. *left-side view B drawn as parallel to centre-line (direction of rake) with scenic elements transferred from plan, rake shown at true rake ratio, with distance of slope as a true measurement;*
4. *front view A showing height and width, yet rake foreshortened, trap in raised and lowered position, sub-stage trap width indicated by vertical dashed lines with trap;*
5. *front view B showing height and width with scenic elements.*

*To plot positions of scenic elements on plan along line a-f: first draw the auxiliary rear view, showing distance of slope to establish true slope, measure and plot from model or as designed, then transfer back through to plan. These points can now be transferred down the page through to front view to establish along a-f; points b,c,d,e.*

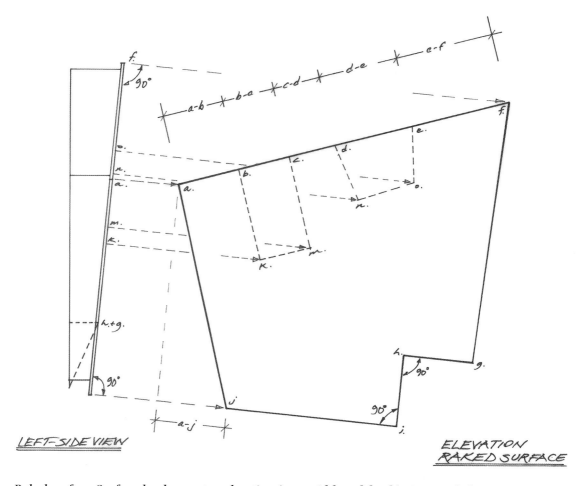

LEFT-SIDE VIEW

ELEVATION
RAKED SURFACE

*Raked surface. Surface development or elevation (true width and depth) views include:*

1. *Left-side view A. Drawing is parallel to the direction of the rake (in this case parallel to centre-line) with gradient 'distance of slope' as a true measurement.*
2. *Elevation of raked surface, true proportions.*

*The process is as follows. Project off from left-side view (at 90 degrees to slope) the corner points a, f, j, i. Refer to plan for plotting a, j, i, g, f. into the elevation. This can be done on plan by extending the horizontal line j-i in both directions, and transferring through perpendiculars all points (a, g, f) down to it. These measurements are then transferred along line j-i in elevation. The rear auxiliary view (parallel to angle) would establish true distance of slope for a-f. Along this true gradient is plotted points a-b, b-c, c-d, d-e, e-f. Once established, these measurements are transferred along the line a-f in development of elevation. In this same drawing, transfer across points n and o, which are to be measured and transferred to line a-f in development of elevation. Letters k, m, n, o have been plotted on left-side view (taken from plan), project across at 90 degrees into development of elevation. Project b and c downwards at 90 degrees off a-f to intersect k and m. Project points n and o along a-f vertically downwards (90 degrees off a-f) to intersect with n and o projected off left-side view.*

# 12 THE ORDERS OF ARCHITECTURE

## TERMS

* Beam, or lintel: that which rests upon the columns or piers.
* Building: a substructure or base, the supporting members and the supported part.
* Columns: slender supports. The column consists of the 'shaft', ornamented at the top by the 'capital', with the 'base' at the bottom. The base is carried on a member: the pedestal when short; the podium when continuous. Column and entablature identify the particular style: the 'Order of Architecture'.
* Entablature: the lintel directly supporting the roof, together with the roof overhang.
* Pediment: triangular front part of a building.
* Piers: isolated supports.
* Tympanum: vertical triangular space within a pediment.
* Wall: continuous support member.

## TUSCAN

A Roman Order with moulding profiles made up of circle arcs and straight lines. The column shaft is not fluted. The base consists of a simple torus placed upon a plain plinth block.

## GREEK DORIC

Of subtle outline and proportion, with a simple capital. Proportions may be based on human dimensions: a man is six times as high as the length of his foot, therefore the column height is six times the base diameter. The column has no base, with a shaft rising from a three-step stylobate. The shaft is typically scored with twenty elliptical channels, each meeting in a sharp edge or arris. The capital is very simple: a heavy square slab called an 'abacus', below which is an 'echinus'. Below the echinus are raised bands or annulets. There are grooves on the shaft just below the echinus, called scamilli. Architraves are typi-

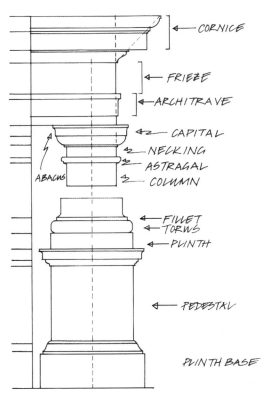

TUSCAN ORDER

CORNICE

FRIEZE

ARCHITRAVE

CAPITAL
NECKING
ASTRAGAL
COLUMN

ABACUS

FILLET
TORUS
PLINTH

PEDESTAL

PLINTH BASE

*Tuscan order is named from Tuscany in Italy. A Roman Doric column except that it has no ornament and lacks refinement seen in the other Roman orders. Shaft is not fluted, the base being a simple torus nesting upon a plain plinth block.*

179

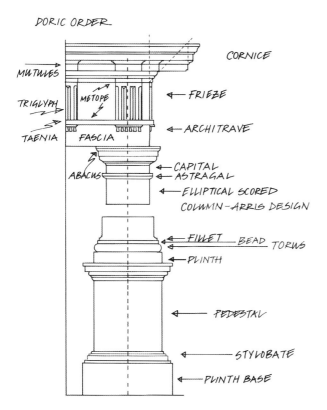

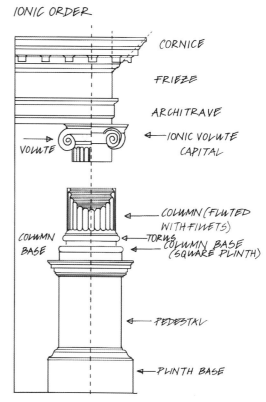

*Greek Doric column – the Doric is the oldest of the Greek orders, and considered of the most refined of outline and proportion. The column is found with twenty elliptical scored channels, ending in arris or sharp edges.*

*Greek ionic volute – a lighter order in proportions to the Doric. The column is scored by twenty-four semi-circular flutes with fillets as separates. The capital is either a cushion capital or a volute capital, which is turned 45 degrees.*

cally plain, very deep, and at the top there is a terminating fillet called the taenia, and a flat band: the regula, from which are suspended peg-like forms called guttae, beneath each triglyph. Within the frieze are square flat spaces called metopes, with the width of the metope determining the spacing of the columns.

## ROMAN DORIC

Resembling Greek Doric with lighter proportions, a base is added to the columns with alteration of mouldings on the capital. The columns have necking and astragal, with channels stopping below the astragal. Two distinct entablatures: one has mutules; the other has in place of mutules a series of small supporting block dentils. The corner triglyph is positioned over the centre of the corner column, not at the corner of the frieze as in the Greek Order.

## IONIC

The Ionic Order is lighter in proportion than the Doric. There are two distinct types: Attic-Ionic (the base of Attic-Ionic consists of an upper torus below a large scotia, and at bottom a smaller torus, which is sometimes omitted) and Asiatic-Ionic.

The principal difference lies in the column base and cornice (the base of Asiatic-Doric consists of a torus resting upon a double scotia, which is carried by a square plinth). Column height is based on 8 to 10 diameters. Columns are scored by twenty-four semicircular flutes, separated by fillets. The capital is a distinctive feature: the Ionic capital is not intended as corner to a building, as the sides are different from front and back, and there are volutes positioned on the corner on both of the outside faces connecting on a diagonal. The architrave is plain or divided into two or three plain surfaces. The frieze is a flat surface typically receiving sculpture.

## ROMAN IONIC

Roman Ionic has a measure of bold ornament with a heavy entablature. The cornice is large and supported by dentils. Mouldings are semi-circular in section.

## GREEK CORINTHIAN

Corinthian is influenced by acanthus leaves. Greek Corinthian consists of a capital used with certain members of Greek Ionic. Roman acanthus is more like the natural leaf. A Corinthian capital resembles an inverted bell, separated from the shaft of the column by a torus and conge. Leaves spring up from the torus to appear as though coming from beneath the bell.

## ROMAN CORINTHIAN

The typical capital consists of two rows of acanthus leaves, with eight leaves in either row. Springing out from the leaves are the stems and tendrils, which form corner volutes.

## COMPOSITE ORDER

This term refers to architecture that is composed of parts of the other Orders, generally the Ionic and Corinthian Orders. Proportions are practically the same as the Corinthian, but with less refinement, yet ornamented.

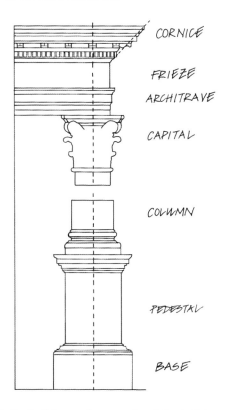

*Greek Corinthian order – a mix of Corinthian capital with the Greek Ionic. The main reference from other orders is the capital being highly ornate in its acanthus leaf decorative carving. The shaft may be fluted.*

## COLUMN ENTASIS

The column at its base is of a larger diameter than at its top, with the shaft not diminishing proportionally to the height. An effect of swelling occurs at the centre of the shaft, with a curvature called 'entasis'. The curvature begins one-third of the way up the shaft (in most Orders), while the lower third is cylindrical (except in Greek Doric, where the entasis starts its curvature at the bottom). Without curvature towards the centre, the shaft would appear as weak. The optical effect of entasis prevents this happening.

# GLOSSARY

**Abacus** The topmost division of the capital of a column. The crowning member of the capital forming a seat for the horizontal members, or a springing for arched members. In the Tuscan, Doric, and Ionic Orders it is rectangular, but it is curved inwards in the Corinthian and Composite.

**Above** That which is above stage level noting height.

**Abutment of an arch** The mass of masonry that resists the thrust of the arch, against which the ends of the arch rest.

**Act drop**, *see* Cloth

**Acting area** The performance area made visible to the audience, where actors or performers deliver the narrative or express themselves.

**Acute angle** Any angle less than 90 degrees.

**Aisle** 1. The side portion of a building, separated from the centre portion usually by columns or piers. 2. The passage between seating and architecture or designed set of a specific dimension (typically 1100mm in width) in accordance with health and safety rules, allowing the audience to enter and exit a performance or auditorium.

**Angles** A figure formed by two rays that have the same origin. The rays are called the sides or arms of the angle. The origin of the rays is the vertex of the angle. When two straight lines intersect, the point of intersection is said to be located definitely. The point of intersection for a line 'a' and a line 'b' is 'ab' or '0'.

**Angle iron** A structural iron whose cross section is in the form of a letter L.

**Annulets** The band of small mouldings at the bottom of the Echinus of the Greek Doric capital.

**Antae** A pilaster attached to a wall.

**Apex** The highest point of a triangle; at its point of intersection forming the tip.

**Approximate ellipse** A shape that is elliptical in appearance, but does not have true focii.

**Apron** 1. The finished board placed immediately below a window stool or internal window sill. 2. The area downstage of the proscenium allowing actors to break the fourth wall.

**Arcade** A series of arches.

**Arch with orders** An arch consisting of several concentric rings in thick walls. The opening is in the middle of the thickness of the wall and the rings increase in size to the two faces of the wall, thus allowing for a better distribution of the light.

**Architectural Order** An entablature supported by columns, with the relative parts proportioned. The three main Orders are Doric, Ionic, and Corinthian, to which are usually added the Tuscan and Composite.

**Architrave** 1. The ornamental mouldings round a door or window opening, usually covering the joint between the plaster and framing. 2. The lowest part of the entablature, or epistylium, that rests on the capital of the column.

**Architrave cornice** An entablature without frieze.

**Architrave of an entablature** The lower division of the entablature.

**Arris** The edge formed by the intersection of two surfaces.

**Astragal** A small moulding of circular section.

**Attic** 1. That part of the classic structure that occurs above the cornice level. 2. The space immediately under the roof of a house.

**Back projection screen** A translucent material suspended from a fly bar, upon which light projection is directed either from down-stage or from up-stage.

**Backing** Refers to the scenic elements positioned offstage; these are viewed through openings in the set, giving the impression of a space beyond such as a garden, another room, or hallway. Backing serves as masking as it hides the theatre or venue beyond from audience view.

**Backstage** The area up-stage of a proscenium arch or similar aperture through which the audience views a performance or part of a performance.

**Balcony** A platform projecting from the building wall.

**Bar/Fly bar/Line set** A series of metal pipes suspended from the Grid, attached through cables to a pulley and counter-weight system for flying. 'LX Bar' refers to a bar specifically assigned for lighting purposes.

**Base** The lower member of a column or a building.

**Base board** The finishing board covering the plaster wall where it meets the floor. (*See* Skirting board.)

**Batten** A length of wood used for fastening other boards together, typically 3in (7.6cm) × 1in (2.5cm). Attached to the upper horizontal of a cloth on both sides through which a sash is fixed to attach it to a fly bar. **Batten out:** to apply battens vertically to a cloth with horizontal battens. **Batten pocket:** the hem in the base horizontal of a cloth allowing a pipe or batten to reside, giving a cloth a solid horizontal at the base.

**Bay** 1. A comparatively small projecting portion of a building. 2. One division of an arcade or the space between two columns.

**Beam** A large horizontal structural member supporting floors.

**Bevel** An inclined edge of a piece of timber, cut by sawing or planing the edge.

**Blacks** The serge or velvet cloths used for masking, typically in the form of borders, legs and full black.

**Blocking** The directorial movement of actors into required positions throughout a performance.

**Bond**   The connection between bricks or stones of a masonry wall formed by overlapping the pieces.

**Border**   A drop of material, generally serge or velvet, attached to a fly bar for the purpose of masking, lighting and scenic elements suspended above the stage, out of audience view. Of matching fabric when used with legs, borders may be constructed and clad in hard or soft material applied with scenic art treatment. The border always hangs in front (down-stage) of the leg, although both are generally attached to the same fly bar.

**Box set**   A three-sided construct, boxing in the acting area, with the fourth side as a 'fourth wall' through which the audience views the set.

**BP (Back Projection Screen or Rear Projection Screen)**   A manufactured material that forms a drop cloth specifically used for back projecting; the projector is positioned up-stage of the screen.

**Brace**   **Stage brace:** a wooden shaft, which can extend and retract, with a hook at one end and a metal flat plate at the other; it functions as a support for scenery, attached to a flat and onto the floor, set at an angle. It is generally fixed to the venue floor with stage weights. **French Brace:** a frame in triangular form supporting scenery.

**Brail**   This is used to divert a scenic element being flown, by means of a length of rope or sash rigged to one of the flying lines.

**Brail line**   A length of sash or rope, rigged to one of the flying lines, for diverting a flown scenic element.

**Break down**   To age a scenic element or costume, to treat it to give it a sense of being worn, weathered, or aged.

**Breast**   To divert a flown unit by means of a separate rope or sash slung across from stage left to stage right, to deflect all fly lines away from a foul happening. (*See* Foul.)

**Breast line**   The rope or sash used to breast a scenic piece.

**Bridging**   A cross-bracing built between joists and studs to add stiffness to floors and walls.

**Buttress**   An enlargement or projection of a wall to resist the thrust of an arch.

**Carriage**   The framing timber that directly supports the stair steps.

**Casement**   1. A window whose frame is hinged at the side to swing out or in. 2. A small hollow moulding. 3. A hinged or pivoted sash.

**Casement lights**   Windows with a pivoted or hinged sash.

**Castor**   A wheel attached within a truck or scenic unit to facilitate it being wheeled across the stage.

**Caulicoli**   The stalks that spring from the second row of leaves of the Corinthian capital and extend up to form the volutes under the corners of the abacus.

**Ceiling**   A frame construct with canvas cover, used as a ceiling within a set. It may also be clad, with sheet ply attached to the frame.

**Centre-line**, *see* Line.

**Chamfer**   A narrow inclined surface along the intersection of two surfaces; to bevel.

**Cloth**   Canvas material with a seamed pocket at the base for a bar, and either fixed to a fly bar with sandwich battens or with fabric binding as ties. **Drop cloth:** refers to any flown cloth. **Framed cloth:** refers to a wood or metal frame upon which a canvas is stretched. **Front cloth:** a down-stage cloth used to mask a scene up-stage, a scene may be played down-stage of a front cloth. **Painted cloth:** a scenic art treated cloth. **Sky cloth:** a painted or dyed cloth depicting a sky. **Ground/Stage cloth:** a floor cloth upon which actors perform. **Star cloth:** a black cloth with lighting effect, whereby small lights are planted into the cloth, from behind.

**Coffer**   A deeply recessed panel usually in a ceiling or dome.

**Colonnade**   A continuous series of columns.

**Complementary angles**   Two angles whose sum is equal to 90 degrees (each is complementary to the other).

**Composite**   One of the 'Orders' of Architecture. The last of the five Roman Orders and composed of parts of the other Orders, hence its name.

**Conge**   A moulding in the form of a quarter circle, often called a scotia, the feature joining the base or capital to the shaft of a column.

**Corbel**   A bracket formed on a wall by building out successive courses of masonry; a wooden bracket.

**Corinthian**   The most ornate of the three main Architectural Orders. The distinguishing feature is the capital, which is richly carved in two tiers of eight acanthus leaves.

**Cornice**   The part of a roof that projects beyond the wall; the upper main division of a classical entablature; the top part of the entablature; horizontal projecting mouldings at the top of the framing, or at the junction of wall and ceiling, or on façades of buildings.

**Corona**   The plain centre member of a classical cornice.

**Counterweight**   A weight used in the flying counterweight system to enable scenic units to fly in and out with ease as they are operated manually.

**Court**   An open space surrounded partly or entirely by a building.

**Cresting**   The ornamental finish of a roof ridge or the top of a wall.

**Crossover**   An area often designed into the set, which enables an actor or crew-member to make the journey around the set from left to right without being in view to the audience. The crossover may be part of the venue, where doors lead off left and right giving access across the stage behind the up-stage wall.

**Cupola**   A small cylindrical or polygonal structure on top of a dome.

**Curtain – Tab:**   the curtain that, through being flown, may start and/or end a scene or act. **Safety/Iron curtain:** the flown dividing wall made of a fireproof material, sealing the opening to a proscenium, preventing fire spreading from one side of the iron to the other. **Blacks:** suspended serge or velvet cloth used to create a black box appearance within a space; may consist of borders and legs, a full black (spanning the distance of a fly bar), and blacks running up-stage to down-stage (in the wing area, left and right of the acting area). **House curtain:** the main house curtain which divides the auditorium from the stage; it may function as a swagged or tracked curtain, or as a drop (flown). **Curtain track:** a tracking system attached to a bar, or other, suspended above stage level, from which cloths or curtains are attached. **Curtain up:** the start of the performance.

**Cyclorama**    The cloth up-stage which offers a plain background; it may curve in a part circle or arc, upon which lighting is projected from down-stage or up-stage or both. It is fixed to a bar and often stretched tight.

**Dais**    A low platform or rostrum upon which a performer stands, typically with a throne or chair.

**Dead**    The 'dead' refers to a measurement from the base of a suspended scenic element, fixed above stage level, to the stage level. The distance between floor and base of unit, noting its height above stage. the correct marked position for the height of a suspended scenic element, typically a tape fixed by the fly-man to the fly-line noting its required position.

**Deck**    The stage level.

**Dentils**    Rectangular supporting blocks beneath the cornice of an entablature.

**Depth of stage**    The measured distance from down-stage through to up-stage, generally along the centre-line.

**Designer**    The individual responsible for the creation of a visual or design for set and costume.

**Development**    Drawing of the surface of an object unfolded or rolled out on a plane.

**Dip trap**    These small traps positioned to the side of the stage, in the floor, are used to contain lighting plug sockets.

**Director**    The individual responsible for the physical manifestation of text through directing; working with actors/performers to make physical the narrative. The role includes co-conceptualizing how performance is presented to an audience.

**Distress**    To make look worn, aged, or faded by time.

**Dock doors/Scene dock**    The access route through to on-stage; the facility entrance through which scenic design and technical equipment enters the stage. The area defined by the entrance, possibly housing the space for storage off the main stage area.

**Doric**    The earliest of the three Greek Orders. It is the simplest in design and had no base. The shaft was usually fluted and had a plain capital consisting of a square abacus and an echinus. Triglyphs, metopes and guttae are characteristic of this Order.

**Dormer**    A structure projecting from a sloping roof, usually to accommodate a window.

**Dowel**    A cylindrical pin, commonly used to prevent sliding between two contacting flat surfaces.

**Down-stage**    The acting area nearest the audience or in the direction of the audience, meaning an actor will walk towards the audience. **Down-centre:** in the direction of the audience yet near the stage centre-line. **Down-left:** in the direction of the audience yet to the actors' left when they are facing the audience. **Down-right:** in the direction of the audience yet to the actors' right when they are facing the audience. **Down and off:** referring to a door hinge and direction of its pivot to open; hinging on the down-stage edge and opening in the direction of off-stage.

**Drift**    The measured distance between the scenic element and the bar it is suspended from.

**Drip mould**    A moulding designed to prevent rain water from running down the face of a wall; used also to protect the bottom of doors and windows from leakage.

**Echinus**    The half-round moulded part of a column capital directly below the abacus.

**Elevations**    Drawings of the scenic units such as a wall, in a plane dimension (2D) showing true height, width and depth. Elevations may be Front, Side, Rear and Top.

**Ellipse**    A continuous curved line having two diameters called axes (singular: axis). An ellipse has two focus points (focii); the sum of the distances from the focii to any point on the curve is always constant. An inclined cut through a cone or cylinder is a true ellipse. **Approximate ellipse:** an ellipse that is elliptical in appearance, but does not have true focii.

**Entablature**    The horizontal members carried by the columns in classical architecture, consisting of architrave, frieze, and cornice.

**Entasis**    The gradual swelling or bulbous shape at the middle of the shaft of a column.

**Entrance**    The way through to the acting area from off stage; the entry point.

**Escutcheon plate**    The protective metal plate at the keyhole. Sometimes merely an ornamental plate around an opening for the key.

**Extrados**    The name applied to the upper or outside curving line of an arch.

**Fenestration**    The distribution or arrangement of windows in a wall.

**Figure**    A plane figure is bounded by lines or sides.

**Fillet**    A small flat moulding, rectangular in section view.

**Finial**    The ornamental termination of a pinnacle, consisting of turned or carved form.

**Fit-up**    The act of constructing a set on-stage prior to actors arriving for the technical rehearsal.

**Flange**    The upper and lower cross parts of a steel 'I' beam; a projecting rib.

**Flat**    The combination of a constructed frame and surface material applied, used as scenery in a design. **Book flat:** a folding flat which through a hinge closes like a book. **Cut out flat:** a flat with a shape or profile to one or several sides, perhaps to give the impression of a townscape silhouette, a ground row with foliage or other. **Double-sided flat:** a frame with cladding or canvas covering both sides (both to be treated by scenic art). **French flat:** a composite of flats or scenic frames which when assembled form a unit that is in its entirety suspended from a fly bar, usually with door and window openings included. **Profiled flat:** a flat with cut-away shaped edges.

**Floor (ground) plan**    The horizontal section through a building showing scaled size and location of rooms; also doors and windows in the walls.

**Flown**    To fly a unit or bar upwards or downwards above a stage.

**Fly floor**    The platform upon which operators stand to fly scenic units; a permanent platform above the stage to left and right.

**Fly in**   The act of lowering a scenic unit using the flying system or other means such as winch.

**Fly out**   The act of raising a unit or bar using the flying system.

**Fly tower**   The area above the stage floor which houses the grid, the bars and system to fly elements out of sight.

**Flying system**   The combination of lines, pulleys, counterweight and bars operated either through manual or electrical means to suspend scenic elements.

**Forestage**   The stage area typically down-stage of the proscenium opening, often called the 'apron'.

**Foul**   Where scenic elements in flying become entangled or caught up with one another.

**Free standing**   A flat that stands alone with only brace supports.

**Frieze**   1. That part of the entablature between the cornice and architrave. 2. The top part of a wall, between the ceiling cornice and the picture rail.

**Frieze panel**   The top panel of a door with five or more panels.

**Front projection**   The effect of projecting light upon the face surface of a scenic element, the light directed from down-stage through to up-stage.

**Gable**   The triangular portion of an end wall formed by a sloping roof.

**Gable roof**   A roof sloping up from two walls only.

**Gain**   The mortice or notch cut out of timber to receive the end of a beam.

**Gargoyle**   A projecting ornamental water-spout to throw water clear of the walls below.

**Gauze**   A cloth with mesh-like structure, allowing for a transparent effect when light illuminates the area up-stage of it, yet when lit from only down-stage it will appear as opaque. A gauze is typically positioned down-stage of a cloth to soften the cloth visual effect, as it creates a softer impression or makes the actual cloth appear less immediate to the eye. **Shark's tooth gauze:** an oblong weave mesh structure. **Filled gauze:** a double weave that fills in the mesh effect, giving a textured fill, not permitting transparent effects from down-stage through to up-stage.

**Geometry**   The study of shapes, the most common being circles, angles, plane figures, and solids. Shapes can be simple, as in a triangle, square, or cone. The basis of a shape is a point and where two points exist there is a line, and with a collection of points there is either potential for a plane or the formation of a shape. The dimension of a geometric figure determines whether it has length, area, volume, or none of the three. Dimension is the most important property of space. Geometry is formed of four building blocks: points, lines, planes, and space.

**Get-in**   The act of moving scenic elements into the theatre and onto the stage.

**Get-out**   The act of removing the scenic elements from the stage or theatre.

**Girder**   A large horizontal structural member, used to support the ends of joists and beams, or to carry walls over openings.

**Glaze**   A medium applied to a surface, such as paint, to seal it or give it surface finish (matt, satin and gloss).

**Grade**   The level of the ground around a building; it may be inclined.

**Grid**   The structure at the top of the fly tower where bars reach their full height.

**Gridded**   The position for scenic elements where they are in the grid, where the bar they are attached to reaches its highest point above the stage.

**Groined vaulting**   A ceiling formed by several intersecting cylindrical vaults.

**Grommet**   A metal fixture attached to the top rail of a flat, through which a fly-line will pass, to then become attached at the flat's base and at the other end of the line to the fly bar.

**Ground plan**   The venue or theatre architectural floor plan, noting that which makes contact with floor surface as permanent, above the stage and below stage level. The plane surface of the floor/deck is a true elevation, giving true width and depth. Height measurements may be noted by numerical notation.

**Ground row**   1. The floor/deck level lighting, which illuminates or directs lighting upwards onto a backcloth, up-stage wall. 2. A constructed frame clad in opaque material, which hides lighting set up-stage of it. May be positioned down-stage of a cloth to break its base horizontal, and may feature profile or cut-out edges.

**Guttae**   Drop-like ornaments under the triglyph and mutule in the Doric entablature.

**Hanging iron**   The hardware attached to the base rail of a flat, to which a fly-line will be fixed.

**Hanging stile**   The vertical part of a door or casement window to which the hinge is fastened.

**Hatching**   The shading of an imaginary cut surface by a series of parallel lines.

**Head of Construction**   The individual responsible for the build of a set and all scenic elements.

**Head room**   The vertical clearance on a stairway or in a room.

**Header**   A border purposely positioned down-stage near the proscenium opening, which frames the opening horizontally. Also used above a door opening or arch opening.

**Hearth**   The vitreous portion of a floor in front of a fireplace.

**Herring-bone**   The name given to masonry work when laid up in a zigzag pattern. It is usually found in brickwork and in wood flooring.

**Hip-roof**   One sloping up from all ways of a building.

**Hood**   The small roof over a doorway, supported by brackets or consoles.

**Housing**   The part cut out of one member so as to receive another. The housing of the stair step into the wall string.

**Incise**   To cut into, as letters incised or carved into stone.

**Intercolumniation**   The clear space between columns.

**Intrados**   The name applied to the lower or inside curving line of an arch.

**Ionic**   One of the Orders of Architecture, characteristic of which is the scroll, or volute capital.

**Jamb**   The inside vertical face of a door or window frame.

**Joist**   The framing timbers that are the direct support of a floor.

**Key-stone**   The centre top stone of an arch.

**Lancet window**   A high, narrow window pointed like a lance at the top.

**Line**   Line has no set thickness, but has length; it can be straight or curved. A straight line is the shortest distance between two points. **Hemp line or cable:** used to suspend scenic elements off a fly bar. **Brail line:** fixing a cross line from stage left to right, to shift a bar's steel cables into a position either slightly down-stage or slightly up-stage. **Centre-line:** the middle of the stage running from down-stage through to up-stage. **Set of lines:** the three or four steel cables attached to a bar which connect it through to the flying system. **Spot line:** a single line positioned to facilitate rigging a scenic element, generally of a light-weight nature, to a block on the grid, allowing the dropping in of that element to the stage. **Trip line:** a line attached to the bottom of a cloth that facilitates it being picked up from the base. **Setting line:** a down-stage edge or imaginary line running left to right, perpendicular to the centre-line, typically registered with a permanent feature of architecture. A line which is further down-stage of scenic elements and furniture positions, used to mark positions on plan, in rehearsal, and for plotting scenic elements once on-stage. **Sight-lines:** the positions of seating which determine the audience viewpoint, at their most extreme.

**Line segment**   A straight line segment is the portion of a line that lies between two points on a line, 'A' and 'B'. Whereas a line has infinite length, a segment has a finite length. Line segment is denoted by 'AB'. When two points are given, the straight line passing through these points is said to be located definitely. Only one straight line can pass through two points.

**Lintel**   The horizontal structural beam supporting the wall over an opening.

**Lobby**   The entrance hall or waiting room.

**Loggia**   A hall within a building but open on one side, this being usually supported by a colonnade.

**Mantel**   The shelf and other ornamental work around a fireplace.

**Mark**   To apply tape, usually a coloured electrical tape, to the floor of a rehearsal room or the stage for the positions of props, furniture and set. **Mark out:** to define the set design upon a floor using tape, in full size.

**Marquetry**   An ornamental surface built up of small pieces of wood to form a pattern, of inlaid work.

**Masking**   The elements typically designed, which mask off views to off-stage, above and to the sides. Traditional masking is in the form of borders and legs.

**Medallion**   A round or elliptical raised surface, usually for ornamental purposes.

**Meeting rail**   The horizontal rails of window frames that fit together when the window is shut.

**Metope**   The part of the frieze between the triglyphs of the Doric Order.

**Mezzanine**   A low secondary storey contained in a high storey.

**Mitre**   A beveled surface cut on the ends of mouldings, so that they may meet at points where they change direction.

**Module**   An accepted division for measuring proportions of the Orders of Architecture. It is taken as half of the base diameter of the column.

**Mouldings**   Long piece of wood, or other material, of which the rectangular sections have been shaped into varied contours for ornamentation. Common mouldings are: beads, chamfers, flutes, hollows, lamb's tongue, nosing, ogee, rounds and scotia.

**Mullion (or munnion)**   The large vertical division of a window opening. In grouped windows it is the member that separates the sash of each unit.

**Multiple set**   Various settings or locations as defined by a change in scenic elements.

**Muntins**   The small members that divide the glass in a window frame.

**Mutule**   A modillion rectangular in section; a square block carrying the guttae in the Doric cornice.

**Nave**   The main or central portion of a church auditorium.

**Necking**   The middle member of a simple column capital.

**Newel**   The post where the handrail of a stair starts or changes direction.

**Niche**   A recess in a wall, often to accommodate a piece of statuary.

**Nosing**   The proud wood feature or moulding applied to an edge, which gives a half-round finish to stair treads.

**Notation**   To use notation means to letter or number the diagrams at points or intersections.

**Obtuse angle**   An angle greater than 90 degrees, but less than 180 degrees.

**Off-stage**   The area beyond (up-stage, left or right) the acting area as defined by the design. 'Off' is typically outside the visible performing area, or the act of removing a scenic element or actor to outside the performance area.

**On-stage**   The area defined by the acting area, as designed.

**Oriel window**   A small projecting upper-storey window; a small bay.

**Orientation**   The direction that a building faces.

**Pane**   1. A panel. 2. A sheet or square of glass cut to the required size.

**Panel**   A thin, wide piece framed by other pieces of thicker framing; any flat surface sunk below the level of the surroundings.

**Parapet**   1. The part of a wall projecting above a roof. 2. The strip in a double-hung window frame that keeps the upper and lower sash apart.

**Parts**   The thirty equal divisions into which the module is divided for convenience.

**Party wall**   A division wall common to two adjacent pieces of property.

**Pediment**   A triangular, or segmental, ornamental head to an opening, or over the entablature at the ends of buildings and porticos in Classical architecture.

**Permanent set**   A fixed design remaining on-stage throughout the performance.

**Perpendicular**   A straight line set at 90 degrees to another straight line.

**Pier**   A rectangular masonry support, either free standing or built into a wall.

**Pilaster**   When an attached pier becomes very high in proportion to its width, it is called a pilaster.

**Piling**   Wooden or concrete posts driven into soft earth to provide a safe footing for heavy loads.

**Pipe**   Bar, fly bar or line set.

**Pitch of roof**   A term applied to the angle of slope. It is found by dividing the height by the span.

**Plan** *see* Ground plan.

**Plane**   A boundless surface in space; it has length like a line yet it also has width, but no thickness. A plane surface is a flat surface.

**Plinth**   The block that forms the bottom member of a column base.

**Plumb**   Vertical; parallel to a plumb line.

**Podium**   The body of a continuous pedestal.

**Point**   A point has position, but it has no dimension; a way to describe a specific location in space. It is a dot at a specified location.

**Polygon**   A regular or irregular figure bounded by more than four sides.

**Porch**   A covered shelter on the outside of the house.

**Portal**   An opening formed through top header and side legs, typically a fixed structure as one flat (*See* Proscenium).

**Practical**   Meaning workable: a prop or scenic element such as a door, window, and drawer in a desk, which is functional.

**Preset**   The setting up of a show in advance of the audience entering.

**Priming**   The first coat of paint, applied to fill the surface, as preparation to receiving subsequent coats.

**Production Manager**   The individual responsible for production realization.

**Properties**   Furniture and other handled objects that an actor will generally interact with on-stage.

**Proscenium**   The front opening or frame of a theatre stage, including the arch over the stage.

**Purlins**   Structural members spanning from truss to truss and supporting the rafters of a roof.

**Quadrilateral**   A four-sided figure, not necessarily with 90 degree corners. Any face bounded by four edges: a square and rectangle belong to a class of quadrilaterals called parallelograms (meaning parallel marks or lines). In the square and rectangle there are right angles; if in these figures you change the direction of two opposite sides as regards the other two, there will no longer be any right angles, but there will be two acute and two obtuse angles in each figure. This distorted figure becomes a rhombus, and from the rectangle a rhomboid is formed.

**Quick change room**   A designed allocated space off-stage for an actor to make a costume change within.

**Rail**   The horizontal top member of a balustrade. Also the horizontal members of windows and doors.

**Rake**   Inclined surface set off the horizontal of 0 degrees; also called gradient, slope, incline, and grade.

**Ramp**   A gradient or incline usually of a narrow width not below 600mm to allow access for actors or audience, or any incline supported by a rostrum.

**Ray**   A portion of a line, which starts at a given point and extends indefinitely in one direction. The point is called the 'origin' of the ray.

**Rebate**   A recessed angle to receive a window or door frame.

**Reflex angle**   An angle greater than 180 degrees, but less than 360 degrees.

**Repertory**   Where plays are performed one after the other or prepared to run as alternate performances.

**Return**   The turning back of a moulding into the wall on which it is located or around a corner of the building.

**Reveal**   The projection of a frame or moulding beyond the wall that carries it. Also the jamb of a window or door frame between the window or door and the face of the wall.

**Revolve**   A circular turntable device, which enables the set or actors to rotate from a central pivot.

**Right angle**   A 90-degree angle, that is, a square corner.

**Riser**   The vertical rise of a step.

**Rostrum**   An elevated platform on-stage.

**Sash**   The separate, lighter frame to a window, carrying the glass. It may be fixed, hinged, pivoted, or sliding. (*See* Casement.)

**Sash and frame**   A boxed frame with vertically sliding sashes. The boxes at the sides, in which the balance weights move, consist of the pulley stile, inner and outer linings, and the back lining. The outer (top) sash slides between the outer lining and the parting beads, and the inner (bottom) sash, between the parting beads, and the guide bead. Cast-iron or lead balance weights are attached to sash cords that pass over pulleys, and are nailed to the edges of the sash.

**Sash beads**   1. Beads forming the joint between a pivoted sash and the frame. 2. Beads forming a stop or guide for a sash.

**Scale rule**   An instrument used for measurement. Using a scale rule to produce a drawing gives the appearance of actual size, either reduced or enlarged from its actual size, yet proportionally accurate.

**Scotia**   A concave moulding.

**Scratch coat**   The first coat of plaster, which is scratched or scored to form a good bond for the second coat.

**Section**   A cut-through object, to produce an elevation of the object as observed in section, giving structural internal information as if sliced in two.

**Serge**   A thick wool.

**Setting**   The entire design for a scene, act or play.

**Shaft**   The part of the column between the base and the capital.

**Shop floor**   The working floor area where carpenters or metal workers build.

**Sight-lines**, *see* Lines.

**Sill**   1. The stone or wooden member across the bottom of a door frame or window frame opening on the outside of the building. 2. The bottom timber or metal strip spanning the opening in a door or a flat. Used to add structure to the framing.

**Skirting**  The base board applied to the wall surface, where the floor meets the wall. (*See* Base board.)

**Sky cloth**  A painted open sky effect upon a cloth.

**Soft masking**  Borders and legs made of black cloth such as serge or velvet.

**Solid**  A solid has three dimensions: length, width, and thickness (depth).

**Solid newel stairs**  Spiral, or winding, stairs in which the inside ends of the stone steps are worked into a cylinder, forming a continuous cylindrical newel.

**Smoke chamber**  The part of the flue directly above the fireplace.

**Snow drop**  A bag, suspended above the stage, filled with material, which when released will drop the contents onto the stage floor.

**Space**  Points, lines, and planes lie within space. Space is a collection of all points, having no shape, and no limits. Space is three-dimensional: it has length, width and height. (Height is length in a different direction.)

**Span**  The distance between supports of a joist, beam.

**Specifications**  The written or printed descriptions of materials and workmanship, which accompany the working drawings of a building.

**Spiral stairs**  A circular staircase with the treads consisting of winders only, round a central newel.

**Stage weight**  A heavy metal weight, shaped to accommodate the stage brace, used to secure scenic elements to the floor.

**Stile**  The vertical members of a built-up part such as a door, window, panel.

**Stool**  The wooden shelf across the bottom and inside of a window.

**Straight angle**  An angle of 180 degrees formed by a straight line.

**Strike**  To dismantle or deconstruct a set for removal, as in repertory or for get-out.

**String**  The supporting side timber at the end of stair steps.

**Style (of architecture)**  The distinguishing characteristics as fixed by the Order used or by the type of roof, windows, doors, walls and other details in combination.

**Stylobate**  The stepped base of a Greek temple.

**Supplementary angles**  Two angles whose sum is equal to 180 degrees; each is supplementary to the other.

**Surface**  A surface may have dimension in several directions, but has no thickness. A flat surface is often referred to as a plane; if it lies flat and level it is a horizontal plane; if the surface is up and down it is a vertical plane; if it lies at an angle it is an inclined plane.

**Tabs**  Stage curtains that part in the middle and track off left and right.

**Tab track**  A solidly constructed track for heavy curtains.

**Taenia**  The flat division band between the architrave and the frieze of the Doric Order.

**Teaser**  The border suspended between tormentors to provide top masking (*see* Header).

**Technical Director**  The individual responsible for all technical aspects of the stage.

**Terrace**  A raised bank of earth.

**Thimble**  The short horizontal pipe leading through a chimney wall into a flue.

**Threshold**  The stone, wood, or metal piece directly under a door.

**Throat**  The opening from a fireplace into the smoke chamber.

**Tongue**  A projecting bead cut on the edge of one board to fit into a corresponding groove on the edge of another piece.

**Tormentor**  A flat, positioned near to the proscenium and set parallel to the centre-line, which masks off-stage; it may include an opening through which actors enter.

**Torus**  Of a doughnut shape.

**Tracery**  Ornamental curving bars across an opening. They usually occur in Gothic buildings and are cut from stone.

**Track**  A metal trough suspended from the fly bar, or other, through which run either roller/wheels or gliding mechanisms to facilitate scenery or cloths being tracked on-stage. It may be set into the deck to facilitate scenic elements such as a table or desk to glide across the stage through a pulley system beneath stage floor level.

**Trammel**  The tool used to describe an ellipse based on connecting the major and minor axes to two points called '0', established along the trammel edge. When drawing on paper the trammel is a strip of paper. When drawing full-scale in the workshop, the trammel is a length of wood.

**Transom**  The horizontal bar dividing an opening into parts. It is also applied to a small window built over a door.

**Trap**  An opening, either hinged or with a removable lid, to allow access to sub-stage.

**Tread**  The horizontal board or surface of a step.

**Trellis**  An ornamental lattice made up of wooden strips to support vines.

**Triglyph**  A block, with perpendicular grooves, repeated at regular intervals in the Doric Order. It has two full and two half-grooves, or flutes.

**Trim**  The finishing frame around an opening.

**Trip**  The method used to fold a cloth in half before flying it out; extra lines are attached to the base batten of a cloth so it may be raised from its base horizontal as well as the top horizontal, through two sets of pick-up lines.

**Trisect**  To divide into three equal parts.

**Truck**  A constructed platform usually only high enough to mask the internal wheels or castors, upon which set design is constructed or positioned, enabling it to exit the stage.

**True ellipse**  An ellipse that has two focus points (focii) of which the sum of the distances from the focii to any point on the curve is always constant. An inclined cut through a cone or cylinder is a true ellipse.

**Truss**  A steel or aluminum framework made up of triangular units for supporting loads over long spans.

**T-square**    A drawing instrument for ruling parallel horizontal lines.

**Tuscan**    The simplest of the five Orders of Architecture. It is the Roman modification of the Doric, but without the triglyphs, and flutes in the columns.

**Under-stage**    The sub-stage area, beneath the deck or floor level.

**Up-stage**    The direction away from the audience.

**Vault**    An arched ceiling or roof.

**Veneer**    A thin covering of valuable material over a less expensive body.

**Venetian window**    A window frame with two mullions and three pairs of sashes. It has a large centre light and two narrow side lights.

**Vertex**    The point at which the two arms of an angle meet.

**Vestibule**    A small entrance room.

**Vista**    The view down an avenue or a path between shrub planting.

**Volute**    A scroll in spiral form, featured in the Ionic capital.

**Wainscot**    An ornamental or protective covering of walls, often consisting of wood panels.

**Weatherboarding**    The finished horizontal boarding of an outside wall.

**Winch**    A motorized mechanism that rolls cable or chain. It is used to facilitate lowering and raising heavy weighted objects or to draw back a truck or platform, if positioned on (or slightly above) stage level.

**Windows**    The various types are classified as: fast sheets, sliding sashes, pivoted sashes, casement windows, and Yorkshire lights, and they may be of wood or steel. The frames are divided into two classes: solid and cased, or boxed. Other terms are: sash and frame, mullion, Venetian, bay, bow, French, double or storm, hospital or hopper, oriel, bull's eye, dormer windows, skylights, lay-lights, and lantern lights. Windows may also be named according to their architectural characteristics, and the number of divisions in the frame. In addition, there are many patented forms of steel windows, and combinations of the above types. The area of glass should equal about one-eighth of the floor space. The sizes are measured according to the wall opening.

**Window board**    1. The inside window base board. 2. A horizontal shelf fixed to the inside of the sill to a window frame.

**Window frame**    A solid or cased frame carrying the sashes.

**Wood blocks**    Small blocks used for flooring. A common size is 9in × 3in × 1.25in. They are bedded in a mastic solution on cement over concrete.

**Wing**    A section of a building extending out from the main part.

**Yoke**    The horizontal top member of a window frame.

# FURTHER READING

Blurton, J., *Scenery: Draughting and Construction* (A&C Black Ltd., 2001)

Corkhill, T., *A Concise Building Encyclopaedia* (Sir Isaac Pitman & Sons Ltd., 1934)

Dorn, D., & Shanda M., *Drafting for the Theatre* (Southern Illinois University Press, 1992)

Field, W.B., *Architectural Drawing* (McGraw-Hill Book Co. Inc., 1922)

Giesecke, Mitchell & Spencer, H.C., *Technical Drawing* (The MacMillan Co., 1958, Revised 1962)

Harris, M.P., *An Illustrated Dictionary of Traditional Theatre Terms* (The Margaret Harris Estate, 2001)

Hilton, F., *Building Geometry and Drawing* (Longman Scientific & Technical, 1973)

Neat, D., *Model Making: Materials and Methods* (The Crowood Press, 2008)

Orton, K., *Model Making for the Stage: A Practical Guide* (The Crowood Press, 2004)

Reekie, F., & McCarthy, T., *Reekie's Architectural Drawing* (Hodder Headline Group, 1976)

Southern, R., *Proscenium and Sight-lines: A complete system of scenery planning* (Faber and Faber Ltd., 1939)

Talbot, A., *Handbook of Doormaking, Windowmaking, and Staircasing* (Sterling Publishing Co., Inc., 1980)

Thorne, G., *Stage Design: A Practical Guide* (The Crowood Press, 1999)

Troubridge, E., & Blaikie, T., *Scenic Art and Construction: A Practical Guide* (The Crowood Press, 2002)

Walmsley, B., *Construction Geometry* (Centennial College Press, 2nd edition 1981)

Winslow, C., *The Oberon Glossary of Theatrical Terms* (Oberon Books Ltd., 1991)

http://www.archive.org (mechanical drawing – all media types)

# INDEX

andiron/dog-iron  153
angle-poise lamp  27
angles  51–54, 55, 57
arches  79–81
architrave  146, 157
arcs  62, 65–66
astragal  158
audience
   auditorium  91–91
   stairs  160–161, 166
   ramps  178
   relationship to set design  5, 14
   sight line  14, 41, 97, 99–100, 139, 156–157, 169
axonometric projection  113, 126–130, 160, 164
back stage  91
baluster/spindle  160, 166
balustrade  160–162, 166
bay window  158
bookcase drawing  147
borders  93, 96–97, 99, 101
brick  153
British equity/raked stages  171
building geometry  14
bullnose  160–161, 167
calculator  26
cames  158
captions  7
cartridge paper  25, 141–142
casement window  158
casing  158
chair  27
chandelier  101, 135
chimney  153
circle
   arcs  62
   constructing segment of  circle
     passing through segmental arc
     65–66
   defined  60–61
   dimensioning  112
   drawing circle to meet point on
     ends of lines  63–64
   hexagon inside circle  58
   hexagon outside a circle
     58–59
   in a triangle  63
   in axonometric projection
     126–127, 128–129
   in isometric projection  133
   in squares  78–79
   octagon inside and outside a
     circle  59
   pentagon inside a circle  59
   radius  155
   square inside and outside a circle
     58
   template  20
   to construct quadrant  53
   to construct shapes within
     57–60
circle template  21
circlehead/window  158
cladding  146

cloister vault form  74–79
compass
   beam compass  19
   compass types  18–19
   dividers  19–20, 119
   handling and maintenance
     18–19
   transferring measurements
     119–120
computer aided design CAD  13, 91, 95
concrete  153
cone  72–73
construction department
needs and responsibility  10–11, 112, 130
corbel  151
costing  43
curtail  160–161, 167
cutting-plane/views  128, 149–150
cyclorama  94, 97, 99
damper  153
dead  101
design
   anticipating problems  42
   creative and practical decision
     making  5, 100, 157
   effective communication  8
   effective communication  8
   fireplace  151–154
   flats  148–151
   leadership  8, 12
   performance demands  11, 119
   plotting design on plan and
     section  100–103
   plotting masking as scenic units
     on plan  103
   presentations  5–6
   raked stage  168–177
   raked stage  168–177
   scenic elements  146–147
   staircase  160–167
   useful references for
     construction 8
   windows  154–159
   working in the model box  14, 40
   working to a brief  8, 11
dimensioning
   45 degree intersecting  111
   accuracy  110
   arrow system  111, 148
   curved shapes  112
   dimension lines  110–111
   examples  138, 147–150, 152, 155, 165, 176, 177
   explained  109–112
   extension lines  110
   measurements  105, 110–115, 112
   methods  110
   notes on dimensioning  111
   plotting dimensions  111

pointer lines  111, 163, 165
type of line  137
use of numerals in dimensioning
   112
director  42
dividers  19
dog  153
dog-leg  161
door
   architrave/door surround  90
   four panel/orthographic  147
   head  90
   jamb  90, 169
   model form  6
   profile  90
   sight-line to masking
     168–169
   to draw  68
   to establish mitre  89–90
door arch/drawing  146
door architrave  90
dormer  158
double curtail  160
double-flight  161
draughting studio  26–30
drawing
   a graphic language  10, 122, 137–145
   a guide for construction  9
   aim  8, 10–11, 42, 143
   anticipating problems  42, 143
   centre-line in objects  110
   computer aided design CAD
     13, 91, 95
   'construction' drawings  9–10, 13, 134
   detail  13
   drawing of lines  140–145
   engineering  13
   enlargement and reduction
     83–84, 125
   facilitates costing  9
   flying on section  102–103
   'for construction' drawings
     40, 143
   from plan to elevations  122
   ink drawings  143–144
   key things to remember  43, 143
   meaning of technical drawing
     6, 12, 91
   multi-views  10, 109, 113–114, 120, 123–124, 143
   page border and title block
     137, 142
   plan and section views/garden
     unit  149–150
   planning orthographic layout
     120–125
   plotting design on plan and
     section  100–103, 137–145
   plotting measurements off
     centre-line and setting-line
     41, 95

preliminaries  8, 40, 42–43
presentation medium  9
presentational  40, 133–134
proportion  12, 37, 119
registration of drawings  40
rough drawings into sketch
   model  143–144
rough layout drawings  40–42, 122
shaping ideas  9, 43, 122
sight-lines  41, 168–169
square  51–52
surface development  69–74
thinking through relationships
   7, 42, 51, 95, 122, 143
three regular views  113–114
time management  43
title block  103, 137, 142–143, 145
to scale  45–47
transfer method for symmetry
   85–86
drawing board
   maintenance  17, 22
   paper positioning  25, 51
parallel motion  16
practical application  6, 14, 27, 49, 51
sizes  16
types  16–17
drawing lines
   angled lines  51, 140
   drawing inclined and parallel
     lines  141
   drawing parallel lines  141
   drawing vertical and parallel
     lines  141
   horizontal lines  51, 140
   title block  142–143
   vertical lines  51, 140
drawing up  49–53, 143, 178–177
drift  150
dye-line print  10, 25, 27–28, 107
dye-line print as model  6
ellipse
   drawing with trammel
     75–76
   string method  76–78
   through intersecting lines
     77–78
   to draw semi-ellipse  82–83
   with circles as foundation  78
enlargement and reduction
   83–84, 125
enlarging and reducing  83–84
eraser
   brush  23–24
   electric  23
   putty eraser  22
   technical drawing eraser  23
erasing shield  23, 141
exercises
   approach  8

drawing exercises 48–90
explained 7
fire irons 153
fireback 154
fireplace
 backing 152
 chimney breast 152
 cross section 152
 explained 151–154
 fireplace terms 153–154
 grate 152
 hearth 152
 mantle 152
 notes about 151–153
 structure 130, 152
 views/orthographic 152
flattage
 cladding 146, 150
 construction 150
 drawing up 143
 flown 148
 meaning and detailing 13, 146
 notes about flats 150–151
 plotting on plan 95
 plotting on section 103
 rails/stiles 146, 150
 reveal 151, 154
 scenic flat explained 146, 150
 touring 151
 window 154–157
 with curve 151
 with fireplace 151–154
flexible curve 26
flown scenery 148
flue 153
fly bars 94, 96, 99–101, 103, 151
fly floor 94
flying 101, 102–103
flying flats 148
flying ironmongery 150
folding gate rostrum 170, 174
form 10–11
freehand sketching
 advantages 32
 axonometric 35
 circles and arcs 38
 dividing a line 37
 drawing parallel lines 37
 elevations 113–114
 estimating a dimension 37
 freehand ellipse 39
 isometric 35
 materials 32
 multi-view 32, 113–114
 negative and positive shape 31
 oblique and foreshortening 35
 perspective 35
 prop drawings 42
 proportions in life study 37–37
 purpose 8, 31
 relationship to model 8
 rough sketch 8
 technique 35, 37
 types of line 32
French curve 26
French window 158
furniture 95
garden unit plan and sections 149–150
geometric shape
 angle 39
 cone 39
 cylinder 39
 pyramid 39
 quadrilateral 39, 51
 sphere 39
 triangle 39
glazing 158
going 167
gradient 168
grate 153
ground plan
 centre-line 40, 95
 dash lines explained 95
 explained 91–96, 118
 facility and restrictions 13, 91–93, 95
 flying 102–103
 from plan to elevations 122
 head clearance 95
 iron/safety curtain 91–94
 off-stage features 98
 overhead features 98
 plotting measurements off centre-line and setting-line 41
 purpose 13, 91, 92–93, 122
 raked stage 168–177
 scenic unit rigging for flying 103
 setting-line 41, 100
 shading within lines 95
 sight-lines 41, 92
 sight-lines for masking on plan 103
 size 16
 solid lines explained 91
 sub-stage 95
 theatre stage floor/deck 91
 title block for page 103
 to acquire 7, 91
 transferring ideas from model to 14
handrail 161–164, 166–167
headroom 166
hearth 153
hexagon 58–59
explained 7, 8
ink drawing 143–144
iron/safety curtain 91, 94–96
isometric projection 113, 115, 130–132
jalousie window 158
jamb 153
jamb 158
landing 161–163, 166
landing guard 161–162
legs 93, 96–97, 99, 101
letter guide 26
lettering
 consistency 105–107
 explained 104–112
 guidelines 106–108
 inclined lettering 105–106
 line spacing 108
 notes on lettering 105–106
 practice study groups 108
 Roman script 107–108
 sign writing 104
 spacing and composition 107–108
 stroke method 104–105
 text spacing 105–106
 type of line 137
 vertical lettering 105–106, 108
 word spacing 108
lettering guide 26, 107
lettering template 109
light box 28
lighting bars 100, 103
lighting design 42, 103
line type
 axes line 138
 break line 140, 149–150
 characteristics explained 137–145
 construction line 137–138
 dash line 91, 126, 137, 139
 density by pencil pressure 137
 dimension line 140
 finished/object lines 137–139
 guidelines/text 140
 hidden line 137–139, 162
 medium line thickness 137
 object/finished line 137–139
 overhead line 137–139, 162
 page border 137, 142
 page layout line 137
 projection line 138–139
 section line 140, 162
 sightline 139
 thick line type 137
 thin line type 137
lines
 axes line 138
 break lines 137–140, 149–150
 centre line 40–41, 95, 114, 124, 137, 140
 construction lines 7, 137
 curtain line 138
 dash lines 91, 126, 137, 139
 dimension lines as arrows 111, 138, 140
 dimension lines as intersection 138, 140
 dimension lines explained 110–111, 138
 drawing angled lines 140
 drawing inclined and parallel 141
 drawing of lines 140–145
 drawing parallel lines 141
 drawing perpendicular lines 141
 drawing vertical and parallel 141
 drawing vertical lines 140
 drop/back cloth line 138
 establish a perpendicular 56
 extension lines explained 110, 137–138
 finished lines 7, 137
 gauze line 138
 guidelines/text 140
 hidden lines in orthographic 126
 hidden lines on plan 91, 96, 124, 137–138
 line characteristics 137–145
 overhead lines on plan 91, 137
 page border line 138, 142
 pencil lead line type 32
 pointer lines 111, 138
 projection lines 138–139
 section lines 137–140, 149–150
 setting line 40–41, 95
 shaded within 95, 98
 sightline 139
 solid lines on plan 95
 to bisect 55
 to divide a line freehand 37
to divide into equal units/parts 20, 56
lintel 153
lintel 158
mantelpiece 152–153
marble 153
masking 41, 97, 99, 103, 169
masking tape 17, 24, 25, 146
masonry 153
meeting rail 159
model
 centre-line 40
 from technical drawing/elevation into model 6, 143
 furniture plotting off centre-line and setting line 95
 in relation to presentational drawings 134
 integration into architecture 5
 model box 14
 model ideas transferred to plan and section 40–41
 plotting measurements off centre-line and setting line 41
 presentational 9, 134
 purpose of 5, 6, 10, 134
 relationship to sketch 8
 sketch model 6, 9, 14, 40, 42–43, 143–144
 white card 5, 6, 8, 40
mortar 153
mortice and tenon 159
mouldings
 astragal 87
 baseboard 133, 152
 cavetto 87–89
 conge 86–89
 convex, concave, compound 86–89
 cornice 133, 152
 cyma recta 87–89
 cyma reversa 87–89
 cymas 87–89
 dado/chair rail 152
 door moulding/casing 89–90, 133
 elliptical ovolo 87–88
 fillet or listel 86–89
 mitre at angle 89
 mitre joins 89–90
 ovolo 86–89
 picture rail 133, 152
 reduce the width of mitre moulding 89
 reduced head and larger jamb 89
 same size mitre join 89
 scotia 86–89
 torus 87–88
mullion 159
muntin 147, 159
newel post 160–163, 165–167
nosing 166–167
notes
 accompanying text 42, 136
 box 40
 for construction 134
numerals 106, 108–114, 137
octagon 59
off stage area 91
orders of architecture 179–181, 185
orthographic projection
 auxiliary views explained 125–126, 134, 178

bookcase 147
bottom view 118
cross section 128, 130, 133, 135, 147, 152, 155–157, 162
cutting plane views 149–150, 162
detail views explained 125
dimensions 119, 135
door 147
elevations 113, 117, 119, 144
elevations/garden unit 149–150
explained 112–136
fireplace 152
four views/dresser 123
from plan to multi-views for scenic elements 122
front view of set on-stage 125
front view/elevation 113, 117–118, 123, 126–130, 134–135
geometric form as 115
glass box approach 116–117
half front and section 90, 133
half views explained 124
hidden lines meaning 126–130
house, multi-views 124
line type 116
multi-views 10, 109, 113–114, 120, 123–124
page layout for four views 123
page layout for six views 120–122
partial views explained 124
plan 118, 120, 123, 129
rakes/ramps 168–177
rear view 119
reverse and repeat explained 124
section views/garden unit 149–150
section/cross section view 128, 130, 133, 135
shading 116
side views 113, 117–120, 123, 126–130, 134–135
six views of an object 116, 119, 129
staircase 162–163, 165
three regular views 117–118
top view 113, 117, 123, 126–130, 134–135
transferring measurements within 118–120
wall with arch opening 147
window 154–157
overmantle 153
package of drawings 5, 9, 134, 151
page border and title block 137, 142–143
pane 159
panel/door 147
paper
  cartridge paper 25, 141–142
  tracing paper 25, 40, 142
  detail paper 25, 40
  film 25
  graph 32, 42
  positioning on board 26
  storage and good practice 25–26, 28
  alignment 141
  sizes 16, 48
paper alignment 141,

pedestal leg table 86
pelmet 159
pencils
  for rough layout drawing 40
  graphite maintenance 22
  mechanical pencil or clutch 21
  mechanical propelling pencil 21
  points and lines 32
  rotary sharpener, how to use 21–24
  wood pencil and how to sharpen 22
pentagon 59
photocopying 28, 107
pick-up cables 103, 150
pitch 167
plan chest 28
ply sheeting/dimensioning 151
polygons 52
production
  health and safety 12
  risk assessment 12
  management of 8, 12, 42, 91, 171
profile flat 148
proportional drawing 83–84
proscenium opening 92, 94, 97, 99
protractor 21
quadrilaterals 51
rail/window 159
rails/flats 146, 151
rake ratios 172–178
rake/ramp 101, 178
raked stage
  aligning plan and section 174
  auxiliary view 176
  calculate rake ratio from drawn gradient /slope 172–178, 174
  calculating rake ratios 172–178
  construction concerns 168, 175
  determining height at any point 174–175
  develop plan then section 175
  develop section then plan 175
  direction of the rake 168–177
  distance of slope 172
  elevation for raked stage 174
  establish height of rake 174
  folding gate rostrum 170, 174
  front view 177
  gradient 168
  guidelines for treads and ramps to a rake 178
  health and safety 171, 178
  masking off 168–169
  notes about raked stages 172–178
  percent incline 172
  ply wood sheeting rake floor 174
  rake and actors 171
  ramps/rake and audience 171
  ratio equation explained 167–168
  risk assessment 171
  run 169, 174
  section views 176
  side views 176, 177
  structure 170

theatre ground plan 169–170, 172–178, 177
theatre section view 168, 171–172, 178
  to draw a rake 178–174
  true view elevation of surface 175–178
recce 13–14, 151
rectangle 52
right angle curve 61–62
rise 160, 164, 167
riser 67–69, 160–165, 163, 166–167
rough layout drawings
  from model to pan and section 40–41
  planning the page 40
run 160, 164
sandpaper block 18, 23
sash 159
sash window unit 130
scale
  advice 46
  dividing a line using scale rule 57
  drawing to scale 45–46
  figurative exercise 46
  for section view 133
  plotting at scale 46
  preferred scale for theatre 45
  proportional relationships 37–37, 124
  to fit the page 120–122, 124
  understanding scale 44–45
scale rule 15, 20, 44, 110, 119
set-squares
  bisecting a line 57
  for inking 20
  handling 49–51
  maintenance 22
  types and use 15–16, 20, 48, 50–51, 140
sight-lines 41, 92, 94, 97, 99–100, 168–169
sill 156, 159
site-specific 14
stage area 91
stage floor/deck 91
staircase unit
  axonometric views 160, 164
  balustrade 6, 160–162
  drawing up 67–69, 166
  entrance step type 160
  explained 160–167
  headroom 166
  health and safety 160–161, 164, 166,
  landing 166
  notes about staircases 166
  orthographic views 162–163, 165, 166
  staircase type 161, 164
  staircase/unit 6
  terms 166–168
  turn in direction 161–162
  width 166
stars shapes 64–69
stile 159
stiles/flats 146, 151
straight continuous 161, 164
string 161–163, 167
structural concerns 9
structure 10–11, 130
subdivisions
  doors 68
  proportional 66–68

staircase tread and riser subdivisions 67–69
sub-stage 94, 96
surface development
  cone 71–72
  cylinder 69–70
  octagonal tube 71–72
  pyramid 70–72
technical sketch 12
theatre architecture
  auditorium 91–92, 100
  facility 13, 98, 100
  iron/safety curtain 91, 94–96, 100
  lighting bars 100
  plan 91–96
  relationship to design 5
  section 96–100
  sightlines explained 97, 99, 139, 156–157, 169
theatre section
  bar allocation and title block 103
  bar numbering 103
  explained 94, 96
  facility 13, 91, 94
  flying 102–103
  meaning and use 13, 94, 96–98
  off-stage features 98
  overhead features 98
  raked stage 168–177
  shading within lines 98
  sight-lines 41, 94, 96, 168–169
  size 16
  solid lines 98
  sub-stage 7–96, 100
  title block for page 103
  to acquire 7, 91
  transferring ideas from model to 14
title block 103, 137, 142–143
tools, instruments and equipment 15–30, 119
touring demands 151
tracery panel 65
transfer method 85–86
transom 159
traps 92, 94–95
tread 67–69, 102, 160–161, 166–167
triangles 66–67
t-square 16–18, 22, 24, 26, 48–49, 51, 140–141
well 161
winder 161, 167
window seat 159
window unit
  architrave 155
  cased sash frame 155
  casement 156–157
  doors in model 6
  elevations 154–157
  explained 154–157
  glazing panels/panes 154–155, 156–157
  mullions 154
  orthographic/views 154–157
  rail 155
  reveal 154
  sash 154–155
  stile 155
  terms 157–159